TABLE OF CONTENTS

INTRODUCTION

Whether you've been playing Fantasy Football for one year or over thirty years, the objective is the same: winning! I'm one of the lucky ones who have been playing this hobby/sport for over 30 years (yes, before the internet). Whether I'm playing against my high school buddies or playing against some of the top Fantasy Football experts in the country, I have the same high energy drive to win. So, in my early years of playing Fantasy Football, I had a difficult time trying to grasp why my team and some of my buddies' teams would be one of the highest scoring teams each year and not make the playoffs. So, being a number cruncher in real life, I decided to investigate the problem and discovered that some of the high scoring players in our league were very inconsistent. One of those players was Shaun Alexander in 2002. He was on my team and he scored 17 touchdowns that season. My team ended 7-7 in the 14 game regular season and missed the playoffs! What happened? Well, my investigation showed since the scoring method was touchdown-only his inconsistency destroyed me! Alexander only scored touchdowns in six games and the other eight, he scored zero touchdowns!

Every season, there are players like this. At the end of the season, it shows these players as being ranked in the Top 10 or Top 20, but yet their lack of consistency kills your Fantasy teams. This book is a collection of articles focusing on each of main Fantasy positions (quarterback, running back, wide receiver and tight end). These articles will provide many different angles of analysis and forecasting based on the Clutch Games system that was created in 2002. In addition, they will be a Consistency Profile for over 175 players that will provide Fantasy owners with a snapshot of each player's consistency over the past three seasons and how consistent they are in various game scenarios (i.e., home vs. away, good defense vs. bad defense).

The Clutch Games system was created as a tool to add to your arsenal when you get ready to dominate your league(s). I believe this tool will help any level of Fantasy player. And I will personally help any Fantasy player who purchases this book with direction and guidance towards understanding and utilizing this tool for their upcoming season. You can email me at bob@bigguyfantasysports.com. Over the past 15 years, I have helped many Fantasy players go from dead last in their league to making the playoffs and some even won their championships the following year. This tool can help you win as well by helping you understand and identify who the most consistent players are in your league with your scoring method.

In addition, you can utilize the same tools that I have used to win my leagues. The Consistency Report allows you to input your league's scoring methods and determine which players are the most consistent in your league. Go to www.BigGuyFantasySports.com and start improving your teams today!

Thank you again for buying this book and I look forward to helping you to achieve a consistent season of success!

KEY TERMS

I felt it was important to define some obvious and not-so-obvious terms that will be used throughout the book. I will mention my email here and as well as throughout the book, so if you have a question about anything, please don't hesitate to email me at bob@bigguyfantasysports.com.

Clutch Game
A player earns a Clutch Game every time his total Fantasy points for a given game exceed the Clutch Factor for the given game.

Clutch Factor
This is a calculated value for each position (QB, RB, WR and TE) based on the league's scoring method and the number of teams in your league. Every player who exceeds this position-specific factor in a given week earns a Quality Game for the given week. This factor usually identifies (on average) the top 12 quarterbacks, 24 running backs, 36 wide receivers and 12 tight ends each week.

Clutch Rate (CR)
This is determined by dividing the number of Clutch Games earned by the number of games played in a given time period (season, month, etc.). Players are ranked as follows:

> Good – CR over 60 percent
> Very good – CR over 70 percent
> Excellent – CR over 80 percent
> Elite – CR over 90 percent

Expected Clutch Rate (ECR)
This is the Clutch Rate or Consistency Rate that I'm expecting the player to earn in the current season.

Good Defense
Team defense is ranked in the Top 10 of the NFL for the week or at year-end.

Average Defense
Team defense is ranked 11th through 22nd of the NFL for the week or at year-end.

Bad Defense
Team defense is ranked 23rd through 32nd of the NFL for the week or at year-end.

HISTORY OF CLUTCH GAMES

The Head-to-Head (H2H) format in Fantasy football leads to the need for consistency. If you have been playing Fantasy football for any length of time, you know how frustrating it can be to win by 30 points one week and then lose by two points the next. How many times have you been one of the highest scoring teams in the league, but you missed the playoffs by one or two games?

Many will call it "bad luck" and that's partially true. Injuries to key players, bad weather, etc. are situations that affect our fantasy teams, but are uncontrollable. However, there is one aspect of fantasy football that you can control. The consistency of your team! If you're scratching your head and asking, "How can you control consistency", you're not alone. The topic and its application are still fairly unfamiliar to Fantasy football world.

Reasoning and Methodology

It's called Clutch Games. Basically, it is the awarding of a Clutch Game to a player each week when they exceed the average points scored in your league for that position. The more Clutch Games a player is awarded each year, the more consistent that player is and the more beneficial they are to your Fantasy team.

It is very similar to the Quality Starts concept used for pitchers in Fantasy baseball. A pitcher earns a Quality Start every time they pitch more than six innings and give up less than three earned runs in a game. The more Quality Starts a pitcher has in a year, the more consistent and more valuable they are to their team. However, Quality Starts do not affect a Fantasy baseball team as much, since its roto-style with accumulative stats. However, in a H2H fantasy baseball format, it can be very important.

So, during the 2002 season, I started to research the concept of consistency in Fantasy football. I knew that just taking the average points (total points/number of games) for each player wasn't really valid, because if two players each rushed for 1,280 yards, they both averaged 80 yards per game. There appears to be no difference between the two players for valuation purposes. BUT, if Player A rushes for exactly 80 yards every week and Player B rushes for 120 yards one week and 40 yards the next week, Player A will probably win you more Fantasy games in the long run. Therefore, it was important to use a game-by-game basis for my valuations.

Next step was to set the Clutch Factor. This was the average points that a player needed to meet or exceed to be awarded a Clutch Game for that scoring method and the league size for that week. This was very important as well since basing Clutch Games on just one typical scoring really only help those Fantasy owners using that method. Therefore, a Fantasy owner can input their scoring method into the Consistency Report (http://www.bigguyfantasysports.com/index.php/tools/clutch-report-intro) and determine who the most consistent players are based on their scoring method. Each Clutch Factor is calculated for each specific position (QB, RB, WR, TE), using a standard amount of players each season for consistency.

HISTORY OF CLUTCH GAMES (cont.)

Clutch Rating (CR)

Once the factor is set, then your fantasy players will earn a Clutch Game for each week that they exceed the related Clutch Game factor. Therefore, the more Clutch Games earned by a player, the more consistent the player is and then, finally, the more consistent the player is then the more beneficial that fantasy player is to your Fantasy team!

The average of the Clutch Games earned divided by the total games played equated to the Clutch Success Rate (CR). A top consistent fantasy player will have a CR of more than 70%. The elite studs of the fantasy world will normally be over an 80% CR.

Summary

By adding the Clutch Game Score system to your arsenal of Fantasy tools, you will see why it's so important in a Head-to-Head format to have good AND consistent Fantasy players on your team. This season start dominating your Fantasy league with consistency instead of luck!

IMPROVING YOUR TEAM WITH CONSISTENCY

The Clutch Games system was created to show how building your team with more consistent players can actually make your Fantasy football experience more rewarding. It doesn't matter whether that reward is monetary or simply the pride from dominating your friends in your Fantasy league, the reward is always sweeter in victory.

With the consistency idea being fairly new and uncommon in the fantasy football world, I've had a number of Fantasy owners say to me, "Sure, it sounds great on paper, but what can I do to see where my team would have been last season had my team been more consistent throughout the regular season?"

No problem, folks! Below is a method of how you can use your team in your league to see where you and the rest of your league owners would have been record-wise if your team was more consistent.

IMPROVING YOUR FANTASY TEAM'S RECORD IN 2016

PLEASE, TRY THIS AT HOME!!!

Take your league that you played in and do the following:

1. List each team's actual record and their team average points per week (game).
2. Take your team first and use your team's average weekly score and replace it in each of your weekly games.
3. Now, determine how many games you would have won or lost.
4. This revised won/loss record is called your team's Consistency Record.
5. Now, complete these same above four tasks on all of the other teams in your league.

Did you notice how some of the team's Consistency Record was better than their actual record? However, this would have only occurred with the teams whose average score was higher than the league average score. Teams below the league average can NOT be helped by consistency, because being "consistently bad" is still….well, bad.

IMPROVING YOUR TEAM WITH CONSISTENCY (cont.)

I have listed below an example league to show you how a more consistent team will normally improve their record.

	Actual Record	Avg. Pts. Per Week	Consistency Record	Change
Team 1	8-6	129.6	12-2	+4
Team 2	9-5	129.3	11-3	+2
Team 3	12-2	125.4	12-2	0
Team 4	11-3	116.9	11-3	0
Team 5	9-5	114.7	9-5	0
LEAGUE AVERAGE		109.6		
Team 6	8-6	107.8	7-7	-1
Team 7	5-9	106.4	4-10	-1
Team 8	4-10	102.0	4-10	-1
Team 9	7-7	101.2	5-9	-2
Team 10	4-10	97.3	4-10	0
Team 11	3-11	96.7	3-11	0
Team 12	4-10	87.7	3-11	-1

As you can see above, the teams above the league average either stayed the same or benefited from having a more consistent team, especially Teams 1 & 2, who could have gained four and two wins respectively. The important thing to note is the teams below the league average would receive no benefit at all; in fact, in this case, their records would have been worse, if they were more consistent.

Team 1 was a perfect example of the "bad luck" team during the season. We have all seen this team in our leagues every year. Sometimes it's actually you and sometimes it's not. Personally, we probably could all care less if it's not us, but for argument purposes, let's say it is.

Your team led the league in scoring! It averaged 129.6 points per week, but because you scored 180 points one week and 80 in the next week, your team barely made it over a .500 record. It's sad, but true. The lack of team consistency caused your team to miss the playoffs even though you led the league in scoring.

Another great case in point here is two teams (Team 2 & 5), who each had a 9-5 record, but Team 2 averaged 14.6 points per week more. If their team would have been consistent, they would have been 11-3 and made the playoffs. The lack of consistency in their team cost them the playoffs and even possibly a Fantasy Championship.

As you can see from the chart, Teams 3 & 4 maximized their consistency winning all of the games that they should have. Their team's consistency was much better than Teams 1 & 2. Your goal each year would be to work towards maximizing your consistency with consistent above average scoring from your players. While an element of luck will always exist, good coaching through looking at the matchups and starting the right players are important as well.

IMPROVING YOUR TEAM WITH CONSISTENCY (cont.)

When it comes to the teams who averaged below the league average, let me make this perfectly clear, consistency WILL NOT make a bad team competitive! If your team's weekly average was far below the league average, then your team was extremely lucky to be competitive (i.e., make the playoffs). While there are certainly teams who seem to be on the good luck side of the fence, over time that luck will run out and their below average team won't be able to keep winning.

Therefore, the most important part to creating a playoff bound fantasy team is to draft an above average team, in comparison to the other teams in your league. An important thing to remember is to look at the player's past Clutch Rating for the past one to three seasons. If you're torn between drafting one of two wide receivers and you note that one has been more consistent over the past few years, then by drafting the more consistent player, you may help to improve your team's record in 2016.

I have been playing Fantasy Football for more than 30 years and I can't tell you how many times I have seen high scoring teams, including my own, not make the playoffs. We used to get upset and throw our hands up and curse the "bad luck". Now, you and I can stop cursing and do something about it! We can create a team with an emphasis on consistency!

As the information above shows, a more consistent team can mean one or two or more wins for an above average team. Those additional wins can mean making the playoffs. Making the playoffs means YOU have a chance to win a Fantasy Championship!

ROOKIES VERSUS CONSISTENCY?

The one question that I get asked every year is "Why don't you include rookies in your consistency analysis?" My answer has always been "They're too inconsistent." Or "College talent doesn't always equate to NFL talent." That normally leads to "Well, what about Odell Beckham, Jr. or LeVeon Bell or Ezekiel Elliott?" Good point.

So, I decided this year to back up my theory with facts. I accumulated the number of draft choices at the offensive positions (QB, RB, WR and TE) since 2010. For the past seven years, there have been 290 of these players drafted in the first four rounds. I did only the first four rounds since that's where most of the NFL starters come from. Yes, there are the Tom Brady's of the world that are drafted in Round 6, but those are few and far between.

The breakdown of the positions and rounds are as follows:

	Rd 1	Rd 2	Rd 3	Rd 4	Total
QB	19	8	9	12	48
RB	10	20	16	27	73
WR	27	27	32	35	121
TE	3	12	16	17	48
Total	59	67	73	91	290

Next, I accumulated all the rookies who exceeded a 60% Clutch Rating (how consistent the player was during the season) in their rookie season since 2010.

	90% - 100%	80% - 89%	70% - 79%	60% - 69%	Total
QB	0	1	1	2	4
RB	2	2	5	2	11
WR	1	2	2	2	7
TE	0	0	0	1	1
Total	3	5	8	7	23

As you can see above, since 2010, only 23 TOTAL rookies have ever exceeded a 60% Clutch Rating in their rookie season. Around 65% of those players had a Clutch Rating between 60-79%, while only 35% were over an 80% Clutch Rating. In summary, it's very rare that a rookie has a Clutch Rating over 80% in his first season. Let's look at the breakdown by position.

	90% - 100%	80% - 89%	70% - 79%	60% - 69%	Total
QB					8.33%
RB					15.07%
WR					5.79%
TE					2.08%
Total	1.03%	1.72%	2.76%	2.41%	7.93%

ROOKIES VERSUS CONSISTENCY? (continued)

The chart shows that only one percent of all position players drafted in the past seven years have earned a Clutch Rating over 90% in their rookie season. The other Clutch Rating categories don't show much success as well with success ratings between 1.72% and 2.76%. In total, less than 8% of all rookies since 2010 earned over a 60% Clutch Rating.

If you're wondering, who were these 23 rookies, who earned over a 60% Clutch Rating in their first season, then you're in luck! We'll start with the quarterbacks. Remember, only four quarterbacks out of the 48 (8.33%), drafted in the first four rounds since 2010, have earned over 60% Clutch Rating. Robert Griffin and Marcus Mariota both earned a 67% Clutch Rating while Cam Newton had an extraordinary 81% in 2011.

Many would have expected Jared Goff or Carson Wentz to earn over 60% in 2016 since they were drafted #1 and #2 overall, but neither one made it. Wentz was the closest at 31%. However, the newest addition to this list at quarterback was a fourth-round pick named Dak Prescott. After an injury to Tony Romo in the preseason, Dak stepped in and had a tremendous rookie season with the second-highest season ever for a rookie quarterback at 75% Clutch Rating. This led to Romo's retirement and now Dak will lead the Cowboys going forward.

Rd	Pick	Team	Name	Year	CR
1	1	CAR	Cam Newton	2011	81%
4	135	DAL	Dak Prescott	2016	75%
1	2	WAS	Robert Griffin	2012	67%
1	2	TEN	Marcus Mariota	2015	67%

The running backs lead all positions with 11 rookies having exceeded the 60% Clutch Rating. This equated to 15.07% of all the drafted running backs since 2010. Of those 11, only one exceeded a 90% Clutch Rating until 2016 and he was LeVeon Bell. In 2016, first round pick, Ezekiel Elliott not only reached the 90% rating, he exceeded Bell's rookie season record of 92% with a 93% Clutch Rating.

ROOKIES VERSUS CONSISTENCY? (continued)

Interestingly, Jordan Howard did earn over a 60% Clutch Rating in 2016, as a rookie. He earned a 73% Clutch Rating for the season. However, since he was drafted in the fifth round, he was not eligible for inclusion in the analysis. As I mentioned before, it does happen sometime, but they are few and far between.

Rd	Pick	Team	Name	Year	CR
1	4	DAL	Ezekiel Elliott	2016	93%
2	48	PIT	Le'Veon Bell	2013	92%
2	61	GNB	Eddie Lacy	2013	87%
1	31	TAM	Doug Martin	2012	81%
1	10	STL	Todd Gurley	2015	77%
6	173	WAS	Alfred Morris	2012	75%
2	36	JAX	T.J. Yeldon	2015	75%
1	3	CLE	Trent Richardson	2012	73%
5	155	BUF	Karlos Williams	2015	73%
2	37	CIN	Giovani Bernard	2013	69%
5	160	STL	Zac Stacy	2013	64%

The wide receivers are second in total rookies over 60% with seven. This equated to only 5.79% of all the drafted running backs since 2010. However, the biggest difference between the wide receivers and running backs is the success AFTER their rookie season. Almost all these receivers have had continued success after their consistent rookie season and remain as some of the top receivers heading into 2016. The newest addition to this list from 2016 was not first-round rookies like Wil Fuller or Corey Coleman, but was a second-round pick named Michael Thomas. It never hurts to get drafted by the New Orleans Saints when you're a wide receiver and Thomas was 2016's beneficiary.

Rd	Pick	Team	Name	Year	CR
1	12	NYG	Odell Beckham	2014	92%
2	47	NOR	Michael Thomas	2016	80%
1	4	CIN	A.J. Green	2011	80%
1	6	ATL	Julio Jones	2011	75%
3	76	SDG	Keenan Allen	2013	71%
1	7	TAM	Mike Evans	2014	60%
2	61	JAX	Allen Robinson	2014	60%

All by his lonesome at the tight end position is Jordan Reed. He is still the only tight end since 2010, who earned over a 60% Clutch Rating in his rookie season. He earned a 67% Clutch Rating in 2013. That's right. No Rob Gronkowski (38%), Jimmy Graham (55%), Julius Thomas (0%); Tyler Eifert (20%) or Travis Kelce (0%). So, if there are any rookie tight ends that you are targeting, please make sure you are drafting in the very late rounds or you're drafting in a dynasty league.

ROOKIES VERSUS CONSISTENCY? (continued)

The facts show what many Fantasy owners already know, drafting rookies early is risky. The chance of drafting a rookie, who earns over a 60% Clutch Rating, is only 7.93%. Your chance of drafting a rookie who earns over an 80% Clutch Rating is less than 2.80%. Let's be honest, you want the players that you draft in the first two rounds of your Fantasy draft to have an 80% Clutch Rating or higher. So, who would you draft? A proven veteran or a rookie? The facts above have already answered the question for you.

QUARTERBACKS

Each major position (QB, RB, WR and TE) tracked for consistency purposes will have the following sections: Year in Review, Consistently Clutch and the Consistency Profiles. The Year in Review is exactly that, a review of the top four tiers on Fantasy consistency at each position. The Consistently Clutch article will highlight how consistent the top Fantasy players have been for the past three seasons. Finally, the Consistency Profiles will provide you with a profile of each player's consistency for each of the top returning Fantasy players.

The quarterback position for Fantasy Football purposes was easily the most waited on position to draft last year. Most of the top picks produced like Aaron Rodgers, Andrew Luck, and even, Tom Brady in his limited number of games. This tier of players has distanced themselves from the other quarterbacks though. Their consistency speaks for itself.

There were a ton of quarterbacks over 300 points (4pts per passing TD) in 2016. There were actually 18 for the second straight year. Heck, even Joe Flacco had 298 points and Tom Brady had 294 in only 12 games. So, obviously, the passing game is still alive and kicking in the NFL!

So, this must have been a banner year for quarterback consistency, right? Well, not so much. While there were certainly some of the "regular" studs near the top of the consistency charts, there were many "regulars" who were not.

I might be drafting Aaron Rodgers, Tom Brady or Andrew Luck, if they are available to me in the fifth or sixth round of my Fantasy drafts this season. If I miss out on them, I'll wait until the sixth round or later to draft someone like Kirk Cousins or Derek Carr. In summary, there are consistent quarterbacks out there in 2017. You can wait to draft them for better value.

As you continue to read the articles and the Consistency Profiles for the quarterbacks allow yourself to make your own decision. Remember the Clutch Games is a tool to help you when you're preparing for your Fantasy draft or with your lineup decisions.

If you have any questions, please don't hesitate to email me at bob@bigguyfantasysports.com or hit me up on Twitter @bob_lung.

2017 PREVIEW – QUARTERBACKS

Let's look at those quarterbacks ranked in their projected Tier for 2017 and show you their 2016 total points and consistency and where they ranked in those categories in 2016. Scoring method is the standard 4 points per TD passing and 6 for rushing plus 1 point for every 20 yards passing and 10 yards rushing.

So, let's start with the top tier of quarterbacks.

TIER ONE

Player Name	Total Points	Pts Rank	Total CG	Total GP	CR %	2016 Rank	2017 Tier	2017 Rank
Aaron Rodgers	435.30	1	14	16	88%	1	QB1A	1
Tom Brady	294.10	20	9	12	75%	5	QB1A	2
Andrew Luck	369.10	4	12	15	80%	3	QB1A	3

As I mentioned above, these three have separated themselves from the rest. Their combination of total points and consistency gives me confidence to draft them earlier than the other quarterbacks in 2017. I expect all three of them to earn an Expected Clutch Rate (ECR) of 80%+. So, how early should you draft them? Well, each league is different, but in a standard 12-team league, I believe the fourth round is the earliest to draft Rodgers followed by Brady and Luck in the fifth round. If you miss out on them because someone drafted them in the first through third rounds, don't worry. There are plenty of solid consistent quarterbacks to draft in rounds six through eight.

TIER TWO

Player Name	Total Points	Pts Rank	Total CG	Total GP	CR %	2016 Rank	2017 Tier	2017 Rank
Drew Brees	407.40	2	11	16	69%	6	QB1B	4
Matt Ryan	403.90	3	13	16	81%	2	QB1B	5
Kirk Cousins	367.85	5	11	16	69%	7	QB1B	6
Derek Carr	309.55	14	9	15	60%	10	QB1B	7
Marcus Mariota	314.00	13	10	15	67%	8	QB1B	8
Dak Prescott	335.55	6	12	16	75%	4	QB1B	9
Russell Wilson	324.35	10	7	16	44%	19	QB1B	10
Cam Newton	303.35	17	6	15	40%	22	QB1B	11
Ben Roethlisberger	301.35	18	9	14	64%	9	QB1B	12

2017 PREVIEW – QUARTERBACKS (continued)

Tier Two are the remaining QB1's with a B rating. This equates to these quarterbacks having an ECR between 67% - 80%. Now, as you can see from the 2016 Clutch Rates and rankings, that not every quarterback in the QB1B Tier earned over 67%. We're looking at you, Russell Wilson and Cam Newton!!! But, both quarterbacks have the ABILITY to earn that Clutch Rate and have done so in the past. Therefore, I have them ranked 10th and 11th, where other experts have them much higher. Drew Brees almost made the QB1A list, but his age and the loss of Brandin Cooks scares me a little. He's still ranked fourth overall, so I'm not that concerned. Some of my favorite undervalued quarterbacks heading into 2017 are in this list. They are Kirk Cousins and Marcus Mariota. If you can draft them in rounds seven or eight, there's great value to be had!

TIER THREE

Player Name	Total Points	Pts Rank	Total CG	Total GP	CR %	2016 Rank	2017 Tier	2017 Rank
Matthew Stafford	335.05	7	8	16	50%	13	QB2A	13
Philip Rivers	334.00	8	8	16	50%	14	QB2A	14
Jameis Winston	321.30	11	7	16	44%	20	QB2A	15
Eli Manning	288.45	21	5	16	31%	30	QB2A	16
Andy Dalton	316.70	12	7	16	44%	21	QB2A	17
Carson Palmer	305.65	16	8	15	53%	12	QB2A	18
Blake Bortles	325.15	9	8	16	50%	15	QB2A	19
Tyrod Taylor	307.15	15	7	15	47%	18	QB2A	20
Carson Wentz	266.10	24	5	16	31%	31	QB2A	21

The next Tier are those quarterbacks, who can earn an ECR between 50% - 67%. Any quarterback too close to 50% is not worth drafting, even as a backup. As you can see, these quarterbacks were in closer to 50% than 67%. If I was going to pick a backup from this group, my favorites would be Stafford, Manning, Dalton and Palmer. Mostly because of experience and the weapons around them to earn a Clutch Game when your starter is having a bye week. The remaining quarterbacks are young and inexperienced and that has led to much inconsistency in their past. One or two of them may improve their consistency in 2017, but I'm not willing to take that risk.

TIER FOUR

Player Name	Total Points	Pts Rank	Total CG	Total GP	CR %	2016 Rank	2017 Tier	2017 Rank
Ryan Tannehill	244.75	25	5	13	38%	25	QB2B	22
Sam Bradford	274.15	22	6	15	40%	23	QB2B	23
Joe Flacco	298.15	19	5	16	31%	29	QB2B	24
Brian Hoyer	95.55	32	3	6	50%	16	QB2B	25
Alex Smith	270.50	23	5	15	33%	26	QB2B	26
Trevor Siemian	237.75	26	4	14	29%	32	QB2B	27
Josh McCown	75.10	35	2	5	40%	24	QB2B	28

This Tier is basically a hot mess of quarterbacks! Names like Tannehill and Flacco have been around for years and still couldn't find consistency if it hit them in the face. None of these quarterbacks are worth drafting, unless it's a two-quarterback league and even then, they're marginal.

Well, there is your preview of the quarterbacks for 2016 and a preview of their consistency expectations for 2017. If you didn't make the playoffs and you had Cam Newton or Russell Wilson on your team and can't understand why, I hope this helped clear things up.

CONSISTENTLY CLUTCH - QUARTERBACKS

Aaron Rodgers leads the quarterbacks over the past three seasons. However, only Drew Brees has earned the honored, Triple Double, with three straight seasons of double-figure Clutch Games.

It's one thing to be clutch during one season in Fantasy Football. However, it's those players who are consistently clutch that make up the real Fantasy studs. These players are the ones that should be drafted in the early rounds of most drafts. A consistently clutch player has normally remained consistently healthy as well, which is just as important as their consistent performance.

The Top 24 most consistent quarterbacks and the number of Clutch Games earned each year are listed below. They start at the horribly inconsistent, Colin Kaepernick and end with the most consistent quarterback, Aaron Rodgers. It is divided into three tiers with a three-year and two-year totals and associated rank. I'll analyze each tier and provide some insight on the players within that tier.

Tier One – The Elite (Ranks 1 - 4)

Player Name	2014	2015	2016	Total	3 yr rank	2 yr total	2 yr rank
Aaron Rodgers	13	9	14	36	1	23	1
Drew Brees	12	10	11	33	2	21	4
Tom Brady	9	13	9	31	3	22	2
Andrew Luck	13	6	12	31	4	18	8

These four quarterbacks are definitely in a class by themselves. Yes, I know that Russell Wilson, Matt Ryan and others are "close" to them in Clutch Games. But are they, really? Tom Brady missed four games last year due to deflated balls and Andrew Luck missed half of 2015 due to injury. If Brady and Luck played all 16 games in those seasons, it's really not that close. If you can draft any of these four in your 2017 drafts, around the fourth or fifth round, you will have consistency on your side. I would highly recommend it. All of them are capable of 12+ Clutch Games in any given season. I can't guarantee that for the other quarterbacks in Tier's Two and Three.

Tier Two – The Above Average (Ranks 5 – 15)

Player Name	2014	2015	2016	Total	3 yr rank	2 yr total	2 yr rank
Russell Wilson	11	11	7	29	5	18	9
Matt Ryan	8	7	13	28	6	20	5
Carson Palmer	5	14	8	27	7	22	3
Ben Roethlisberger	9	8	9	26	8	17	10
Cam Newton	8	11	6	25	9	17	11
Matthew Stafford	8	9	8	25	10	17	12
Eli Manning	9	10	5	24	11	15	17
Blake Bortles	4	11	8	23	12	19	6
Kirk Cousins	4	8	11	23	13	19	7
Andy Dalton	6	10	7	23	14	17	13
Philip Rivers	8	7	8	23	15	15	18

CONSISTENTLY CLUTCH – QUARTERBACKS (continued)

This tier is made up of quarterbacks who have the "potential" to earn double-digit Clutch Games in a season. In fact, if you look at the list of quarterbacks, in this tier, you will see eight out of the eleven earned double-digit Clutch Games, at least once over the past three seasons. However, in the other years, they failed miserably. No one failed as bad as Russell Wilson last season. After "appearing" that he was going to join the elite crowd in Fantasy quarterbacks, Wilson earned only seven Clutch Games and destroyed many Fantasy teams in 2016. The loss of a running game and a porous offensive line were much of the contributing factors, but Wilson looked lost at times last year. I believe there some room for improvement in 2017, but I'll probably stay clear from him just to be safe.

There are some of these quarterbacks that I believe can regain double-digit consistency in 2017. I'll start with Matt Ryan. He truly figured it out last season. By not focusing on Julio Jones on every passing play, his Falcons and his consistency could be more successful. This was Ryan's most consistent season ever and that was with Julio Jones only catching six touchdowns! The team remained intact in the offseason and Ryan should stay consistent again in 2017. Kirk Cousins was my "man-crush" heading into 2016 and he delivered with a very consistent season (11 Clutch Games). Don't worry about him losing DeSean Jackson and Pierre Garcon, he'll be just fine. I assume there won't be many believers in 2017, but he should be very focused to earn that big contract in 2018, so grab him as your backup or a late-round starter.

Tier Three – The Average (Ranks 16 – 24)

Player Name	2014	2015	2016	Total	3 yr rank	2 yr total	2 yr rank
Derek Carr	4	8	9	21	16	17	14
Joe Flacco	8	6	5	19	17	11	23
Ryan Tannehill	8	5	5	18	18	10	25
Alex Smith	5	7	5	17	19	12	20
Jay Cutler	10	7	0	17	20	7	27
Marcus Mariota	DNP	6	10	16	21	16	15
Jameis Winston	DNP	9	7	16	22	16	16
Ryan Fitzpatrick	4	10	2	16	23	12	21
Colin Kaepernick	7	3	6	16	24	9	26

Most of these quarterbacks barely hover around the average level. However, there are two quarterbacks in this group, that I believe have the ability to earn double-digit Clutch Games in 2017 and will be in Tier Two next season for sure. Let's start with the only quarterback who has earned double-digit Clutch Games, Marcus Mariota. Mariota missed one game in 2016, so he could have been better. However, Mariota accomplished this with an excellent running game in Tennessee. I would expect him to continue that consistency in 2017 and finish as a Top 12 quarterback.

Derek Carr is easily the second quarterback with potential to earn double-digit Clutch Games in 2017. He was well on his way in 2016 to double-digit Clutch Games when an injury ended his season. He will be a Top 12 Fantasy quarterback in 2017 as well, just don't overpay for him. I'm a tad worried about his ADP being too high heading into August. There are your most consistent quarterbacks over the past three seasons. Keep this information handy as you prepare for your drafts this season. Clutch is good but consistently clutch is great!

CONSISTENCY PROFILES – QUARTERBACKS

The Consistency Profiles were created for the same reason that we have Fantasy profiles: to have a quick summary of a player's performance at a glance. The following Consistency Profiles for the quarterbacks are listed in alphabetical order by last name for easy reference. Each player's profile will have the following information:

1. Three-year historical breakdown per season of the following:
   a. Fantasy points total
   b. Clutch Games earned
   c. Games played
   d. Clutch Rating (CR – Clutch Games/Games Played)

2. Tier Draft Rank (Expected Clutch Rate)
   a. This number ties to the Tier Draft List in this book. This is where I have ranked the quarterback based on Fantasy points and consistency for the 2017 redraft leagues. The Tiers equate to Expected Clutch Rate (ECR) in this manner:
      i. QB1A = 80%+ ECR
      ii. QB1B = 67-80% ECR
      iii. QB2A = 50-67% ECR

3. Clutch Games by Week for 2016
   a. "+" means a Clutch Game was earned that week
   b. "B" means it was the player's Bye Week.

4. Three-year historical breakdown of the player's consistency by the following game scenarios:
   a. Home versus a good defense (Top 10 NFL defensive ranking)
   b. Home versus an average defense (NFL defense rankings 11-22)
   c. Home versus a bad defense (Bottom 10 NFL defensive rankings)
   d. Totals for all home games
   e. Away versus a good defense (Top 10 NFL defensive ranking)
   f. Away versus an average defense (NFL defense rankings 11-22)
   g. Away versus a bad defense (Bottom 10 NFL defensive rankings)
   h. Totals for all away games

These profiles are designed to allow quick access to how consistent a player has been over the past one, two or three seasons. In addition, the game scenarios will assist you when you're making those tough decisions on your weekly lineups. You can focus on how consistent your players have been over the past three seasons in those scenarios and change your lineup accordingly.

These profiles' descriptions will change as we get closer to the August draft dates but the historical information will not change until the season begins. If you want to access this information by inputting your own league's scoring method, you can go to the Tools section on www.BigGuyFantasySports.com on any device and have this information at your fingertips at any time.

CONSISTENCY PROFILES – QUARTERBACKS

BLAKE BORTLES

Bortles looked destined to improve on his consistency in 2016 after a Top 5 season in 2015. He didn't. But, he wasn't as bad as some people may think. He ended 2017 ninth in total points but, only had a 50% Clutch Rate (tied for 13th). Two more Clutch Games and he's in the Top 10 in consistency. He's not a QB1 this year but he's one of the best backup QB's, for sure.

3 YEAR CONSISTENCY HISTORY

		Total FP	RANK	QG	GP	QSR	RANK
Blake Bortles	2016	325.15	9	8	16	50%	T13
	2015	386.40	4	11	16	69%	T5
	2014	214.25	24	4	14	29%	30

CLUTCH GAMES BY WEEK - 2016

Player Name	1	2	3	4	5	6	7	8	9	10	11	12	13	14	15	16	17	Total
Blake Bortles		+		+	B			+	+	+		+				+	+	8

CONSISTENCY VS DEFENSES (2015-2016)

	Good Defenses (Top 10)				Average Defenses				Bad Defenses (Bottom 10)				Total			
	FPG	QG	GP	QSR	FPG	QG	GP	QSR	FPG	QG	GP	QSR	FPG	QG	GP	QSR
Home	19.14	2	6	33%	20.25	2	4	50%	24.68	4	6	67%	21.49	8	16	50%
Away	16.78	1	4	25%	24.94	5	8	63%	25.26	4	4	100%	22.98	10	16	63%

SAM BRADFORD

Bradford is as boring of a Fantasy quarterback as he appears to be in person. Ranked 22nd two years in a row in total points and his consistency is well…. boring. He should remain the starter in Minnesota with Teddy Bridgewater nowhere near ready to play. This is only good news for Kyle Rudolph and his owners. Not even worth a backup spot on your team.

3 YEAR CONSISTENCY HISTORY

		Total FP	RANK	QG	GP	QSR	RANK
Sam Bradford	2016	274.15	22	6	15	40%	T22
	2015	252.15	22	5	14	36%	28
	2014	DNP	DNP	DNP	DNP	DNP	DNP

CLUTCH GAMES BY WEEK – 2016

Player Name	1	2	3	4	5	6	7	8	9	10	11	12	13	14	15	16	17	Total
Sam Bradford		+			+	B				+				+		+	+	6

CONSISTENCY VS DEFENSES (2016)

	Good Defenses (Top 10)				Average Defenses				Bad Defenses (Bottom 10)				Total			
	FPG	QG	GP	QSR	FPG	QG	GP	QSR	FPG	QG	GP	QSR	FPG	QG	GP	QSR
Home	17.13	1	3	33%	20.30	1	3	33%	17.78	1	2	50%	18.48	3	8	38%
Away	20.30	1	1	100%	13.01	0	4	0%	26.98	2	2	100%	18.04	3	7	43%

CONSISTENCY PROFILES – QUARTERBACKS (continued)

TOM BRADY

Tom Brady has to be an alien! He's past 40 now and he's just as good as ever and that was with marginal receivers outside of Julian Edelman. Now, he gets Brandin Cooks for 2017! He's certainly a Top 3 pick at quarterback this year. His consistency has been over 75% for two straight years, so what's not to like?

3 YEAR CONSISTENCY HISTORY

		Total FP	RANK	QG	GP	QSR	RANK
Tom Brady	2016	294.10	20	9	12	75%	T4
	2015	398.80	2	13	16	81%	3
	2014	334.15	10	9	16	56%	11

CLUTCH GAMES BY WEEK - 2016

Player Name	1	2	3	4	5	6	7	8	9	10	11	12	13	14	15	16	17	Total
Tom Brady					+	+	+	+	B		+	+		+		+	+	9

CONSISTENCY VS DEFENSES (2014-2016)

	Good Defenses (Top 10)				Average Defenses				Bad Defenses (Bottom 10)				Total			
	FPG	QG	GP	QSR	FPG	QG	GP	QSR	FPG	QG	GP	QSR	FPG	QG	GP	QSR
Home	22.99	5	8	63%	24.21	6	7	86%	28.01	5	6	83%	24.83	16	21	76%
Away	18.88	3	8	38%	22.83	6	9	67%	24.85	5	6	83%	21.98	14	23	61%

DREW BREES

People will talk about the Big Three of Rodgers, Brady and Luck. However, Brees should always be included with these three. His consistency has floated around the 70% mark for three straight years. He ended last season ranked second in total points. While he lost Brandin Cooks in the off-season, the receiving core is just fine and the Saints added Adrian Peterson. No worries.

3 YEAR CONSISTENCY HISTORY

		Total FP	RANK	QG	GP	QSR	RANK
Drew Brees	2016	407.40	2	11	16	69%	T6
	2015	367.90	6	10	15	67%	8
	2014	375.40	3	12	16	75%	3

CLUTCH GAMES BY WEEK - 2016

Player Name	1	2	3	4	5	6	7	8	9	10	11	12	13	14	15	16	17	Total
Drew Brees	+		+		B	+	+	+	+	+	+	+			+		+	11

CONSISTENCY VS DEFENSES (2014-2016)

	Good Defenses (Top 10)				Average Defenses				Bad Defenses (Bottom 10)				Total			
	FPG	QG	GP	QSR	FPG	QG	GP	QSR	FPG	QG	GP	QSR	FPG	QG	GP	QSR
Home	28.68	6	6	100%	23.85	6	11	55%	30.42	5	7	71%	26.98	17	24	71%
Away	21.85	3	5	60%	22.36	4	7	57%	21.6	7	11	64%	21.88	14	23	61%

For the most current Fantasy Football Consistency information, visit www.BigGuyFantasySports.com

TEDDY BRIDGEWATER.
His 2016 was lost and it's not looking any better for Bridgewater to play, let alone start in 2017. He'll continue to work hard to get back but for now, outside of dynasty leagues, he's not worth drafting for any reason. We wish Teddy the best and hope to see him on the field in 2018.

3 YEAR CONSISTENCY HISTORY

		Total FP	RANK	QG	GP	QSR	RANK
Teddy Bridgewater	2016	DNP	DNP	DNP	DNP	DNP	DNP
	2015	245.75	23	4	16	25%	35
	2014	216.85	22	6	13	46%	20

TIER DRAFT RANK – N/A
NO VALUE: Bridgewater still isn't guaranteed that he can play at all in 2017. Therefore, at this point, he's not worth drafting unless it's a deep dynasty league.

CLUTCH GAMES BY WEEK – 2016

Player Name	1	2	3	4	5	6	7	8	9	10	11	12	13	14	15	16	17	Total
Teddy Bridgewater																		0

CONSISTENCY VS DEFENSES (2014-2016)

	Good Defenses (Top 10)				Average Defenses				Bad Defenses (Bottom 10)				Total			
	FPG	CG	GP	CR	FPG	CG	GP	CR	FPG	CG	GP	CR	FPG	CG	GP	CR
Home	12.43	1	4	25%	21.47	3	6	50%	15.55	2	5	40%	17.08	6	15	40%
Away	18.03	2	4	50%	14.23	2	5	40%	12.62	0	5	0%	14.74	4	14	29%

DEREK CARR
Derek had a very good season going last year until an injury took him down for Week 17 and the playoffs. There were swirling MVP talks at one point for him, but the numbers below don't show that, in my opinion. Even if Carr earns a Clutch Game in Week 17, he's still only at a 63% Clutch Rate. Not bad, but it wouldn't help his 10th place ranking. Don't reach for him in 2017.

3 YEAR CONSISTENCY HISTORY

		Total FP	RANK	QG	GP	QSR	RANK
Derek Carr	2016	309.55	14	9	15	60%	10
	2015	328.15	12	8	16	50%	T18
	2014	244.20	20	4	16	25%	31

TIER DRAFT RANK – QB1 – B
AT VALUE: Carr's current ADP is QB8/pick 74. He moved up this summer and is at a fair value. If you can grab him there, he's right at value.

CLUTCH GAMES BY WEEK - 2016

Player Name	1	2	3	4	5	6	7	8	9	10	11	12	13	14	15	16	17	Total
Derek Carr	+	+		+	+			+		B	+	+	+			+		9

CONSISTENCY VS DEFENSES (2015-2016)

	Good Defenses (Top 10)				Average Defenses				Bad Defenses (Bottom 10)				Total			
	FPG	QG	GP	QSR	FPG	QG	GP	QSR	FPG	QG	GP	QSR	FPG	QG	GP	QSR
Home	18.31	3	7	43%	24.37	5	5	100%	20.85	2	4	50%	20.84	10	16	63%
Away	17.10	1	4	25%	19.15	2	6	33%	24.2	4	5	80%	20.29	7	15	47%

For the most current Fantasy Football Consistency information, visit www.BigGuyFantasySports.com

CONSISTENCY PROFILES – QUARTERBACKS (continued)

KIRK COUSINS

If you read last year's guide, you know Cousins was my undervalued quarterback. I showed you his second half of 2015 and said he was due for a solid season. He even impressed me as he ended the season fifth in total points and sixth in consistency. But, even with that, his ADP is still currently QB11. Huh? So, he's still undervalued...so draft him again in 2017 and smile!

3 YEAR CONSISTENCY HISTORY

		Total FP	RANK	QG	GP	QSR	RANK
Kirk Cousins	2016	367.85	5	11	16	69%	T6
	2015	348.10	9	8	16	50%	T18
	2014	118.50	36	4	6	67%	43

> **TIER DRAFT RANK – QB1 – B**
>
> **UNDERVALUED**: With Cousins' ADP at QB11/pick 86, it's hard to not see great value. Top 6 in consistency and total points last year and he's still playing for a long-term deal in 2018.

CLUTCH GAMES BY WEEK – 2016

Player Name	1	2	3	4	5	6	7	8	9	10	11	12	13	14	15	16	17	Total
Kirk Cousins		+	+	+		+	+	+	B	+	+	+	+			+		11

CONSISTENCY VS DEFENSES (2015-2016)

	Good Defenses (Top 10)				Average Defenses				Bad Defenses (Bottom 10)				Total			
	FPG	QG	GP	QSR	FPG	QG	GP	QSR	FPG	QG	GP	QSR	FPG	QG	GP	QSR
Home	18.68	1	2	50%	22.42	4	8	50%	24.17	5	6	83%	22.61	10	16	63%
Away	16.71	2	6	33%	25.29	6	8	75%	25.83	1	2	50%	22.14	9	16	56%

ANDY DALTON

Dalton improved in total points last year by going from 19th to 12th. However, his consistency went the other way. Going from fourth to 21st with only a 44% Clutch Rate. So, he's a little tougher to judge in 2017. His current ADP of QB17 says he's undervalued as a backup and that's where I would draft him in 2017. He could be your starter if he regains his 2015 numbers.

3 YEAR CONSISTENCY HISTORY

		Total FP	RANK	QG	GP	QSR	RANK
Andy Dalton	2016	316.70	12	7	16	44%	21
	2015	287.60	19	10	13	77%	4
	2014	269.80	18	6	16	38%	23

> **TIER DRAFT RANK – QB2 – A**
>
> **AT VALUE**: Dalton's current ADP is QB17/pick 117. He's lost some consistency due to injuries for him and his receivers. He's a solid backup at this spot.

CLUTCH GAMES BY WEEK – 2016

Player Name	1	2	3	4	5	6	7	8	9	10	11	12	13	14	15	16	17	Total
Andy Dalton	+	+			+	+	+	+	B				+					7

CONSISTENCY VS DEFENSES (2014-2016)

	Good Defenses (Top 10)				Average Defenses				Bad Defenses (Bottom 10)				Total			
	FPG	QG	GP	QSR	FPG	QG	GP	QSR	FPG	QG	GP	QSR	FPG	QG	GP	QSR
Home	19.48	3	7	43%	17.61	4	8	50%	19.74	4	8	50%	18.92	11	23	48%
Away	20.19	3	7	43%	19.06	5	10	50%	21.41	3	5	60%	19.95	11	22	50%

For the most current Fantasy Football Consistency information, visit www.BigGuyFantasySports.com

CONSISTENCY PROFILES – QUARTERBACKS (continued)

JOE FLACCO

There's nothing to see here, especially with his back issues causing to miss 3-6 weeks before the season starts. He may be elite because he won a Super Bowl, but he will NEVER be elite in Fantasy Football. I honestly don't think I would even draft him as a backup. I may desperately pick him up on a bye week if my only other option is a Browns quarterback.

3 YEAR CONSISTENCY HISTORY

		Total FP	RANK	QG	GP	QSR	RANK
Joe Flacco	2016	298.15	19	5	16	31%	T29
	2015	203.85	24	6	10	60%	T12
	2014	314.30	14	8	16	50%	16

TIER DRAFT RANK – QB2 – B

AT VALUE: Flacco's back injury is a cause for concern. I'd stay completely away until he proves he's 100% healthy. Back issues can linger for a long time!

CLUTCH GAMES BY WEEK – 2016

Player Name	1	2	3	4	5	6	7	8	9	10	11	12	13	14	15	16	17	Total
Joe Flacco		+		+				B		+			+	+				5

CONSISTENCY VS DEFENSES (2014-2016)

	Good Defenses (Top 10)				Average Defenses				Bad Defenses (Bottom 10)				Total			
	FPG	QG	GP	QSR	FPG	QG	GP	QSR	FPG	QG	GP	QSR	FPG	QG	GP	QSR
Home	25.33	2	2	100%	19.28	3	9	33%	22.70	6	10	60%	21.48	11	21	52%
Away	14.80	1	5	20%	15.34	2	11	18%	24.48	4	5	80%	17.39	7	21	33%

BRIAN HOYER

Hoyer has been the ultimate journeyman quarterback, jumping from team to team, to replace the starter until someone better comes along to replace him. His next stop in 2017 is San Francisco. He gets Kyle Shanahan as new head coach, but there's no "Julio Jones" receivers around to throw to. He's not worth much of anything this year or next or the next.

3 YEAR CONSISTENCY HISTORY

		Total FP	RANK	QG	GP	QSR	RANK
Brian Hoyer	2016	95.60	32	3	6	50%	16
	2015	203.70	25	4	12	33%	28
	2014	205.15	25	2	14	14%	38

TIER DRAFT RANK – QB3 – C

AT VALUE: With a current ADP of QB27, there isn't much to see here. Maybe some value in a 2 QB league as a backup, but that's about it in 2017.

CLUTCH GAMES BY WEEK – 2016

Player Name	1	2	3	4	5	6	7	8	9	10	11	12	13	14	15	16	17	Total
Brian Hoyer			+	+	+													3

CONSISTENCY VS DEFENSES (2016)

	Good Defenses (Top 10)				Average Defenses				Bad Defenses (Bottom 10)				Total			
	FPG	QG	GP	QSR	FPG	QG	GP	QSR	FPG	QG	GP	QSR	FPG	QG	GP	QSR
Home	15.10	0	1	0%	13.35	1	2	50%	0.00	0	0	0%	13.93	1	3	33%
Away	0.00	0	0	0%	23.55	1	1	100%	15.10	1	2	50%	17.92	2	3	67%

For the most current Fantasy Football Consistency information, visit www.BigGuyFantasySports.com

CONSISTENCY PROFILES – QUARTERBACKS (continued)

ANDREW LUCK

Luck came back with a vengeance in 2016 as he ended the season ranked fourth in total points and third in consistency. HOWEVER, his shoulder surgery certainly scares me, because INSIDE SOURCES say it's MUCH WORSE! He could miss games at the start of the season! I would stay away from Hilton and Moncrief as well!

3 YEAR CONSISTENCY HISTORY

		Total FP	RANK	QG	GP	QSR	RANK
Andrew Luck	2016	369.10	4	12	15	80%	3
	2015	161.65	28	6	7	86%	2
	2014	426.35	1	13	16	81%	1

TIER DRAFT RANK – QB1 – B

AT VALUE: Luck's overall ADP is around QB4/pick 44. With the expectation, that he won't start Week 1, I moved him done in the rankings. As of right now, I'm not drafting him. Neither should you!

CLUTCH GAMES BY WEEK – 2016

Player Name	1	2	3	4	5	6	7	8	9	10	11	12	13	14	15	16	17	Total
Andrew Luck	+			+	+	+	+	+		B	+		+	+	+	+	+	12

CONSISTENCY VS DEFENSES (2014-2016)

	Good Defenses (Top 10)				Average Defenses				Bad Defenses (Bottom 10)				Total			
	FPG	QG	GP	QSR	FPG	QG	GP	QSR	FPG	QG	GP	QSR	FPG	QG	GP	QSR
Home	23.89	6	7	86%	24.74	4	6	67%	28.34	6	6	100%	25.56	16	19	84%
Away	22.78	4	6	67%	28.49	6	7	86%	22.55	3	6	50%	24.81	13	19	68%

ELI MANNING

Eli had one of his worst Fantasy seasons in recent history. He barely earned backup quarterback numbers in 2016. His consistency was a horrid 31% and was tied for 29th place! The Giants added Brandon Marshall so there's some hope. However, if the Giants running game doesn't help Manning's cause, his offensive line may not keep him upright long enough to throw.

3 YEAR CONSISTENCY HISTORY

		Total FP	RANK	QG	GP	QSR	RANK
Eli Manning	2016	288.45	21	5	16	31%	T29
	2015	353.90	7	10	16	63%	10
	2014	335.60	8	9	16	56%	10

TIER DRAFT RANK – QB2 – A

AT VALUE: Manning's current ADP is QB16/ pick 114. That used to make him undervalued, but not anymore. Yes, he has the weapons, but he's just too risky for me in 2017.

CLUTCH GAMES BY WEEK – 2016

Player Name	1	2	3	4	5	6	7	8	9	10	11	12	13	14	15	16	17	Total
Eli Manning	+					+		B	+	+		+						5

CONSISTENCY VS DEFENSES (2014-2016)

	Good Defenses (Top 10)				Average Defenses				Bad Defenses (Bottom 10)				Total			
	FPG	QG	GP	QSR	FPG	QG	GP	QSR	FPG	QG	GP	QSR	FPG	QG	GP	QSR
Home	23.18	3	5	60%	19.95	6	10	60%	23.47	6	9	67%	21.94	15	24	63%
Away	12.33	0	5	0%	19.35	3	7	43%	21.18	6	12	50%	18.80	9	24	38%

For the most current Fantasy Football Consistency information, visit www.BigGuyFantasySports.com

CONSISTENCY PROFILES – QUARTERBACKS (continued)

MARCUS MARIOTA

Mariota is certainly showing improvement each year in his total points and more importantly, his consistency. He missed one game and ended the year 13th in total points and ranked eighth in consistency with a 67% Clutch Rate. One more Clutch Game and he's tied with Drew Brees in consistency. His current ADP is QB10 in round 7. This is very good value! Grab him!

3 YEAR CONSISTENCY HISTORY

		Total FP	RANK	QG	GP	QSR	RANK
Marcus Mariota	2016	314.00	13	10	15	67%	8
	2015	193.15	26	6	10	60%	T12
	2014	DNP	DNP	DNP	DNP	DNP	DNP

TIER DRAFT RANK – QB1 – B

UNDERVALUED: Mariota proved that he should upgraded to a QB1 in 2017 and that's where I have him. His current ADP is QB10, He's ranked 7th on the Tier Draft list. Great value!

CLUTCH GAMES BY WEEK – 2016

Player Name	1	2	3	4	5	6	7	8	9	10	11	12	13	14	15	16	17	Total
Marcus Mariota	+	+			+	+	+	+	+	+	+	+	B					10

CONSISTENCY VS DEFENSES (2015-2016)

	Good Defenses (Top 10)				Average Defenses				Bad Defenses (Bottom 10)				Total			
	FPG	QG	GP	QSR	FPG	QG	GP	QSR	FPG	QG	GP	QSR	FPG	QG	GP	QSR
Home	15.98	2	4	50%	13.05	0	1	0%	21.99	5	7	71%	19.24	7	12	58%
Away	11.51	1	4	25%	26.00	4	4	100%	25.24	4	5	80%	21.25	9	13	69%

CAM NEWTON

Newton went from MVP to C.R.A.P.! Let's be honest, Newton at his best in 2015 still only earned a 69% Clutch Rate, so why is he at an ADP of QB7 in Round 5? There's no way I'm drafting him that high in 2017, 2018 or ever! Let someone else remember the MVP season and draft him in Round 5! So, you can just pass him on by and dab in his honor!

3 YEAR CONSISTENCY HISTORY

		Total FP	RANK	QG	GP	QSR	RANK
Cam Newton	2016	303.35	17	6	15	40%	T22
	2015	445.45	1	11	16	69%	T5
	2014	300.25	17	8	14	57%	8

TIER DRAFT RANK – QB1 – B

OVERVALUED: Newton's current ADP is QB7/pick 72 overall. Too rich for my blood! With McCaffery added to the backfield, Newton will run less and that's a bad thing for fantasy.

CLUTCH GAMES BY WEEK – 2016

Player Name	1	2	3	4	5	6	7	8	9	10	11	12	13	14	15	16	17	Total
Cam Newton	+	+				+	B			+		+			+			6

CONSISTENCY VS DEFENSES (2014-2016)

	Good Defenses (Top 10)				Average Defenses				Bad Defenses (Bottom 10)				Total			
	FPG	QG	GP	QSR	FPG	QG	GP	QSR	FPG	QG	GP	QSR	FPG	QG	GP	QSR
Home	18.77	2	5	40%	25.92	4	6	67%	24.00	7	11	64%	23.33	13	22	59%
Away	18.85	2	5	40%	21.81	2	7	29%	26.25	8	11	73%	23.29	12	23	52%

For the most current Fantasy Football Consistency information, visit www.BigGuyFantasySports.com

CONSISTENCY PROFILES – QUARTERBACKS (continued)

CARSON PALMER

I told my readers in 2015 to take Palmer and they were rewarded. I said last year to stay away and hopefully you did. In 2017, Palmer is still a question mark. The Cardinals have a great running back in David Johnson and a solid defense. So, the days of Palmer throwing more is over. He's a solid backup at best, but I wouldn't draft him as a QB1 in 2017.

3 YEAR CONSISTENCY HISTORY

		Total FP	RANK	QG	GP	QSR	RANK
Carson Palmer	2016	305.65	16	8	15	53%	12
	2015	370.95	5	14	16	88%	1
	2014	124.80	31	5	6	83%	-

TIER DRAFT RANK – QB2 – A

UNDERVALUED: Palmer's current ADP is QB21/pick 138. That's good value for a backup pick. He has the weapons around him. If he stays healthy, he can be a solid backup in 2017

CLUTCH GAMES BY WEEK – 2016

Player Name	1	2	3	4	5	6	7	8	9	10	11	12	13	14	15	16	17	Total
Carson Palmer	+	+						+	B	+		+	+		+		+	8

CONSISTENCY VS DEFENSES (2014-2016)

	Good Defenses (Top 10)				Average Defenses				Bad Defenses (Bottom 10)				Total			
	FPG	QG	GP	QSR	FPG	QG	GP	QSR	FPG	QG	GP	QSR	FPG	QG	GP	QSR
Home	20.86	4	7	57%	17.68	2	5	40%	24.58	8	8	100%	21.56	14	20	70%
Away	21.95	2	4	50%	22.04	4	6	67%	21.46	4	7	57%	21.78	10	17	59%

DAK PRESCOTT

There have been very few rookie QB's who earned over a 60% Clutch Rate in their rookie season, let alone 75%! However, the unlikely rookie, Dak Prescott, did just that in 2016! Now Dak heads into his sophomore season. Can he stay this consistent? History tells us yes. Of the three quarterbacks, only RGIII did not earn over 60% the next year. Current ADP is QB13. Perfect!

3 YEAR CONSISTENCY HISTORY

		Total FP	RANK	QG	GP	QSR	RANK
Dak Prescott	2016	335.55	6	12	16	75%	T4
	2015	DNP	DNP	DNP	DNP	DNP	DNP
	2014	DNP	DNP	DNP	DNP	DNP	DNP

TIER DRAFT RANK – QB1 – B

UNDERVALUED: I don't see Prescott being Top 5 in 2017 and neither does anyone else. His current ADP is QB13/pick 97. That's well below the Tier Draft list at QB9 with a QB1-B rating.

CLUTCH GAMES BY WEEK – 2016

Player Name	1	2	3	4	5	6	7	8	9	10	11	12	13	14	15	16	17	Total
Dak Prescott		+	+	+	+	+	B	+	+	+	+	+			+	+		12

CONSISTENCY VS DEFENSES (2016)

	Good Defenses (Top 10)				Average Defenses				Bad Defenses (Bottom 10)				Total			
	FPG	QG	GP	QSR	FPG	QG	GP	QSR	FPG	QG	GP	QSR	FPG	QG	GP	QSR
Home	20.60	1	2	50%	26.25	4	4	100%	22.80	2	2	100%	23.98	7	8	88%
Away	12.50	0	2	0%	13.35	1	2	50%	23.01	4	4	100%	17.97	5	8	63%

For the most current Fantasy Football Consistency information, visit www.BigGuyFantasySports.com

PHILIP RIVERS

Philip Rivers is very consistent and when I say consistent, I mean consistently AVERAGE! Three straight seasons of exactly 50% Clutch Rate and all three seasons, he's been ranked in the Top 12 of total points. So, many Fantasy owners will see that and his new wide receiver Mike Williams and believe he's a QB1. He's not. He's a solid backup, if you need one.

3 YEAR CONSISTENCY HISTORY

		Total FP	RANK	QG	GP	QSR	RANK
Philip Rivers	2016	334.00	8	8	16	50%	T13
	2015	345.50	11	8	16	50%	T17
	2014	330.70	11	8	16	50%	T16

TIER DRAFT RANK – QB2 – A

AT VALUE: River's current ADP is QB14/pick 100. That's solid value! However, I still wouldn't take him any earlier than that as a backup for your Fantasy teams. 50% Clutch Rating is the norm.

CLUTCH GAMES BY WEEK – 2016

Player Name	1	2	3	4	5	6	7	8	9	10	11	12	13	14	15	16	17	Total
Philip Rivers		+		+	+		+		+	+	B	+				+		8

CONSISTENCY VS DEFENSES (2014-2016)

	Good Defenses (Top 10)				Average Defenses				Bad Defenses (Bottom 10)				Total			
	FPG	QG	GP	QSR	FPG	QG	GP	QSR	FPG	QG	GP	QSR	FPG	QG	GP	QSR
Home	17.41	3	9	33%	21.63	3	5	60%	22.98	6	10	60%	20.61	12	24	50%
Away	20.87	5	11	45%	19.42	2	5	40%	22.42	4	7	57%	21.03	11	23	48%

AARON RODGERS

Please disregard the 2015 numbers. Injuries to Jordy Nelson and poor play from Randall Cobb hurt Rodgers greatly that year. The 2016 and 2014 numbers are more in line with a normal Rodgers' type year. He's the #1 QB in 2017. The question is: When is too early to draft him? I believe anywhere before Round 4 is too early. Would rather grab him in the 5th…we'll see!

3 YEAR CONSISTENCY HISTORY

		Total FP	RANK	QG	GP	QSR	RANK
Aaron Rodgers	2016	435.30	1	14	16	88%	1
	2015	347.45	10	9	16	56%	16
	2014	404.95	2	13	16	81%	1

TIER DRAFT RANK – QB1 – A

AT VALUE: It's not a bad thing to get Rodgers at value. If you don't want to have to worry about your QB, he's the man! I would be happier if I could draft him in Round 5 though.

CLUTCH GAMES BY WEEK – 2016

Player Name	1	2	3	4	5	6	7	8	9	10	11	12	13	14	15	16	17	Total
Aaron Rodgers	+	+	+	B	+		+	+	+	+	+	+	+	+		+	+	14

CONSISTENCY VS DEFENSES (2014-2016)

	Good Defenses (Top 10)				Average Defenses				Bad Defenses (Bottom 10)				Total			
	FPG	QG	GP	QSR	FPG	QG	GP	QSR	FPG	QG	GP	QSR	FPG	QG	GP	QSR
Home	27.20	9	10	90%	23.10	7	9	78%	31.09	5	5	100%	26.47	21	24	88%
Away	17.43	3	9	33%	26.74	7	8	88%	25.94	5	7	71%	23.01	15	24	63%

CONSISTENCY PROFILES – QUARTERBACKS (continued)

BEN ROETHLISBERGER

There's no questioning Big Ben's talent. It's his health that has been the problem the past two seasons. His consistency is Top 10 every year in the games that he's played. However, the health history tells me to pass him by in most drafts. His current ADP is QB12. I doubt that I'll draft Ben that high in 2017. But that's a fair value for him.

3 YEAR CONSISTENCY HISTORY

		Total FP	RANK	QG	GP	QSR	RANK
Ben Roethlisberger	2016	301.35	18	9	14	64%	9
	2015	267.55	21	8	12	67%	T8
	2014	369.30	5	9	16	56%	9

> **TIER DRAFT RANK – QB1 – B**
>
> **AT VALUE:** Right now, Ben's ADP is just right! It's sitting at QB12/pick 87! If he can stay healthy, he's worth a pick in Round 8. But that's a BIG IF for Big Ben!

CLUTCH GAMES BY WEEK – 2016

Player Name	1	2	3	4	5	6	7	8	9	10	11	12	13	14	15	16	17	Total
Ben Roethlisberger	+	+		+	+			B	+	+		+	+			+		9

CONSISTENCY VS DEFENSES (2014-2016)

	Good Defenses (Top 10)				Average Defenses				Bad Defenses (Bottom 10)				Total			
	FPG	QG	GP	QSR	FPG	QG	GP	QSR	FPG	QG	GP	QSR	FPG	QG	GP	QSR
Home	23.97	4	6	67%	29.80	7	7	100%	30.12	7	7	100%	28.16	18	20	90%
Away	18.73	3	6	50%	14.74	1	8	13%	18.09	3	8	38%	17.04	7	22	32%

MATT RYAN

In the past, when Ryan constantly threw to Julio Jones all of the time, Ryan's consistency was terrible (see 2014 and 2015). However, when he focuses on spreading the ball around, his team and his consistency is much better! Julio was only 64% in 2016 and yet, Ryan ranked second with a Clutch Rate of 81%! Which Ryan will show up in 2017? Tough call…I'm cautious!

3 YEAR CONSISTENCY HISTORY

		Total FP	RANK	QG	GP	QSR	RANK
Matt Ryan	2016	403.90	3	13	16	81%	2
	2015	303.85	18	7	16	44%	T25
	2014	347.20	7	8	16	50%	13

> **TIER DRAFT RANK – QB1 – B**
>
> **AT VALUE:** Ryan finally found consistency last season. Kyle Shanahan is gone. Can Ryan stay consistent? I say yes. He's ranked QB5, but don't draft him sooner than Round 6 or 7.

CLUTCH GAMES BY WEEK – 2016

Player Name	1	2	3	4	5	6	7	8	9	10	11	12	13	14	15	16	17	Total
Matt Ryan	+	+	+	+		+		+	+		B	+	+	+	+	+	+	13

CONSISTENCY VS DEFENSES (2014-2016)

	Good Defenses (Top 10)				Average Defenses				Bad Defenses (Bottom 10)				Total			
	FPG	QG	GP	QSR	FPG	QG	GP	QSR	FPG	QG	GP	QSR	FPG	QG	GP	QSR
Home	18.09	1	5	20%	24.22	5	7	71%	24.06	10	12	83%	22.86	16	24	67%
Away	19.13	2	5	40%	20.94	4	9	44%	22.22	6	10	60%	21.10	12	24	50%

For the most current Fantasy Football Consistency information, visit www.BigGuyFantasySports.com

ALEX SMITH

The Chiefs didn't draft Patrick Mahomes because Alex Smith needs a ball boy! This may be his last year in Kansas City. He's a decent NFL quarterback, just not a good Fantasy quarterback. He'll have a good game or two, but then disappear for five or six games and repeat. He's not worth drafting unless it's a 2-QB league.

3 YEAR CONSISTENCY HISTORY

		Total FP	RANK	QG	GP	QSR	RANK
Alex Smith	2016	270.50	23	5	15	33%	T26
	2015	309.10	16	7	16	44%	T25
	2014	265.65	19	5	15	33%	24

TIER DRAFT RANK – QB3 – C

AT VALUE: Not sure why Smith's current ADP is QB25/pick 170. But I'm not going to draft him anyways. He could be replaced mid-season. I'll pass.

CLUTCH GAMES BY WEEK – 2016

Player Name	1	2	3	4	5	6	7	8	9	10	11	12	13	14	15	16	17	Total
Alex Smith	+			+	B						+					+	+	5

CONSISTENCY VS DEFENSES (2014-2016)

	Good Defenses (Top 10)				Average Defenses				Bad Defenses (Bottom 10)				Total			
	FPG	QG	GP	QSR	FPG	QG	GP	QSR	FPG	QG	GP	QSR	FPG	QG	GP	QSR
Home	16.43	2	6	33%	20.21	3	8	38%	19.16	2	8	25%	18.80	7	22	32%
Away	17.74	2	10	20%	19.29	5	8	63%	16.68	2	6	33%	17.99	9	24	38%

MATTHEW STAFFORD

The Clutch Rating speaks for itself. 50%, 56% and 50% over the past three years. His total points have been in the Top 8 for the past two years but his consistency is always outside of the Top 12. Nothing much has changed in Detroit, so it's fairly easy to predict that Stafford will be worth just about the same as the past. A solid backup for a 12-team league.

3 YEAR CONSISTENCY HISTORY

		Total FP	RANK	QG	GP	QSR	RANK
Matthew Stafford	2016	335.05	7	8	16	50%	T13
	2015	350.00	8	9	16	56%	16
	2014	309.65	15	8	16	50%	17

TIER DRAFT RANK – QB2 – A

AT VALUE: His ADP is QB15/pick 102, which lines up with the Tier Draft list ranking of QB13. So, he's right at value as a top backup pick in the 10-12th rounds. Don't expect much more.

CLUTCH GAMES BY WEEK – 2016

Player Name	1	2	3	4	5	6	7	8	9	10	11	12	13	14	15	16	17	Total
Matthew Stafford	+		+		+	+	+			B			+	+			+	8

CONSISTENCY VS DEFENSES (2014-2016)

	Good Defenses (Top 10)				Average Defenses				Bad Defenses (Bottom 10)				Total			
	FPG	QG	GP	QSR	FPG	QG	GP	QSR	FPG	QG	GP	QSR	FPG	QG	GP	QSR
Home	18.02	2	7	29%	20.79	5	8	63%	26.42	9	9	100%	22.09	16	24	67%
Away	17.27	2	8	25%	17.88	2	9	22%	23.63	5	7	71%	19.35	9	24	38%

RYAN TANNEHILL

The only consistency Tannehill has going for him is making Jarvis Landry a consistent receiver and his hot wife! And it ends right there! Every year, there have been expectations for him to continue to improve and every year, he doesn't. Two straight years of Clutch Rating's under 40% is pitiful with the weapons he has. He's a good #2 QB in a 2-QB league, but that's about it.

3 YEAR CONSISTENCY HISTORY

		Total FP	RANK	QG	GP	QSR	RANK
Ryan Tannehill	2016	244.75	25	5	13	38%	25
	2015	314.60	14	5	16	31%	32
	2014	335.30	9	8	16	50%	14

TIER DRAFT RANK – QB2 – B

AT VALUE: His current ADP is QB22/ pick 142. He's at value, because he's barely a backup quarterback at this point in his career. He won't be on my teams in 2017.

CLUTCH GAMES BY WEEK – 2016

Player Name	1	2	3	4	5	6	7	8	9	10	11	12	13	14	15	16	17	Total
Ryan Tannehill		+	+					B		+		+		+				5

CONSISTENCY VS DEFENSES (2014-2016)

	Good Defenses (Top 10)				Average Defenses				Bad Defenses (Bottom 10)				Total			
	FPG	QG	GP	QSR	FPG	QG	GP	QSR	FPG	QG	GP	QSR	FPG	QG	GP	QSR
Home	21.31	5	10	50%	16.90	2	9	22%	25.19	2	4	50%	20.26	9	23	39%
Away	19.10	4	11	36%	17.63	2	4	50%	21.16	3	7	43%	19.49	9	22	41%

TYROD TAYLOR

There was a time when I believed this kid had a future as a solid Fantasy quarterback and other times, when I scratched my head. The Buffalo Bills felt the same way in the off-season. One minute, he's gone and the next minute they sign him. Anyways, Taylor, at this point, is a late backup quarterback. He's not terrible, if you need one.

3 YEAR CONSISTENCY HISTORY

		Total FP	RANK	QG	GP	QSR	RANK
Tyrod Taylor	2016	307.15	15	7	15	47%	18
	2015	306.55	17	8	14	57%	15
	2014	0.30	76	0	1	0%	76

TIER DRAFT RANK – QB2 – A

AT VALUE: Taylor's ADP is QB18/pick 12. This is close to where I have him as well. So, in my opinion he is currently at value. Draft as your backup, if you want. I would if he's there.

CLUTCH GAMES BY WEEK – 2016

Player Name	1	2	3	4	5	6	7	8	9	10	11	12	13	14	15	16	17	Total
Tyrod Taylor		+				+	+	+	+	B		+				+		7

CONSISTENCY VS DEFENSES (2015-2016)

	Good Defenses (Top 10)				Average Defenses				Bad Defenses (Bottom 10)				Total			
	FPG	QG	GP	QSR	FPG	QG	GP	QSR	FPG	QG	GP	QSR	FPG	QG	GP	QSR
Home	23.93	4	6	67%	20.53	1	3	33%	21.55	3	6	50%	22.3	8	15	52%
Away	18.07	2	7	29%	17.13	1	2	50%	23.70	4	5	80%	19.95	7	14	50%

For the most current Fantasy Football Consistency information, visit www.BigGuyFantasySports.com

CONSISTENCY PROFILES – QUARTERBACKS (continued)

CARSON WENTZ

Wentz didn't have as bad as a rookie season as Jared Goff, but it wasn't great either. He has been given more weapons at receiver and running back to take some pressure off him. I would expect improvement in his consistency in 2017, but he's still a late backup pick in most Fantasy drafts. If you're in a dynasty league, he's worth much more.

3 YEAR CONSISTENCY HISTORY

		Total FP	RANK	QG	GP	QSR	RANK
Carson Wentz	2016	266.10	24	5	16	31%	T29
	2015	DNP	DNP	DNP	DNP	DNP	DNP
	2014	DNP	DNP	DNP	DNP	DNP	DNP

TIER DRAFT RANK – QB2 – A

AT VALUE: Wentz's ADP is QB19/pick 124. It matches close to the Tier Draft list rankings, but it's still not great. He's a decent backup pick at best.

CLUTCH GAMES BY WEEK – 2016

Player Name	1	2	3	4	5	6	7	8	9	10	11	12	13	14	15	16	17	Total
Carson Wentz	+		+	B	+							+					+	5

CONSISTENCY VS DEFENSES (2016)

	Good Defenses (Top 10)				Average Defenses				Bad Defenses (Bottom 10)				Total			
	FPG	QG	GP	QSR	FPG	QG	GP	QSR	FPG	QG	GP	QSR	FPG	QG	GP	QSR
Home	11.40	0	2	0%	22.80	2	2	100%	18.69	2	4	50%	17.89	4	8	50%
Away	15.73	0	3	0%	16.65	1	4	25%	9.15	0	1	0%	15.37	1	8	13%

RUSSELL WILSON

For the second straight year, Wilson has a season of two different halves. First half = Two of eight in Clutch Games. Second half = five for eight! It was still way below expectations though. He ends the season 10th in total points BUT tied for 19th in consistency. He's ranked QB7 currently and that's way too high for me at this point. Don't draft him this high.

3 YEAR CONSISTENCY HISTORY

		Total FP	RANK	QG	GP	QSR	RANK
Russell Wilson	2016	324.35	10	7	16	44%	T19
	2015	390.60	3	11	16	69%	T5
	2014	367.65	6	11	16	69%	6

TIER DRAFT RANK – QB1 – B

OVERVALUED: Wilson's ADP is QB6/pick 58. Tier Draft list has him at QB10 and that may be too high after last season. The OL is still pretty bad and will continue to cause problems. Stay away.

CLUTCH GAMES BY WEEK – 2016

Player Name	1	2	3	4	5	6	7	8	9	10	11	12	13	14	15	16	17	Total
Russell Wilson				+	B				+	+	+		+		+	+		7

CONSISTENCY VS DEFENSES (2014-2016)

	Good Defenses (Top 10)				Average Defenses				Bad Defenses (Bottom 10)				Total			
	FPG	QG	GP	QSR	FPG	QG	GP	QSR	FPG	QG	GP	QSR	FPG	QG	GP	QSR
Home	23.38	4	6	67%	23.57	8	10	80%	19.13	3	8	38%	22.04	15	24	63%
Away	21.56	5	9	56%	27.38	5	8	63%	20.06	2	7	29%	23.06	12	24	50%

JAMEIS WINSTON

Unlike Marcus Mariota, Winston did not improve on his consistency from his rookie season. Winston will have more weapons in 2017, but will that necessarily make him consistent? Doubtful. His current ADP is way too high for me at QB8. He's ranked ahead of Carr, Prescott and Cousins! Oh yeah, he's ranked ahead of Mariota as well. Please don't draft Winston as your QB1.

3 YEAR CONSISTENCY HISTORY

		Total FP	RANK	QG	GP	QSR	RANK
Jameis Winston	2016	321.30	11	7	16	44%	T19
	2015	317.15	13	9	15	60%	T12
	2014	DNP	DNP	DNP	DNP	DNP	DNP

TIER DRAFT RANK – QB2 – A

OVERVALUED: Winston's ADP is QB9/pick 77. Ooff! Someone is basing their rankings off his total points ranking, I guess. Based on consistency, he's way overvalued! Not worth it at all!

CLUTCH GAMES BY WEEK – 2016

Player Name	1	2	3	4	5	6	7	8	9	10	11	12	13	14	15	16	17	Total
Jameis Winston	+		+			B	+		+	+	+					+		7

CONSISTENCY VS DEFENSES (2015-2016)

	Good Defenses (Top 10)				Average Defenses				Bad Defenses (Bottom 10)				Total			
	FPG	QG	GP	QSR	FPG	QG	GP	QSR	FPG	QG	GP	QSR	FPG	QG	GP	QSR
Home	21.54	1	4	25%	19.65	3	6	50%	18.44	2	5	40%	19.75	6	15	40%
Away	16.92	1	3	33%	19.50	2	5	40%	24.24	7	8	88%	21.39	10	16	63%

RUNNING BACKS

Each major position (QB, RB, WR and TE) tracked for consistency purposes will have the following sections: Year in Review; Consistently Clutch and the Consistency Profiles. The Year in Review is exactly that, a review of the top four tiers on Fantasy consistency at each position. The Consistently Clutch article will highlight how consistent the top Fantasy players have been for the past three seasons. Finally, the Consistency Profiles will provide you with a profile of each player's consistency for each of the top returning Fantasy players.

The running back position in Fantasy football has really changed over the years. The Running Back by Committee (RBBC) scenario for most teams over the last 15 seasons has greatly decreased the overall Fantasy points by many individual players. However, this couldn't be more prevalent in the top Fantasy players. For example, in 2002, there were eight Fantasy running backs that exceeded 300 points in a PPR scoring system and one player who exceeded 400 Fantasy points (Priest Holmes). In 2003, there were five backs over 300 points and two over 400 points (Priest Holmes and LaDainian Tomlinson).

The running back position had lost its stranglehold on the Fantasy owners over the years. The draft theory of grabbing two running backs in the first two rounds is still dead, but the ZERO RB theory is also dead! As I have mentioned over the past couple of years, you can see the trends below regarding the decline of the super-stud backs (scoring based on PPR).

2002 – 2008 – Number of RB's over 300 points in one season = 31 running backs
2002 – 2008 – Number of RB's over 400 points in one season = 5 running backs

2015 – 2009 – Number of RB's over 300 points in one season = 20 running backs
2015 – 2009 – Number of RB's over 400 points in one season = ZERO running backs

But, rejoice, 2016 was slightly better with our first running back (David Johnson) over 400 points since 2006 when Ladainian Tomlinson and Steven Jackson both did it! There were two running backs over 300 points with Ezekiel Elliott and LeVeon Bell. Bell earned over 300 points in only 12 games, so 400 points for Bell in a season isn't out of the question.

So, as we head into 2017, the No RB approach has died before it really had life. Not that I believed in it anyways. The top three picks once again in Fantasy draft are running backs. Finding quality consistent backs after that can be troublesome. This is where the Clutch Games and consistency play a key role in identifying the consistently excellent backs that can help you win a championship versus the very good, yet inconsistent, backs that will cause you headaches.

This is where the Clutch Games and consistency play a key role in identifying the consistently excellent backs that can help you win a championship versus the very good, yet inconsistent, backs that will cause you headaches.

As you continue to read the articles and the Consistency Profiles for the running backs, allow yourself to make your own decisions. Remember the Clutch Games is a tool to help you when you're preparing for your Fantasy draft or with your lineup decisions. Having an arsenal of tools will win you championships. I can provide you with those tools. If you have any questions, please don't hesitate to email me at bob@bigguyfantasysports.com or hit me up on Twitter @bob_lung.

2017 PREVIEW – RUNNING BACKS

Let's look at those running backs ranked in their projected Tier for 2017 and show you their 2016 total points and consistency and where they ranked in those categories in 2016. So, let's start with the top tier of running backs.

TIER ONE

Player Name	Total Points	Pts Rank	Total CG	Total GP	CR %	2016 Rank	2017 Tier	2017 Rank
David Johnson	411.80	1	15	16	94%	2	RB1A	1
LeVeon Bell	317.40	3	12	12	100%	1	RB1A	2
Ezekiel Elliott	327.40	2	14	15	93%	3	RB1A	3
Melvin Gordon	254.60	7	11	13	85%	6	RB1A	4
LeSean McCoy	297.30	4	13	15	87%	5	RB1A	5

This Tier consists of running backs that can obtain an Expected Clutch Rate (ECR) of 80+% in 2017. All five of them accomplished this in 2016 and should be capable of doing it again. David Johnson and LeVeon Bell are locks for the #1 and #2 overall in most Fantasy drafts this year. Ezekiel Elliott concerns me a little bit as the Cowboys lost two offensive lineman in the offseason. I believe he'll hit the 80% ECR, I just believe he'll slip a bit. Melvin Gordon and LeSean McCoy should be late first round picks after the WR1A wide receivers come off the board. In summary, if you can get any of these backs in the first round, you are off to a good start.

TIER TWO

Player Name	Total Points	Pts Rank	Total CG	Total GP	CR %	2016 Rank	2017 Tier	2017 Rank
DeMarco Murray	295.90	5	14	16	88%	4	RB1B	6
Devonta Freeman	286.10	6	11	16	69%	8	RB1B	7
Jordan Howard	232.10	10	11	15	73%	7	RB1B	8
Todd Gurley	200.20	15	11	16	69%	10	RB1B	9
Lamar Miller	193.10	19	9	14	64%	12	RB1B	10
Jay Ajayi	217.30	11	7	15	47%	28	RB1B	11
Frank Gore	216.30	12	11	16	69%	9	RB1B	12

These running backs in this Tier (RB1B) have an ECR of 67-80% in 2017. As you will note above, most of them earned this Clutch Rate in 2016. DeMarco Murray earned an 88% Clutch Rate last season, but I have a difficult time putting Murray in the RB1A range as long as Derrick Henry is healthy. Murray's current ADP is RB10/pick 23. I believe he should be ranked higher than that as evident by his ranking of RB6 above.

The one back that scares me the most is Jay Ajayi. He ended the year ranked 11th in total points last season, but his HORRID Clutch Rate of 47% screams "Stay Away"! There's no reason to believe that's going to change. Same offense, same head coach, etc. says he's not consistent enough to be picked as a RB1. In fact, I would pick Frank Gore ahead of Ajayi, if he wasn't so damn old! My thought is if you get to a draft day decision between Ajayi and a consistent wide receiver, take the receiver.

2017 PREVIEW – RUNNING BACKS (continued)

TIER THREE

Player Name	Total Points	Pts Rank	Total CG	Total GP	CR %	2016 Rank	2017 Tier	2017 Rank
Tevin Coleman	191.10	20	8	13	62%	16	RB2A	13
Isaiah Crowell	209.10	14	9	16	56%	19	RB2A	14
C.J. Anderson	102.50	45	4	7	57%	18	RB2A	15

This is a small section of RB2's, who are above the rest and have the ability to earn between an ECR of 60-67% this year. Tevin Coleman on most other teams is an RB1, but with Devonta Freeman in the way, Coleman maintains a solid RB2 status. His 62% Clutch Rate last year is amazing considering sharing time with Freeman. Isaiah Crowell is a forgotten man in Fantasy because he plays for the Browns. However, a new and improved offensive line could improve his solid Clutch Rate of 56% in 2017. If he earns just one or two more Clutch Games, he's in the RB1B Tier. C.J. Anderson is on the fence with me. He has the ability to up his game but he needs to stay healthy and keep Jamaal Charles from cutting into his carries.

TIER FOUR

Player Name	Total Points	Pts Rank	Total CG	Total GP	CR %	2016 Rank	2017 Tier	2017 Rank
Spencer Ware	199.90	16	7	14	50%	22	RB2B	16
Mark Ingram	242.20	8	8	16	50%	21	RB2B	17
Danny Woodhead	27.10	94	1	2	50%	25	RB2B	20
Theo Riddick	161.80	25	6	10	60%	17	RB2B	21
Mike Gillislee	125.60	38	5	15	33%	45	RB2B	22
Latavius Murray	210.20	13	9	14	64%	11	RB2B	23
Carlos Hyde	196.10	18	8	13	62%	15	RB2B	24

This section has some running backs, who prior to 2016 had some very consistent seasons. Mark Ingram and Danny Woodhead were once in the RB1 Tiers. Ingram would have been there again, except the Saints signed Adrian Peterson in the offseason. Woodhead is now in Baltimore and with Kenneth Dixon being a head-case, could be a very consistent PPR back for the Ravens. His current ADP is RB37, so there's a ton of value to be had. Mike Gillislee in New England this year also provides a ton of value. His current ADP is RB34 and is certainly worth a look come draft time. Latavius Murray and Carlos Hyde have both earned over 60% last season, but their situations on their respective teams is shaky at best.

Well, there are your Expected Clutch Rate rankings for the running backs in 2017 with some 2016 data to support their cause. If you didn't make the playoffs and you had Mark Ingram or Matt Forte on your team and can't understand why, I hope this helped clear things up.

CONSISTENTLY CLUTCH – RUNNING BACKS

The running backs are much like the Consistently Clutch quarterbacks, there are fewer elite Fantasy players when it comes to consistency. Many Fantasy owners may be surprised to see DeMarco Murray as the #1 Consistently Clutch running back, but even more surprised to see there are FIVE Clutch Games separating him from second place!

It's one thing to be clutch during one season in Fantasy Football. However, it's those players who are consistently clutch that make up the real Fantasy studs. These players are the ones that should be drafted in the early rounds of most drafts. A consistently clutch player has normally remained consistently healthy as well, which is just as important as their consistent performance.

The Top 26 most consistent running backs and the number of Clutch Games earned each year are listed below. They are divided into four tiers with a three-year and two-year totals and associated rank. I'll analyze each tier and provide some insight on the players within that tier.

Tier One – The Elite (Ranks 1 - 3)

Player Name	2014	2015	2016	Total	3 yr rank	2 yr total	2 yr rank
DeMarco Murray	16	9	14	39	1	23	2
LeSean McCoy	11	10	13	34	2	23	3
LeVeon Bell	16	4	12	32	3	16	11

Before anyone has a fit about the Tier One not having David Johnson it, please remember this is a three-year total and Johnson has only played for two years. If you note below in Tier Two, you will see Johnson is ranked #1 over two years. Looking at Tier One, you will see three very different Fantasy backs at different points in their careers.

DeMarco Murray went from elite to average to elite in three seasons and yet, he's still #1 by five Clutch Games. He's 29 years old, heading into his seventh season with 84 games played with only one missed game in the past three seasons. LeSean McCoy is FIVE MONTHS YOUNGER than Murray, however, he's entering his ninth season with 117 games played and has missed four games the past three years. Are you surprised McCoy is younger? I know I was. If I had to pick between the two, I'm picking Murray. The question will be their respective ADP's heading into 2017. If McCoy is a round or two later, he may be a better value but I'm assuming he won't be.

LeVeon Bell is the youngest of the three, but he missed most of 2015 due to an injury. If he played all 16 games, he would be ranked #1 easily. His suspension hurt him last season as well. However, when he's on the field, he's one of the few running backs who's a lock for a Clutch Game in a PPR format every week. He and Murray are the only two running backs to ever have a "Perfect Season" for consistency (both in 2014). Bell is still my choice for the #1 overall pick in 2017.

CONSISTENTLY CLUTCH – RUNNING BACKS (continued)

Tier Two – The Above Average (Ranks 4 – 10)

Player Name	2014	2015	2016	Total	3 yr rank	2 yr total	2 yr rank
Matt Forte	15	11	6	32	4	17	9
Mark Ingram	10	11	8	29	5	19	7
Lamar Miller	12	8	9	29	6	17	10
Frank Gore	7	10	11	28	7	21	5
Devonta Freeman	2	12	11	25	8	23	4
Jeremy Hill	10	8	7	25	9	15	14
David Johnson	DNP	10	15	25	10	25	1

Yes, I know that Matt Forte had the same number of Clutch Games as LeVeon Bell. Do you think he should be still ranked as a Tier One? I know I don't. He's heading towards retirement and Bell is in his prime. Big difference! Forte was a Tier One consistency running back for many years and one of my favorite picks every season. However, his time is done. Let someone else take him.

There is no question in my mind that David Johnson is worthy of an early first round pick. He earned 15 of 16 Clutch Games and was first in total points as the only back with 400+ points. He was almost 80 points ahead of second place! Is he worth a #1 overall pick? It's certainly between him and LeVeon Bell, based on preference. So, sure…pick him #1! I can't say I'd blame you! Devonta Freeman is also a solid first round pick. However, I'm going to put him in the later first round or early second round. Some people will bring up the concern for Tevin Coleman in the mix, but I wouldn't worry. They complement each other, but Freeman is the better back.

Mark Ingram is an intriguing running back for 2017. He earned two straight seasons of double-digit Clutch Games. However, in 2016, he had a slow start and Sean Payton basically benched him and had him share touches with Tim Hightower for much of the middle of the season. Then over the last three weeks, the focus was back on Ingram and he earned three straight Clutch Games. Hightower has signed by the 49ers leaving Ingram as the main back. He should be undervalued in 2017 and should be back in double-digit Clutch Games.

Tier Three – The Average (Ranks 11 – 19)

Player Name	2014	2015	2016	Total	3 yr rank	2 yr total	2 yr rank
Latavius Murray	4	9	9	22	11	18	8
Giovani Bernard	8	8	5	21	12	13	23
Isaiah Crowell	7	5	9	21	13	14	17
Todd Gurley	DNP	10	11	21	14	21	6
Chris Ivory	7	9	5	21	15	14	18
Doug Martin	5	11	5	21	16	16	12
Jonathan Stewart	6	9	6	21	17	15	15
Rashad Jennings	6	9	5	20	18	14	19
Eddie Lacy	12	7	1	20	19	8	42

CONSISTENTLY CLUTCH – RUNNING BACKS (continued)

This Tier is a weird combination of running backs. There are some who have had that one big year but two other marginal ones like Doug Martin and Eddie Lacy. Of these players, I would not expect Martin and Lacy to regain that double-digit Clutch games in 2017. A few of the remaining backs have some potential to be solid RB2's. Some believe Latavius Murray, who went to Minnesota in the offseason, is one of them. However, I'm worried that Sam Bradford and company aren't going to provide the offensive protection around Murray like the Raiders did. So, I'm staying away from him. Jonathan Stewart, Isiah Crowell, and Giovani Bernard are decent, but just aren't that guaranteed RB2 consistency that I'm looking for.

Pssst, don't tell anyone but Todd Gurley earned double-digit Clutch Games last season in a PPR format and has the sixth most Clutch Games over the past two years. Did he live up to expectations last year? Nope, not even close! However, that makes him way undervalued heading into this season. He would be a perfect RB2! Keep an eye on his ADP this summer.

Tier Four – The Below Average (Ranks 20 - 26)

Player Name	2014	2015	2016	Total	3 yr rank	2 yr total	2 yr rank
Theo Riddick	4	9	6	19	20	15	16
Darren Sproles	6	7	6	19	21	13	24
C.J. Anderson	8	5	4	17	22	9	38
LeGarrette Blount	3	4	10	17	23	14	20
Darren McFadden	7	10	0	17	24	10	33
T.J. Yeldon	DNP	9	7	16	25	16	13
Jamaal Charles	10	4	1	15	26	5	57

This Tier is a hot mess. Running backs who have been average enough to make it here, like Darren Sproles, Theo Riddick, and CJ Anderson. Only Anderson has any hope to earn double-digit Clutch Games in 2017, but that's only IF he can stay healthy for 16 games and that's not likely. T.J. Yeldon showed he can be fairly consistent, like in 2015, but the Jags went out and grabbed Chris Ivory to screw that up in 2016. Ivory is still there, so I wouldn't expect either one to be consistent unless an injury occurs with one of them. Jamaal Charles and LeGarrette Blount could end up with a team where they can be successful, but based on their history, I'm not taking any chances on either one in 2017.

There are your most consistent running backs over the past three seasons. Keep this information handy as you prepare for your drafts this season. Clutch is good but consistently clutch is great!

CONSISTENCY PROFILES – RUNNING BACKS

The Consistency Profiles were created for the same reason that we have Fantasy profiles: to have a quick summary of a player's performance at a glance. The following Consistency Profiles for the running backs are listed in alphabetical order by last name for easy reference. Each player's profile will have the following information:

1. Three-year historical breakdown per season of the following:
   a. Fantasy points total
   b. Clutch Games earned
   c. Games played
   d. Clutch Rating (CR – Clutch Games/Games Played)

2. Tier Draft Rank (Expected Clutch Rate)
   a. This number ties to the Tier Draft List in this book. This is where I have ranked the running back based on Fantasy points and consistency for the 2017 redraft leagues. The Tiers equate to Expected Clutch Rate (ECR) in this manner:
      i. RB1A = 80%+ ECR
      ii. RB1B = 67-80% ECR
      iii. RB2A = 60-67% ECR
      iv. RB2B = 50-60% ECR

3. Clutch Games by Week for 2016
   a. "+" means a Clutch Game was earned that week
   b. "B" means it was the player's Bye Week.

4. Three-year historical breakdown of the player's consistency by the following game scenarios:
   a. Home versus a good defense (Top 10 NFL defensive ranking)
   b. Home versus an average defense (NFL defense rankings 11-22)
   c. Home versus a bad defense (Bottom 10 NFL defensive rankings)
   d. Totals for all home games
   e. Away versus a good defense (Top 10 NFL defensive ranking)
   f. Away versus an average defense (NFL defense rankings 11-22)
   g. Away versus a bad defense (Bottom 10 NFL defensive rankings)
   h. Totals for all away games

These profiles are designed to allow quick access to how consistent a player has been over the past one, two or three seasons. In addition, the game scenarios will assist you when you're making those tough decisions on your weekly lineups. You can focus on how consistent your players have been over the past three seasons in those scenarios and change your lineup accordingly.

These profiles' descriptions will change as we get closer to the August draft dates but the historical information will not change until the season begins. If you want to access this information by inputting your own league's scoring method, you can go to the Tools section on www.BigGuyFantasySports.com on any device and have this information at your fingertips at any time.

CONSISTENCY PROFILES – RUNNING BACKS

AMEER ABDULLAH

Abdullah missed most of last year due to injury. However, he's still the lead back in Detroit in 2017. He will have more value in a standard than PPR due to Theo Riddick. However, The Lions signed Matt Asiata in the offseason, so he could steal his goal-line carries. With this signing, Abdullah won't be consistent enough to be a RB2.

3 YEAR CONSISTENCY HISTORY

		Total FP	RANK	CG	GP	CR	RANK
Ameer Abdullah	2016	26.80	95	1	2	50%	26
	2015	121.10	44	3	16	19%	73
	2014	DNP	DNP	DNP	DNP	DNP	DNP

TIER DRAFT RANK – RB3 - C

OVERVALUED PICK: Abdullah needs to first stay healthy. Right now, he's at value with an ADP of RB23/pick 61. But only as a backup on your team and not as your RB2.

QUALITY GAMES BY WEEK – 2016

Player Name	1	2	3	4	5	6	7	8	9	10	11	12	13	14	15	16	17	Total
Ameer Abdullah	+									B								1

CONSISTENCY VS DEFENSES (2015-2016)

	Good Defenses (Top 10)				Average Defenses				Bad Defenses (Bottom 10)				Total			
	FPG	CG	GP	CR	FPG	CG	GP	CR	FPG	CG	GP	CR	FPG	CG	GP	CR
Home	6.70	1	3	33%	6.80	0	3	0%	7.63	0	3	0%	7.04	1	9	11%
Away	3.17	0	3	0%	5.23	0	3	0%	19.77	3	3	100%	9.39	3	9	33%

JAY AJAYI

Ajayi is the perfect example of inconsistency at running back. This is proved by his 11th place rank in total points but a Clutch Rate of only 47% with a ranking of 28th. This running back should be completely ignored during your Fantasy drafts in 2017 unless he falls into the fourth or fifth round, which won't happen.

3 YEAR CONSISTENCY HISTORY

		Total FP	RANK	CG	GP	CR	RANK
Jay Ajayi	2016	217.30	11	7	15	47%	28
	2015	40.70	84	1	9	11%	85
	2014	DNP	DNP	DNP	DNP	DNP	DNP

TIER DRAFT RANK – RB1 – B

OVERVALUED PICK: Ajayi has a current ADP of RB7/pick 14. In order for Ajayi to be in the Top 7 RB's, he needs to add four more Clutch Games to his 2016 total. That's not happening.

QUALITY GAMES BY WEEK – 2016

Player Name	1	2	3	4	5	6	7	8	9	10	11	12	13	14	15	16	17	Total
Jay Ajayi						+	+	B	+		+	+	+			+		7

CONSISTENCY VS DEFENSES (2016)

	Good Defenses (Top 10)				Average Defenses				Bad Defenses (Bottom 10)				Total			
	FPG	CG	GP	CR	FPG	CG	GP	CR	FPG	CG	GP	CR	FPG	CG	GP	CR
Home	9.10	0	2	0%	23.63	3	4	75%	10.7	1	2	50%	16.76	4	8	50%
Away	11.53	2	3	67%	12.15	1	4	25%	0.00	0	0	0%	11.89	3	7	43%

For the most current Fantasy Football Consistency information, visit www.BigGuyFantasySports.com

CONSISTENCY PROFILES – RUNNING BACKS (continued)

CJ ANDERSON

Anderson was high on the ADP chart in 2016, but injuries and poor quarterback play were his demise. He comes into 2017 healthy and ready to go, but the Broncos decided to sign Jamaal Charles as a safety net. I believe he is a decent RB2 if drafted in fourth or fifth round. Keep an eye on the preseason to see how much time he shares with Charles before drafting.

3 YEAR CONSISTENCY HISTORY

		Total FP	RANK	CG	GP	CR	RANK
CJ Anderson	2016	102.50	45	4	7	57%	18
	2015	145.30	31	5	15	33%	53
	2014	211.30	11	8	15	53%	20

TIER DRAFT RANK – RB2 – A

UNDERVALUED: Anderson's value revolves around the quarterback play in Denver and the health of Charles. Anderson has his work cut out for him, but I feel can do the job.

QUALITY GAMES BY WEEK – 2016

Player Name	1	2	3	4	5	6	7	8	9	10	11	12	13	14	15	16	17	Total
CJ Anderson	+	+		+			+				B							4

CONSISTENCY VS DEFENSES (2014-2016)

	Good Defenses (Top 10)				Average Defenses				Bad Defenses (Bottom 10)				Total			
	FPG	CG	GP	CR	FPG	CG	GP	CR	FPG	CG	GP	CR	FPG	CG	GP	CR
Home	11.09	4	9	44%	17.70	3	5	60%	18.55	3	4	75%	14.58	10	18	56%
Away	8.48	2	6	33%	11.34	2	7	29%	11.05	2	6	33%	10.35	6	19	32%

MATT ASIATA

The Lions signed Asiata in the offseason to help with short yardage/goal-line tasks. The only thing this does is hurt Abdullah's value. With Abdullah's injury issues, there is the possibility that Asiata provides a solid handcuff to Abdullah, but since Abdullah should be drafted as a backup on your Fantasy team, Asiata is a waiver wire pickup at this point.

3 YEAR CONSISTENCY HISTORY

		Total FP	RANK	CG	GP	CR	RANK
Matt Asiata	2016	134.50	35	4	16	25%	56
	2015	43.40	82	0	16	0%	98
	2014	192.20	15	6	15	40%	32

TIER DRAFT RANK – RB5 – D

UNDRAFTABLE: At this point in time, Asiata is not worth drafting. This could change in the off-season if Abdullah gets hurt. Even so, I'd stay away and pick him up on the waiver wire.

QUALITY GAMES BY WEEK – 2016

Player Name	1	2	3	4	5	6	7	8	9	10	11	12	13	14	15	16	17	Total
Matt Asiata					+	B	+					+		+				4

CONSISTENCY VS DEFENSES (2014-2016)

	Good Defenses (Top 10)				Average Defenses				Bad Defenses (Bottom 10)				Total			
	FPG	CG	GP	CR	FPG	CG	GP	CR	FPG	CG	GP	CR	FPG	CG	GP	CR
Home	9.26	2	8	25%	4.31	0	8	0%	11.84	3	7	43%	8.33	5	23	22%
Away	8.94	2	5	40%	7.09	3	12	25%	6.97	0	7	0%	7.44	5	24	21%

For the most current Fantasy Football Consistency information, visit www.BigGuyFantasySports.com

CONSISTENCY PROFILES – RUNNING BACKS (continued)

LeVEON BELL

The toughest decision this Fall for me will be "If I have the #1 overall pick, do I pick Bell or David Johnson?" Right now, I'm leaning towards Johnson, but I can't blame you if Bell is the choice. He's been one of the most consistent running backs for the past three years. He is an almost lock to be above 85% Clutch Rate for 2017.

3 YEAR CONSISTENCY HISTORY

		Total FP	RANK	CG	GP	CR	RANK
LeVeon Bell	2016	317.40	3	12	12	100%	1
	2015	111.20	46	4	6	67%	15
	2014	370.50	1	16	16	100%	1

TIER DRAFT RANK – RB1 – A

AT VALUE: Everyone knows he's the one of the top two RB, so he's not sneaking under anyone's radar. Grab him and smile that you have one of most consistent RB's in your league.

QUALITY GAMES BY WEEK – 2016

Player Name	1	2	3	4	5	6	7	8	9	10	11	12	13	14	15	16	17	Total
LeVeon Bell				+	+	+	+	B	+	+	+	+	+	+	+	+		12

CONSISTENCY VS DEFENSES (2014-2016)

	Good Defenses (Top 10)				Average Defenses				Bad Defenses (Bottom 10)				Total			
	FPG	CG	GP	CR	FPG	CG	GP	CR	FPG	CG	GP	CR	FPG	CG	GP	CR
Home	17.91	5	7	71%	26.26	7	7	100%	26.37	3	3	100%	22.84	15	17	88%
Away	15.33	4	4	100%	29.3	6	6	100%	24.81	7	7	100%	24.16	17	17	100%

GIOVANI BERNARD

Every year, Bernard has been the better value between the Bengals' running backs. However, the Bengals believe Bernard and Jeremy Hill's time is about done since they drafted Joe Mixon in May. I'm sure it will take time for Mixon to assume the starting spot, but will also be based on Bernard's ability to hold him off. Expect a quick start from Gio and then draft him.

3 YEAR CONSISTENCY HISTORY

		Total FP	RANK	CG	GP	CR	RANK
Giovani Bernard	2016	124.30	39	5	10	50%	23
	2015	181.20	16	8	16	50%	31
	2014	187.90	17	8	13	62%	18

TIER DRAFT RANK – RB4 – D

UNDERVALUED: Bernard's current ADP is RB52/pick 156. That's a little high at this point with Mixon in the mix. Draft as a backup and see if he starts hot and flex him until he cools off.

QUALITY GAMES BY WEEK – 2016

Player Name	1	2	3	4	5	6	7	8	9	10	11	12	13	14	15	16	17	Total
Giovani Bernard		+			+	+	+	+	B									5

CONSISTENCY VS DEFENSES (2014-2016)

	Good Defenses (Top 10)				Average Defenses				Bad Defenses (Bottom 10)				Total			
	FPG	CG	GP	CR	FPG	CG	GP	CR	FPG	CG	GP	CR	FPG	CG	GP	CR
Home	13.57	5	6	83%	11.27	1	6	17%	15.61	5	7	71%	13.59	11	19	58%
Away	12.85	3	6	50%	12.33	6	10	60%	8.68	1	4	25%	11.76	10	20	50%

For the most current Fantasy Football Consistency information, visit www.BigGuyFantasySports.com

LEGARRETTE BLOUNT

Blount had a very consistent season last year for the Patriots. However, in typical Patriots' fashion, they let Blount go instead of paying him. Blount was picked up by the Eagles to be their workhorse back ahead of Ryan Mathews. Mathews hasn't been cut yet, but probably will be. Blount should be a decent backup for your Fantasy teams, but don't reach too high for him.

3 YEAR CONSISTENCY HISTORY

		Total FP	RANK	CG	GP	CR	RANK
Legarrette Blount	2016	234.90	9	10	16	63%	13
	2015	122.60	39	4	12	33%	45
	2014	100.10	45	3	16	19%	72

TIER DRAFT RANK – RB2 – B

AT VALUE: Blount's current ADP is RB34/pick 94. His ADP continues to improve as we get closer to the season. He's a solid RB2/3 on your Fantasy team but I wouldn't reach too high for him.

QUALITY GAMES BY WEEK – 2016

Player Name	1	2	3	4	5	6	7	8	9	10	11	12	13	14	15	16	17	Total
Legarrette Blount	+	+	+			+	+		B	+	+		+	+		+		10

CONSISTENCY VS DEFENSES (2015-2016)

	Good Defenses (Top 10)				Average Defenses				Bad Defenses (Bottom 10)				Total			
	FPG	CG	GP	CR	FPG	CG	GP	CR	FPG	CG	GP	CR	FPG	CG	GP	CR
Home	15.36	4	5	80%	11.98	2	4	50%	15.84	3	5	60%	14.56	9	14	64%
Away	7.53	1	4	25%	10.24	1	5	20%	14.46	3	5	60%	10.97	5	14	36%

DEVONTAE BOOKER

Booker should be the forgotten back in Denver as C.J. Anderson and Jamaal Charles will battle for most of the touches. Booker had his opportunity to grab the starting job and run with it, but failed. His only value would be if injuries take out Anderson and Charles. In my opinion, Booker is undraftable unless it's a very deep league.

3 YEAR CONSISTENCY HISTORY

		Total FP	RANK	CG	GP	CR	RANK
Devontae Booker	2016	148.70	29	4	16	25%	55
	2015	DNP	DNP	DNP	DNP	DNP	DNP
	2014	DNP	DNP	DNP	DNP	DNP	DNP

TIER DRAFT RANK – RB5 – D

UNDRAFTABLE: Booker had the chance last season to prove he could handle the starting role but he failed. He will continue as the backup in Denver behind Anderson and Charles.

QUALITY GAMES BY WEEK – 2016

Player Name	1	2	3	4	5	6	7	8	9	10	11	12	13	14	15	16	17	Total
Devontae Booker							+	+			B					+	+	4

CONSISTENCY VS DEFENSES (2016)

	Good Defenses (Top 10)				Average Defenses				Bad Defenses (Bottom 10)				Total			
	FPG	CG	GP	CR	FPG	CG	GP	CR	FPG	CG	GP	CR	FPG	CG	GP	CR
Home	10.50	1	2	50%	10.10	1	2	50%	13.00	1	4	25%	11.65	3	8	38%
Away	10.70	0	1	0%	4.63	0	3	0%	7.73	1	4	25%	6.94	1	8	13%

For the most current Fantasy Football Consistency information, visit www.BigGuyFantasySports.com

CONSISTENCY PROFILES – RUNNING BACKS (continued)

JAMAAL CHARLES

Charles let tons of Fantasy owners down last year (including myself) by not returning from his 2015 injury. He was released by the Chiefs and picked up by the Broncos in the offseason. So, many questions surround his status at this point in 2017. Is he FINALLY healthy enough to be a solid back again? Will C.J. Anderson hold him off? I believe the answers are still unanswered until preseason.

3 YEAR CONSISTENCY HISTORY

		Total FP	RANK	CG	GP	CR	RANK
Jamaal Charles	2016	13.40	115	1	2	50%	27
	2015	105.10	49	4	5	80%	T4
	2014	257.00	7	10	15	67%	15

TIER DRAFT RANK – RB4 – D

AT VALUE: He's Jamaal Charles and his current ADP is RB46. Which would make him undervalued IF he's 100% healthy this year. It's still not resolved. Until then, stay clear!

QUALITY GAMES BY WEEK – 2016

Player Name	1	2	3	4	5	6	7	8	9	10	11	12	13	14	15	16	17	Total
Jamaal Charles					B	+												1

CONSISTENCY VS DEFENSES (2014-2016)

	Good Defenses (Top 10)				Average Defenses				Bad Defenses (Bottom 10)				Total			
	FPG	CG	GP	CR	FPG	CG	GP	CR	FPG	CG	GP	CR	FPG	CG	GP	CR
Home	21.20	5	6	83%	18.55	1	2	50%	6.85	0	2	0%	17.80	6	10	60%
Away	15.48	4	6	67%	17.43	3	4	75%	17.45	2	2	100%	16.46	9	12	75%

TEVIN COLEMAN

After his injury and losing his job to Devonta Freeman in 2015, Coleman came back strong in 2016 and performed at a solid, consistent RB2 level. He heads into 2017 with little change to the offense in Atlanta, which means he should be a good RB2 on your Fantasy team if he can stay healthy all season. He hasn't done that yet, so be cautious.

3 YEAR CONSISTENCY HISTORY

		Total FP	RANK	CG	GP	CR	RANK
Tevin Coleman	2016	191.10	20	8	13	62%	T15
	2015	48.60	79	1	12	8%	88
	2014	DNP	DNP	DNP	DNP	DNP	DNP

TIER DRAFT RANK – RB2 – A

AT VALUE: Coleman's current ADP is RB20/ pick 55. This is a fair value for him. He ranked 15th last season in consistency, so if he matches those numbers, he's a good value in 2017.

QUALITY GAMES BY WEEK – 2016

Player Name	1	2	3	4	5	6	7	8	9	10	11	12	13	14	15	16	17	Total
Tevin Coleman	+	+	+		+		+				B			+		+	+	8

CONSISTENCY VS DEFENSES (2016)

	Good Defenses (Top 10)				Average Defenses				Bad Defenses (Bottom 10)				Total			
	FPG	CG	GP	CR	FPG	CG	GP	CR	FPG	CG	GP	CR	FPG	CG	GP	CR
Home	9.30	0	1	0%	10.35	1	2	50%	11.28	2	4	50%	10.73	3	7	43%
Away	16.17	2	3	67%	22.50	1	1	100%	22.50	2	2	100%	19.33	5	6	83%

For the most current Fantasy Football Consistency information, visit www.BigGuyFantasySports.com

CONSISTENCY PROFILES – RUNNING BACKS (continued)

ISAIAH CROWELL

Crowell quietly had a nice season amidst the train wreck known as the Cleveland Browns. This offseason the Browns greatly improved their offensive line and other offensive weapons. So, if that leads to just two more Clutch Games and Crowell is the in the RB1 tier. He's an excellent pick as your Fantasy RB2.

3 YEAR CONSISTENCY HISTORY

		Total FP	RANK	CG	GP	CR	RANK
Isaiah Crowell	2016	209.10	14	9	16	56%	19
	2015	137.80	33	5	16	31%	58
	2014	126.40	33	7	16	44%	35

TIER DRAFT RANK – RB1 – B

AT VALUE: Crowell's current ADP is at RB13/pick 32. That's pretty close to where I have him ranked. Oh yeah, it's his contract season, so Isaiah might have a little motivation in 2017.

QUALITY GAMES BY WEEK – 2016

Player Name	1	2	3	4	5	6	7	8	9	10	11	12	13	14	15	16	17	Total
Isaiah Crowell	+	+		+			+	+				+	B	+		+	+	9

CONSISTENCY VS DEFENSES (2014-2016)

	Good Defenses (Top 10)				Average Defenses				Bad Defenses (Bottom 10)				Total			
	FPG	CG	GP	CR	FPG	CG	GP	CR	FPG	CG	GP	CR	FPG	CG	GP	CR
Home	10.07	3	7	43%	10.58	7	12	58%	8.12	1	5	20%	9.92	11	24	46%
Away	7.49	1	7	14%	10.02	5	11	45%	12.10	3	6	50%	9.80	9	24	38%

KENNETH DIXON

Dixon was destined to be the starter in Baltimore heading into this season, but a bad life choice put Dixon into a four-game suspension at the beginning of 2017. This summer, he injured his knee and will now miss the whole season. DO NOT DRAFT unless it's a dynasty league.

3 YEAR CONSISTENCY HISTORY

		Total FP	RANK	CG	GP	CR	RANK
Kenneth Dixon	2016	102.40	46	5	12	42%	37
	2015	DNP	DNP	DNP	DNP	DNP	DNP
	2014	DNP	DNP	DNP	DNP	DNP	DNP

TIER DRAFT RANK – NONE

UNDRAFTABLE: A suspension and subsequent knee injury has put Dixon out for the year. DO NOT DRAFT in 2017!

QUALITY GAMES BY WEEK – 2016

Player Name	1	2	3	4	5	6	7	8	9	10	11	12	13	14	15	16	17	Total
Kenneth Dixon								B		+		+	+	+			+	5

CONSISTENCY VS DEFENSES (2016)

	Good Defenses (Top 10)				Average Defenses				Bad Defenses (Bottom 10)				Total			
	FPG	CG	GP	CR	FPG	CG	GP	CR	FPG	CG	GP	CR	FPG	CG	GP	CR
Home	12.15	1	2	50%	6.75	1	4	25%	0.00	0	0	0%	8.55	2	6	33%
Away	0.00	0	0	0%	8.3	1	3	33%	8.73	2	3	67%	8.52	3	6	50%

For the most current Fantasy Football Consistency information, visit www.BigGuyFantasySports.com

SHAUN DRAUGHN

Draughn did a decent job of filling in for Carlos Hyde last year in San Francisco, but he was released in the off-season and picked up by the Giants. However, the Giants drafted Wayne Gallman and that should mean Draughn will be back out in the free agent market. He's not worth drafting in 2017.

3 YEAR CONSISTENCY HISTORY

		Total FP	RANK	CG	GP	CR	RANK
Shaun Draughn	2016	110.90	42	5	15	33%	46
	2015	74.80	68	4	6	67%	18
	2014	1.90	149	0	5	0%	150

TIER DRAFT RANK – RB5 – D

UNDRAFTABLE: Draughn isn't draftable at this point unless he's signed by a team that could use him. Nothing to see here. Move on.

QUALITY GAMES BY WEEK – 2016

Player Name	1	2	3	4	5	6	7	8	9	10	11	12	13	14	15	16	17	Total
Shaun Draughn	+						+	B			+					+	+	5

CONSISTENCY VS DEFENSES (2015-2016)

	Good Defenses (Top 10)				Average Defenses				Bad Defenses (Bottom 10)				Total			
	FPG	CG	GP	CR	FPG	CG	GP	CR	FPG	CG	GP	CR	FPG	CG	GP	CR
Home	11.75	4	6	67%	8.37	1	3	33%	16.30	1	1	100%	11.19	6	10	60%
Away	7.60	2	4	50%	5.98	1	4	25%	6.50	0	3	0%	6.71	3	11	27%

EZEKIEL ELLIOTT

Not only did Elliott become one of only a few running back rookies to exceed a 60% Clutch Rate in 2016, he beat LeVeon Bell's record of a 92% Clutch Rate in his rookie season. Elliott is still a Top 5 running back, but I believe his consistency may fall off bit since the Cowboys lost two offensive linemen in the offseason. A potential 1-2 game suspension is looming, so be careful.

3 YEAR CONSISTENCY HISTORY

		Total FP	RANK	CG	GP	CR	RANK
Ezekiel Elliott	2016	327.40	2	14	15	93%	3
	2015	DNP	DNP	DNP	DNP	DNP	DNP
	2014	DNP	DNP	DNP	DNP	DNP	DNP

TIER DRAFT RANK – RB1 – A

AT VALUE: Zeke is ranked as the RB3 and overall pick #3. It's hard to argue with that. I'd probably pick Antonio Brown at #3 overall, but that's me! The suspension scares me though.

QUALITY GAMES BY WEEK – 2016

Player Name	1	2	3	4	5	6	7	8	9	10	11	12	13	14	15	16	17	Total
Ezekiel Elliott	+	+	+	+	+	+	B	+	+	+	+	+	+		+	+		14

CONSISTENCY VS DEFENSES (2016)

	Good Defenses (Top 10)				Average Defenses				Bad Defenses (Bottom 10)				Total			
	FPG	CG	GP	CR	FPG	CG	GP	CR	FPG	CG	GP	CR	FPG	CG	GP	CR
Home	14.45	2	2	100%	22.78	4	4	100%	26.90	2	2	100%	21.73	8	8	100%
Away	15.60	1	2	50%	40.90	1	1	100%	20.38	4	4	100%	21.94	6	7	86%

For the most current Fantasy Football Consistency information, visit www.BigGuyFantasySports.com

MATT FORTE

The days of a consistent Matt Forte is over. After two straight years, of 85%+ Clutch Rate, Forte hit the "brick wall" and had a 43% Clutch Rate and missed two games. He's still the main back with Bilal Powell in the wings, so be cautious before drafting him. I believe Forte is a solid backup for 2017 as his ADP is around RB37.

3 YEAR CONSISTENCY HISTORY

		Total FP	RANK	CG	GP	CR	RANK
Matt Forte	2016	185.60	21	6	14	43%	35
	2015	214.70	6	11	13	85%	2
	2014	346.60	3	15	16	94%	5

TIER DRAFT RANK – RB4 – D

AT VALUE: Forte's current ADP sits around RB37/pick 104. That's a good value for him as you're drafting him as your RB3/4 anyways. Just don't reach too high for him. The Jets suck.

QUALITY GAMES BY WEEK – 2016

Player Name	1	2	3	4	5	6	7	8	9	10	11	12	13	14	15	16	17	Total
Matt Forte	+	+					+	+	+	+	B							6

CONSISTENCY VS DEFENSES (2016)

	Good Defenses (Top 10)				Average Defenses				Bad Defenses (Bottom 10)				Total			
	FPG	CG	GP	CR	FPG	CG	GP	CR	FPG	CG	GP	CR	FPG	CG	GP	CR
Home	14.65	2	4	50%	20.50	1	1	100%	7.35	0	2	0%	13.4	3	7	43%
Away	3.20	0	1	0%	19.45	1	2	50%	12.43	2	4	50%	13.11	3	7	43%

DEVONTA FREEMAN

Freeman followed up his monster 2015 season with an expected solid season. The surprise was the emergence of Tevin Coleman hurting Freeman's numbers some. Freeman is still a Top 10 back. I believe the Falcons will maintain the successful running game combo that worked so well for them last season. Freeman is a solid pick in the early – mid second round.

3 YEAR CONSISTENCY HISTORY

		Total FP	RANK	CG	GP	CR	RANK
Devonta Freeman	2016	286.10	6	11	16	69%	T8
	2015	320.90	1	12	15	80%	T4
	2014	89.30	48	2	16	13%	78

TIER DRAFT RANK – RB1 – B

AT VALUE: Freeman's current ADP is RB6/pick 11. That's a little high for me, but it's not a horrible reach. I still believe he's a better second round pick than first round. Don't reach too high.

QUALITY GAMES BY WEEK – 2016

Player Name	1	2	3	4	5	6	7	8	9	10	11	12	13	14	15	16	17	Total
Devonta Freeman			+	+	+		+	+	+		B	+	+		+	+	+	11

CONSISTENCY VS DEFENSES (2015-2016)

	Good Defenses (Top 10)				Average Defenses				Bad Defenses (Bottom 10)				Total			
	FPG	CG	GP	CR	FPG	CG	GP	CR	FPG	CG	GP	CR	FPG	CG	GP	CR
Home	25.87	3	3	100%	16.17	3	3	100%	20.34	6	9	67%	20.61	12	15	80%
Away	10.58	1	4	25%	21.10	4	5	80%	21.43	6	7	86%	18.61	11	16	69%

For the most current Fantasy Football Consistency information, visit www.BigGuyFantasySports.com

CONSISTENCY PROFILES – RUNNING BACKS (continued)

MIKE GILLISLEE

Gillislee was an excellent backup to LeSean McCoy last season in Buffalo. When he had 12 or more touches in a game, he earned a Clutch Game more often than not. This offseason, Gillislee was picked up by the Patriots to replace LeGarrette Blount. Therefore, Gillislee's Fantasy value has increased tremendously. Keep an eye on his ADP, but he should be a good pick.

3 YEAR CONSISTENCY HISTORY

		Total FP	RANK	CG	GP	CR	RANK
Mike Gillislee	2016	125.60	38	5	15	33%	45
	2015	53.60	76	2	5	40%	53
	2014	DNP	DNP	DNP	DNP	DNP	DNP

TIER DRAFT RANK – RB2 – A

UNDERVALUED: Gillislee's current ADP is RB29/pick 78. As of right now's he is way undervalued. His ADP has continued to improve though. Keep an eye on it this summer.

QUALITY GAMES BY WEEK – 2016

Player Name	1	2	3	4	5	6	7	8	9	10	11	12	13	14	15	16	17	Total
Mike Gillislee						+		+	+	B			+				+	5

CONSISTENCY VS DEFENSES (2015-2016)

	Good Defenses (Top 10)				Average Defenses				Bad Defenses (Bottom 10)				Total			
	FPG	CG	GP	CR	FPG	CG	GP	CR	FPG	CG	GP	CR	FPG	CG	GP	CR
Home	7.20	1	4	25%	10.37	1	3	33%	10.27	1	3	33%	9.07	3	10	30%
Away	6.03	1	4	25%	9.60	1	2	50%	11.30	2	4	50%	8.85	4	10	40%

MELVIN GORDON

Gordon became the running back last year that everyone expected him to be. An injury caused him to miss three games, but his consistency was outstanding! He ended the year ranked sixth in consistency at an 85% Clutch Rate while his total points ranked him seventh. He's a definite first rounder in 2017.

3 YEAR CONSISTENCY HISTORY

		Total FP	RANK	CG	GP	CR	RANK
Melvin Gordon	2016	254.60	7	11	13	85%	6
	2015	103.30	50	3	13	23%	68
	2014	DNP	DNP	DNP	DNP	DNP	DNP

TIER DRAFT RANK – RB1 – B

AT VALUE: Gordon's current ADP is RB4/pick 9. This is a fair value for him. Depending on which receivers are available, I might take one of them, but overall Gordon is a 1st round pick.

QUALITY GAMES BY WEEK – 2016

Player Name	1	2	3	4	5	6	7	8	9	10	11	12	13	14	15	16	17	Total
Melvin Gordon	+	+	+	+	+		+	+	+	+	B	+	+					11

CONSISTENCY VS DEFENSES (2015-2016)

	Good Defenses (Top 10)				Average Defenses				Bad Defenses (Bottom 10)				Total			
	FPG	CG	GP	CR	FPG	CG	GP	CR	FPG	CG	GP	CR	FPG	CG	GP	CR
Home	10.90	1	4	25%	17.70	2	4	50%	13.85	3	6	50%	14.11	6	14	43%
Away	11.72	3	5	60%	4.83	1	3	33%	21.83	4	4	100%	13.37	8	12	67%

For the most current Fantasy Football Consistency information, visit www.BigGuyFantasySports.com

FRANK GORE

Signs (age, number of career carries, etc.) point to Gore finally nearing the end of his career. The only problem is Frank Gore doesn't obviously see those signs! At age 33, Gore ended last season ranked 12th in total points and eighth in consistency. If his ADP was RB12, I would be reluctant to pick him that high, but it's currently RB33! Yep, that's great value!

3 YEAR CONSISTENCY HISTORY

		Total FP	RANK	CG	GP	CR	RANK
Frank Gore	2016	216.30	12	11	16	69%	T8
	2015	199.40	14	10	16	63%	19
	2014	162.40	22	7	16	44%	33

TIER DRAFT RANK – RB2 – A

UNDERVALUED: Aging veterans rarely get any love from Fantasy owners. This is normally where the value is! Gore's ADP is RB33/pick 89. His consistency numbers say GREAT VALUE!

QUALITY GAMES BY WEEK – 2016

Player Name	1	2	3	4	5	6	7	8	9	10	11	12	13	14	15	16	17	Total
Frank Gore	+	+	+	+		+	+	+	+	B	+			+	+			11

CONSISTENCY VS DEFENSES (2015-2016)

	Good Defenses (Top 10)				Average Defenses				Bad Defenses (Bottom 10)				Total			
	FPG	CG	GP	CR	FPG	CG	GP	CR	FPG	CG	GP	CR	FPG	CG	GP	CR
Home	11.27	3	6	50%	9.93	3	7	43%	13.47	3	3	100%	11.09	9	16	56%
Away	15.18	6	6	100%	14.35	4	6	67%	15.25	2	4	50%	14.89	12	16	75%

TODD GURLEY

If you drafted Gurley in the early first round last year, you didn't read this book. The second half consistency numbers of Gurley's rookie season pointed to defenses stopping Gurley since the Rams quarterback situation was garbage. However, overall, Gurley's season wasn't that bad. He's a decent RB1, but I would make sure I have a top WR/RB before drafting him.

3 YEAR CONSISTENCY HISTORY

		Total FP	RANK	CG	GP	CR	RANK
Todd Gurley	2016	200.20	15	11	16	69%	T8
	2015	210.60	8	10	13	77%	6
	2014	DNP	DNP	DNP	DNP	DNP	DNP

TIER DRAFT RANK – RB1 – B

AT VALUE: Gurley's current ADP is RB10/ pick 22. That's fair value, but I'm still a little leery since rumors have him not being as involved in the passing game. Keep an eye on this.

QUALITY GAMES BY WEEK – 2016

Player Name	1	2	3	4	5	6	7	8	9	10	11	12	13	14	15	16	17	Total
Todd Gurley			+	+	+	+	+	B	+		+	+		+		+	+	11

CONSISTENCY VS DEFENSES (2015-2016)

	Good Defenses (Top 10)				Average Defenses				Bad Defenses (Bottom 10)				Total			
	FPG	CG	GP	CR	FPG	CG	GP	CR	FPG	CG	GP	CR	FPG	CG	GP	CR
Home	9.75	2	4	50%	15.85	5	6	83%	20.90	5	5	100%	15.91	12	15	80%
Away	11.82	4	7	57%	12.60	3	4	75%	13.03	2	3	67%	12.30	9	14	64%

For the most current Fantasy Football Consistency information, visit www.BigGuyFantasySports.com

CONSISTENCY PROFILES – RUNNING BACKS (continued)

DEREK HENRY

Henry certainly has an interesting spot in the Fantasy world. His numbers below appear boring, at best. However, the hype of him replacing DeMarco Murray is overwhelming. Don't get me wrong, Henry is a talented running back and the Titans made a great draft pick with him. However, don't reach too high for Henry until he officially gets the job.

3 YEAR CONSISTENCY HISTORY

		Total FP	RANK	CG	GP	CR	RANK
Derrick Henry	2016	105.70	44	4	14	29%	52
	2015	DNP	DNP	DNP	DNP	DNP	DNP
	2014	DNP	DNP	DNP	DNP	DNP	DNP

TIER DRAFT RANK – RB3 – C

AT VALUE: IF Henry continues to be drafted at his current ADP32/pick 84, then that's fair value, especially if you drafted Murray. If not, that may be a little high since he can't fill in for byes.

QUALITY GAMES BY WEEK – 2016

Player Name	1	2	3	4	5	6	7	8	9	10	11	12	13	14	15	16	17	Total
Derrick Henry								+				+	B		+		+	4

CONSISTENCY VS DEFENSES (2016)

	Good Defenses (Top 10)				Average Defenses				Bad Defenses (Bottom 10)				Total			
	FPG	CG	GP	CR	FPG	CG	GP	CR	FPG	CG	GP	CR	FPG	CG	GP	CR
Home	11.40	2	4	50%	0.00	0	0	0%	3.15	0	4	0%	7.28	2	8	25%
Away	3.20	0	2	0%	8.95	1	2	50%	11.60	1	2	50%	7.92	2	6	33%

TIM HIGHTOWER

Hightower stole carries away from Mark Ingram over the past couple of years. In the offseason, Hightower went to San Francisco to backup Carlos Hyde. There isn't much value here unless Hyde gets injured or becomes ineffective. The 49ers also drafted Joe Williams, who may be the future.

3 YEAR CONSISTENCY HISTORY

		Total FP	RANK	CG	GP	CR	RANK
Tim Hightower	2016	126.80	37	5	15	33%	44
	2015	86.40	56	4	8	50%	34
	2014	DNP	DNP	DNP	DNP	DNP	DNP

TIER DRAFT RANK – RB5 – D

UNDRAFTABLE: Hightower's current ADP is RB72, so obviously, he's not worth drafting. The rare reason for drafting him very late is to handcuff Carlos Hyde, which isn't a dumb idea.

QUALITY GAMES BY WEEK – 2016

Player Name	1	2	3	4	5	6	7	8	9	10	11	12	13	14	15	16	17	Total
Tim Hightower					B			+	+		+	+			+			5

CONSISTENCY VS DEFENSES (2015-2016)

	Good Defenses (Top 10)				Average Defenses				Bad Defenses (Bottom 10)				Total			
	FPG	CG	GP	CR	FPG	CG	GP	CR	FPG	CG	GP	CR	FPG	CG	GP	CR
Home	9.35	2	4	50%	4.47	1	3	33%	10.20	1	4	25%	8.33	4	11	36%
Away	6.90	1	3	33%	14.98	3	4	75%	8.20	1	5	20%	10.13	5	12	42%

For the most current Fantasy Football Consistency information, visit www.BigGuyFantasySports.com

JEREMY HILL

Just like Giovani Bernard, Hill's days are numbered in Cincinnati. The drafting of Joe Mixon started that countdown. I believe Hill will be hurt the most. Hill's best year was 2014 when his Clutch Rate was 63%, which ranked him 17th that season. I'm not sure he's worth drafting even as a backup since the Bengals backfield seems unsettled.

3 YEAR CONSISTENCY HISTORY

		Total FP	RANK	CG	GP	CR	RANK
Jeremy Hill	2016	176.30	22	7	15	47%	29
	2015	174.30	19	8	16	50%	32
	2014	214.90	10	10	16	63%	17

TIER DRAFT RANK – RB4 – D

AT VALUE: Hill's ADP of RB48/pick 147 is about right for Hill. Maybe he's worth being drafted as your RB4, but I have to believe there are better risks to take at that point in your draft.

QUALITY GAMES BY WEEK – 2016

Player Name	1	2	3	4	5	6	7	8	9	10	11	12	13	14	15	16	17	Total
Jeremy Hill			+				+	+	B			+	+	+	+			7

CONSISTENCY VS DEFENSES (2014-2016)

	Good Defenses (Top 10)				Average Defenses				Bad Defenses (Bottom 10)				Total			
	FPG	CG	GP	CR	FPG	CG	GP	CR	FPG	CG	GP	CR	FPG	CG	GP	CR
Home	13.70	3	6	50%	10.90	5	9	56%	14.59	4	8	50%	12.91	12	23	52%
Away	8.39	2	8	25%	10.23	4	10	40%	16.52	5	6	83%	11.19	11	24	46%

JORDAN HOWARD

If you held a vote for biggest Fantasy surprise last season, Jordan Howard should at least be a nomination, if not the winner. As a backup running back to Jeremy Langford, he probably wasn't even drafted in most Fantasy drafts. However, he ended the season ranked 10th in total points and seventh in consistency with a 73% Clutch Rate. Can he repeat? Second half says yes.

3 YEAR CONSISTENCY HISTORY

		Total FP	RANK	CG	GP	CR	RANK
Jordan Howard	2016	232.10	10	11	15	73%	7
	2015	DNP	DNP	DNP	DNP	DNP	DNP
	2014	DNP	DNP	DNP	DNP	DNP	DNP

TIER DRAFT RANK – RB1 – B

AT VALUE: Howard's current ADP is RB8/pick 16. An early second round pick is fair, but scary, as Howard came out of nowhere. I feel there are more consistent receivers at that spot.

QUALITY GAMES BY WEEK – 2016

Player Name	1	2	3	4	5	6	7	8	9	10	11	12	13	14	15	16	17	Total
Jordan Howard			+	+	+	+		+	B			+	+	+	+	+	+	11

CONSISTENCY VS DEFENSES (2016)

	Good Defenses (Top 10)				Average Defenses				Bad Defenses (Bottom 10)				Total			
	FPG	CG	GP	CR	FPG	CG	GP	CR	FPG	CG	GP	CR	FPG	CG	GP	CR
Home	21.10	2	2	100%	12.33	2	3	67%	21.60	3	3	100%	18.00	7	8	88%
Away	12.20	1	2	50%	13.1	2	2	100%	12.50	1	3	33%	12.59	4	7	57%

For the most current Fantasy Football Consistency information, visit www.BigGuyFantasySports.com

CARLOS HYDE

Hyde had his "best" year last year as he ranked 15th in consistency. However, once again, he couldn't stay healthy all season. The 49ers drafted a running back and picked up Tim Hightower in the offseason. This is a contract year for Hyde, so maybe he'll be a little more motivated in 2017. I'm probably not going to draft him in 2017 as his value is too high.

3 YEAR CONSISTENCY HISTORY

		Total FP	RANK	CG	GP	CR	RANK
Carlos Hyde	2016	196.10	18	8	13	62%	15
	2015	81.30	61	2	7	29%	61
	2014	76.10	59	1	14	7%	85

TIER DRAFT RANK – RB2 – B

OVERVALUED: His current ADP is RB18/pick 49. That's a tad too high for me when you see what the 49ers are doing to push him out. I would stay away from him this year. Draft someone else.

QUALITY GAMES BY WEEK – 2016

Player Name	1	2	3	4	5	6	7	8	9	10	11	12	13	14	15	16	17	Total
Carlos Hyde	+		+	+	+			B			+	+		+		+		8

CONSISTENCY VS DEFENSES (2016)

	Good Defenses (Top 10)				Average Defenses				Bad Defenses (Bottom 10)				Total			
	FPG	CG	GP	CR	FPG	CG	GP	CR	FPG	CG	GP	CR	FPG	CG	GP	CR
Home	20.23	3	3	100%	20.95	2	2	100%	0.00	0	0	0%	20.52	5	5	100%
Away	13.37	2	3	67%	8.07	0	3	0%	14.60	1	2	50%	11.69	3	8	38%

MARK INGRAM

If the Saints don't sign Adrian Peterson in the offseason, Ingram would have ranked as an RB1 as his past consistency shows he can earn those numbers. But, the Saints then drafted Alvin Kamara (Darren Sproles-prototype), so there go the receptions. Based on this, I'm not sure I want to be any part of the Saints' backfield in 2017.

3 YEAR CONSISTENCY HISTORY

		Total FP	RANK	CG	GP	CR	RANK
Mark Ingram	2016	242.20	8	8	16	50%	21
	2015	203.40	12	11	12	92%	1
	2014	193.90	14	10	13	77%	10

TIER DRAFT RANK – RB2 – B

AT VALUE: Ingram's current ADP is RB22/pick 60. If Peterson wasn't there, he would be undervalued. However, it is what it is right now. He could be a decent RB2, but be safe here.

QUALITY GAMES BY WEEK – 2016

Player Name	1	2	3	4	5	6	7	8	9	10	11	12	13	14	15	16	17	Total
Mark Ingram			+	+	B		+		+			+			+	+	+	8

CONSISTENCY VS DEFENSES (2014-2016)

	Good Defenses (Top 10)				Average Defenses				Bad Defenses (Bottom 10)				Total			
	FPG	CG	GP	CR	FPG	CG	GP	CR	FPG	CG	GP	CR	FPG	CG	GP	CR
Home	13.25	3	6	50%	14.99	6	9	67%	17.02	4	5	80%	14.98	13	20	65%
Away	13.60	4	6	67%	18.10	4	5	80%	16.79	8	10	80%	16.19	16	21	76%

For the most current Fantasy Football Consistency information, visit www.BigGuyFantasySports.com

CHRIS IVORY

Ivory came to Jacksonville and was about as ineffective as I expected him to be. In the NFL draft, the Jags picked their future starting running back. Leonard Fournette. This leaves either Chris Ivory or T.J. Yeldon as the odd man out. Either way, Ivory's value is about worthless for fantasy purposes.

3 YEAR CONSISTENCY HISTORY

		Total FP	RANK	CG	GP	CR	RANK
Chris Ivory	2016	100.50	47	5	11	45%	32
	2015	206.70	10	9	15	60%	20
	2014	154.30	24	7	16	44%	34

TIER DRAFT RANK – RB5 – D

UNDRAFTABLE: Ivory's current ADP is RB77, which means he's undraftable at this point. The only way this changes is if Ivory goes to a different team/situation before the season begins.

QUALITY GAMES BY WEEK – 2016

Player Name	1	2	3	4	5	6	7	8	9	10	11	12	13	14	15	16	17	Total
Chris Ivory					B	+			+		+	+				+		5

CONSISTENCY VS DEFENSES (2016)

	Good Defenses (Top 10)				Average Defenses				Bad Defenses (Bottom 10)				Total			
	FPG	CG	GP	CR	FPG	CG	GP	CR	FPG	CG	GP	CR	FPG	CG	GP	CR
Home	4.70	0	2	0%	21.40	1	1	100%	5.00	0	2	0%	8.16	1	5	20%
Away	4.40	0	1	0%	10.90	3	4	75%	11.70	1	1	100%	9.95	4	6	67%

RASHAD JENNINGS

Rashad Jennings can now be talked about in the same company of Emmitt Smith. Of course, I'm talking about the fact that they both won "Dancing with The Stars". Jennings falls behind Paul Perkins (and possible Wayne Gallman) on the depth chart in New York heading into 2017. His Dancing with The Stars trophy may be worth more than his Fantasy value.

3 YEAR CONSISTENCY HISTORY

		Total FP	RANK	CG	GP	CR	RANK
Rashad Jennings	2016	138.40	34	5	13	38%	41
	2015	168.90	21	9	16	56%	27
	2014	140.50	30	6	11	55%	19

TIER DRAFT RANK – RB5 – D

UNDRAFTABLE: Unless your league gives bonus points for reality TV championships, Jennings isn't worth drafting this year. He may sign with another team, so there's that. I'd pass.

QUALITY GAMES BY WEEK – 2016

Player Name	1	2	3	4	5	6	7	8	9	10	11	12	13	14	15	16	17	Total
Rashad Jennings							+	B		+	+		+				+	5

CONSISTENCY VS DEFENSES (2014-2016)

	Good Defenses (Top 10)				Average Defenses				Bad Defenses (Bottom 10)				Total			
	FPG	CG	GP	CR	FPG	CG	GP	CR	FPG	CG	GP	CR	FPG	CG	GP	CR
Home	9.46	2	5	40%	11.22	4	9	44%	11.11	3	8	38%	10.78	9	22	41%
Away	16.03	3	3	100%	11.55	3	6	50%	10.36	4	9	44%	11.70	10	18	56%

For the most current Fantasy Football Consistency information, visit www.BigGuyFantasySports.com

DAVID JOHNSON

Johnson in 2015 showed why he should have been a top pick in 2016 with an outstanding second half. However, as the first running back with over 400 Fantasy points in a PRR since 2006, he proved why he should be your #1 pick in most leagues. The Cardinals will continue to use him as long as he stays healthy. No worries here.

3 YEAR CONSISTENCY HISTORY

		Total FP	RANK	CG	GP	CR	RANK
David Johnson	2016	411.80	1	15	16	94%	2
	2015	211.80	7	10	16	63%	17
	2014	DNP	DNP	DNP	DNP	DNP	DNP

TIER DRAFT RANK – RB1 – A

AT VALUE: When you're worth the #1 overall pick and your ADP is RB1/pick 1, then you're AT VALUE. There aren't too many flaws in his game. He excels at both running and receiving.

QUALITY GAMES BY WEEK – 2016

Player Name	1	2	3	4	5	6	7	8	9	10	11	12	13	14	15	16	17	Total
David Johnson	+	+	+	+	+	+	+	+	B	+	+	+	+	+	+	+		15

CONSISTENCY VS DEFENSES (2015-2016)

	Good Defenses (Top 10)				Average Defenses				Bad Defenses (Bottom 10)				Total			
	FPG	CG	GP	CR	FPG	CG	GP	CR	FPG	CG	GP	CR	FPG	CG	GP	CR
Home	16.92	4	6	67%	19.75	3	4	75%	21.55	5	6	83%	19.36	12	16	75%
Away	19.95	2	4	50%	15.12	5	6	83%	23.88	5	6	83%	19.61	12	16	75%

DUKE JOHNSON

There was a little too much hype for Duke last year as the receiving back in the Browns offense. Maybe people forgot how bad the Browns offense really was. His total points rank with 31st in 2016, but his consistency was ranked 50th. I honestly wouldn't expect much change in 2017.

3 YEAR CONSISTENCY HISTORY

		Total FP	RANK	CG	GP	CR	RANK
Duke Johnson	2016	146.20	31	5	16	31%	50
	2015	164.30	24	5	16	31%	57
	2014	DNP	DNP	DNP	DNP	DNP	DNP

TIER DRAFT RANK – RB4 – D

AT VALUE: Duke is Duke is Duke. No matter how you slice it, Johnson is a third-down back on a bad team. This will allow him to have a few big games and then nothing. I'd stay clear.

QUALITY GAMES BY WEEK – 2016

Player Name	1	2	3	4	5	6	7	8	9	10	11	12	13	14	15	16	17	Total
Duke Johnson			+	+		+		+					B		+			5

CONSISTENCY VS DEFENSES (2015-2016)

	Good Defenses (Top 10)				Average Defenses				Bad Defenses (Bottom 10)				Total			
	FPG	CG	GP	CR	FPG	CG	GP	CR	FPG	CG	GP	CR	FPG	CG	GP	CR
Home	7.62	0	6	0%	8.50	1	8	13%	9.45	0	2	0%	8.29	1	16	6%
Away	8.14	2	5	40%	10.49	4	8	50%	17.77	3	3	100%	11.12	9	16	56%

For the most current Fantasy Football Consistency information, visit www.BigGuyFantasySports.com

ROB KELLEY

The Redskins backfield is like a "poor man's version" of the Saints backfield. A three-headed scenario between Rob Kelley, Chris Thompson and newly drafted, Samaje Perine appears imminent. Sadly, like the Saints, it's difficult to trust anyone out of this group. Regardless of ADP, I'm not sure any of them are worth drafting, except in dynasty leagues.

3 YEAR CONSISTENCY HISTORY

		Total FP	RANK	CG	GP	CR	RANK
Rob Kelley	2016	132.60	36	4	14	29%	51
	2015	DNP	DNP	DNP	DNP	DNP	DNP
	2014	DNP	DNP	DNP	DNP	DNP	DNP

TIER DRAFT RANK – RB5 – D

AT VALUE: Kelley's current is ADP RB43/pick 121. This is a better value for him. His ADP has plummeted this summer. His tenure won't last long, so I'd stay away from this situation.

QUALITY GAMES BY WEEK – 2016

Player Name	1	2	3	4	5	6	7	8	9	10	11	12	13	14	15	16	17	Total
Rob Kelley								+	B		+				+	+		4

CONSISTENCY VS DEFENSES (2016)

	Good Defenses (Top 10)				Average Defenses				Bad Defenses (Bottom 10)				Total			
	FPG	CG	GP	CR	FPG	CG	GP	CR	FPG	CG	GP	CR	FPG	CG	GP	CR
Home	6.90	0	2	0%	10.70	1	2	50%	16.05	1	2	50%	11.22	2	6	33%
Away	2.93	0	3	0%	11.30	2	5	40%	0	0	0	0%	8.16	2	8	25%

EDDIE LACY

After Lacy "fat farmed" his way out of Green Bay, Seattle decided to sign him in the offseason. So, Lacy helps create another three-headed backfield. By competing with Thomas Rawls and C.J. Prosise, Lacy will try to separate himself. This may be just as difficult as separating himself from a Baconator Value Meal. This situation is a risky as a heart attack!

3 YEAR CONSISTENCY HISTORY

		Total FP	RANK	CG	GP	CR	RANK
Eddie Lacy	2016	42.80	74	1	5	20%	64
	2015	144.60	32	7	15	47%	38
	2014	276.60	5	12	16	75%	11

TIER DRAFT RANK – RB3 – C

OVERVALUED: Lacy's current ADP is RB27/pick 71. I think this spot is too high to draft him. I believe the Seahawks play the "hot foot" RBBC all season with no consistency to show for it.

QUALITY GAMES BY WEEK – 2016

Player Name	1	2	3	4	5	6	7	8	9	10	11	12	13	14	15	16	17	Total
Eddie Lacy			+	B														1

CONSISTENCY VS DEFENSES (2014-2016)

	Good Defenses (Top 10)				Average Defenses				Bad Defenses (Bottom 10)				Total			
	FPG	CG	GP	CR	FPG	CG	GP	CR	FPG	CG	GP	CR	FPG	CG	GP	CR
Home	9.33	3	7	43%	16.33	5	7	71%	19.70	3	4	75%	14.36	11	18	61%
Away	9.52	4	9	44%	12.70	2	4	50%	13.82	3	5	60%	11.42	9	18	50%

For the most current Fantasy Football Consistency information, visit www.BigGuyFantasySports.com

MARSHAWN LYNCH

We go from a new Seahawk (Eddie Lacy) to a former Seahawk, Marshall Lynch. The Skittles-maniac, Lynch, came out of retirement to dedicate himself to helping his hometown Raiders to the Super Bowl. Is there enough in the tank to make Lynch viable in Fantasy leagues? I believe yes. My concern is health since he missed a year. At least he's the starter.

3 YEAR CONSISTENCY HISTORY

		Total FP	RANK	CG	GP	CR	RANK
Marshawn Lynch	2016	DNP	DNP	DNP	DNP	DNP	DNP
	2015	80.70	63	4	7	57%	24
	2014	306.30	4	13	16	81%	8

TIER DRAFT RANK – RB2 – B

OVERVALUED: It's tough to value Lynch at this point. He's the main starter for a good offense. PLUS: he hasn't played for more than a year. MINUS: his ADP is RB14 and that's too high for me!

QUALITY GAMES BY WEEK – 2016

Player Name	1	2	3	4	5	6	7	8	9	10	11	12	13	14	15	16	17	Total
Marshawn Lynch																		DNP

CONSISTENCY VS DEFENSES (2014-2016)

	Good Defenses (Top 10)				Average Defenses				Bad Defenses (Bottom 10)				Total			
	FPG	CG	GP	CR	FPG	CG	GP	CR	FPG	CG	GP	CR	FPG	CG	GP	CR
Home	17.25	4	4	100%	14.63	3	4	75%	26.60	2	3	67%	18.85	9	11	82%
Away	13.97	3	3	100%	12.43	2	6	33%	21.07	3	3	100%	14.98	8	12	67%

DOUG MARTIN

Remember, Martin still has three games to serve on his suspension from last year. So, if you plan on drafting him, you better take Charles Sims at some point. Even if Martin comes back in Week Four, there's no guarantee he starts right away. So, I have a better idea. Don't draft any running backs from Tampa Bay.

3 YEAR CONSISTENCY HISTORY

		Total FP	RANK	CG	GP	CR	RANK
Doug Martin	2016	87.50	54	5	8	63%	14
	2015	205.50	11	11	15	73%	10
	2014	80.80	51	5	11	45%	31

TIER DRAFT RANK – RB4 – D

OVERVALUED: Martin's current ADP of RB25/pick 68 seems high for a marginal running back who will be suspended for the first three games. He has shown some decent consistency in the past, but that was the past.

QUALITY GAMES BY WEEK – 2016

Player Name	1	2	3	4	5	6	7	8	9	10	11	12	13	14	15	16	17	Total
Doug Martin	+					B				+	+			+	+			5

CONSISTENCY VS DEFENSES (2014-2016)

	Good Defenses (Top 10)				Average Defenses				Bad Defenses (Bottom 10)				Total			
	FPG	CG	GP	CR	FPG	CG	GP	CR	FPG	CG	GP	CR	FPG	CG	GP	CR
Home	14.03	1	3	33%	9.31	5	9	56%	12.30	3	4	75%	10.94	9	16	56%
Away	6.98	1	4	25%	10.33	4	6	67%	13.60	7	8	88%	11.04	12	18	67%

For the most current Fantasy Football Consistency information, visit www.BigGuyFantasySports.com

CONSISTENCY PROFILES – RUNNING BACKS (continued)

RYAN MATHEWS

Mathews has never been one to stay healthy or be consistent, so that automatically puts him on my "don't draft" list. The fact the Eagles signed LeGarrette Blount in the offseason, makes it that much easier to not draft him. Mathews may end up on another teams as a backup, but there's not much value here.

3 YEAR CONSISTENCY HISTORY

		Total FP	RANK	CG	GP	CR	RANK
Ryan Mathews	2016	144.60	32	5	13	38%	41
	2015	130.50	36	6	13	46%	39
	2014	66.70	68	3	6	50%	26

QUALITY GAMES BY WEEK – 2016

Player Name	1	2	3	4	5	6	7	8	9	10	11	12	13	14	15	16	17	Total
Ryan Mathews	+	+		B	+					+					+			5

CONSISTENCY VS DEFENSES (2015-2016)

	Good Defenses (Top 10)				Average Defenses				Bad Defenses (Bottom 10)				Total			
	FPG	CG	GP	CR	FPG	CG	GP	CR	FPG	CG	GP	CR	FPG	CG	GP	CR
Home	7.87	0	3	0%	1.90	0	3	0%	13.37	4	7	57%	9.45	4	13	31%
Away	14.76	3	5	60%	13.52	4	5	80%	3.60	0	3	0%	11.71	7	13	54%

LESEAN MCCOY

McCoy has been one of the most consistent backs over the past couple of years, with back-to-back Clutch Ratings over 80%. With Mike Gillislee gone, there's even less competition. The Bills will continue to use as much as possible in 2017. You can easily draft McCoy with confidence again this year.

3 YEAR CONSISTENCY HISTORY

		Total FP	RANK	CG	GP	CR	RANK
LeSean McCoy	2016	297.30	4	13	15	87%	5
	2015	180.70	18	10	12	83%	3
	2014	207.40	12	11	16	69%	14

QUALITY GAMES BY WEEK – 2016

Player Name	1	2	3	4	5	6	7	8	9	10	11	12	13	14	15	16	17	Total
LeSean McCoy	+	+	+	+	+	+	B		+		+	+	+	+	+	+		13

CONSISTENCY VS DEFENSES (2015-2016)

	Good Defenses (Top 10)				Average Defenses				Bad Defenses (Bottom 10)				Total			
	FPG	CG	GP	CR	FPG	CG	GP	CR	FPG	CG	GP	CR	FPG	CG	GP	CR
Home	19.44	5	5	100%	17.90	2	2	100%	24.64	5	5	100%	21.35	12	12	100%
Away	19.70	7	7	100%	7.55	1	2	50%	11.47	3	6	50%	14.79	11	15	73%

For the most current Fantasy Football Consistency information, visit www.BigGuyFantasySports.com

CONSISTENCY PROFILES – RUNNING BACKS (continued)

JERICK MCKINNON

Well, here's another three-headed backfield. McKinnon can't be too happy when your front office signs Latavius Murray in the offseason and then proceeds to draft Dalvin Cook in the NFL draft. Once again, we have a team with way too uncertainty regarding anyone's Fantasy value. There's no consistency here to be found.

3 YEAR CONSISTENCY HISTORY

		Total FP	RANK	CG	GP	CR	RANK
Jerick McKinnon	2016	146.40	30	6	15	40%	39
	2015	83.40	58	2	16	13%	82
	2014	94.30	47	3	11	27%	49

TIER DRAFT RANK – RB5 – D

UNDRAFTABLE: Another team, another three-headed backfield to stay away from. Wait until someone pulls ahead of the pack. Then see if they are worth picking up on the waiver wire.

QUALITY GAMES BY WEEK – 2016

Player Name	1	2	3	4	5	6	7	8	9	10	11	12	13	14	15	16	17	Total
Jerick McKinnon				+		B							+	+	+	+	+	6

CONSISTENCY VS DEFENSES (2015-2016)

	Good Defenses (Top 10)				Average Defenses				Bad Defenses (Bottom 10)				Total			
	FPG	CG	GP	CR	FPG	CG	GP	CR	FPG	CG	GP	CR	FPG	CG	GP	CR
Home	7.46	2	7	29%	9.80	3	8	38%	11.45	3	6	50%	9.49	8	21	38%
Away	6.85	2	4	50%	4.93	0	10	0%	6.87	1	7	14%	5.94	3	21	14%

LAMAR MILLER

Miller did okay last year on a team with a terrible quarterback. Not much has changed as the Texans replaced Brock Osweiler with either, Tom Savage or rookie, DeShaun Watson. Either way, it is still going to be difficult for Miller. Be that as it may, Miller doesn't have much competition for touches. I'd rather have him as a RB2, then RB1 though.

3 YEAR CONSISTENCY HISTORY

		Total FP	RANK	CG	GP	CR	RANK
Lamar Miller	2016	193.10	19	9	14	64%	T11
	2015	233.90	3	8	16	50%	30
	2014	229.40	9	12	16	75%	12

TIER DRAFT RANK – RB1 – B

AT VALUE: Miller is what you get. Nothing flashy, but not inconsistent. He's ranked as RB1B because he's one of the few running backs with little competition to steal touches.

QUALITY GAMES BY WEEK – 2016

Player Name	1	2	3	4	5	6	7	8	9	10	11	12	13	14	15	16	17	Total
Lamar Miller	+	+	+	+		+		+	B	+				+	+			9

CONSISTENCY VS DEFENSES (2016)

	Good Defenses (Top 10)				Average Defenses				Bad Defenses (Bottom 10)				Total			
	FPG	CG	GP	CR	FPG	CG	GP	CR	FPG	CG	GP	CR	FPG	CG	GP	CR
Home	16.90	1	1	100%	13.58	3	4	75%	22.25	2	2	100%	16.53	6	7	86%
Away	9.03	1	4	25%	0	0	0	0%	13.77	2	3	67%	11.06	3	7	43%

For the most current Fantasy Football Consistency information, visit www.BigGuyFantasySports.com

TY MONTGOMERY

Yes, being the #1 running back for the Packers gives you the opportunity to be a top Fantasy player. However, it doesn't guarantee consistency. This was evident by Ty Montgomery's move to the backfield from his wide receiver position in 2016. Now, his ADP has him in the RB2 range and I just see it below. Let someone else reach for him.

3 YEAR CONSISTENCY HISTORY

		Total FP	RANK	CG	GP	CR	RANK
Ty Montgomery	2016	142.50	56	5	13	38%	T41
	2015	42.00	121	1	6	17%	115
	2014	187.90	16	8	16	50%	21

TIER DRAFT RANK – RB3 – C

OVERVALUED: Montgomery's ADP is RB17/ pick 48. He's not consistent enough to be my RB2 on my Fantasy teams in 2017. I'll grab someone more proven in that role as my RB2.

QUALITY GAMES BY WEEK – 2016

Player Name	1	2	3	4	5	6	7	8	9	10	11	12	13	14	15	16	17	Total
Ty Montgomery				B		+	+		+					+	+			5

CONSISTENCY VS DEFENSES (2016)

	Good Defenses (Top 10)				Average Defenses				Bad Defenses (Bottom 10)				Total			
	FPG	CG	GP	CR	FPG	CG	GP	CR	FPG	CG	GP	CR	FPG	CG	GP	CR
Home	8.33	1	4	25%	14.30	2	3	67%	12.10	1	1	100%	11.04	4	8	50%
Away	0.00	0	0	0%	11.70	1	4	25%	7.40	0	1	0%	10.84	1	5	20%

DEMARCO MURRAY

Murray went to the Titans last season and many weren't sure how to determine his value. I was even cautious about him after his down season the year before. However, Murray proved he was a consistent Fantasy stud! The Titans used rookie, Derrick Henry to keep Murray fresh all season and it worked very well. Murray is a solid RB1 for 2017.

3 YEAR CONSISTENCY HISTORY

		Total FP	RANK	CG	GP	CR	RANK
DeMarco Murray	2016	295.90	5	14	16	88%	4
	2015	188.10	15	9	15	60%	21
	2014	361.10	2	16	16	100%	1

TIER DRAFT RANK – RB1 – B

UNDERVALUED: Murray's current ADP is RB9/pick 18. This isn't greatly under value but I have him ranked as RB6 due to his consistency. Get Henry as a handcuff to be safe though.

QUALITY GAMES BY WEEK – 2016

Player Name	1	2	3	4	5	6	7	8	9	10	11	12	13	14	15	16	17	Total
DeMarco Murray	+	+	+	+	+	+	+	+	+	+	+	+	B	+	+			14

CONSISTENCY VS DEFENSES (2016)

	Good Defenses (Top 10)				Average Defenses				Bad Defenses (Bottom 10)				Total			
	FPG	CG	GP	CR	FPG	CG	GP	CR	FPG	CG	GP	CR	FPG	CG	GP	CR
Home	15.65	3	4	75%	0	0	0	0%	22.20	4	4	100%	18.93	7	8	88%
Away	16.95	1	2	50%	18.63	3	3	100%	18.23	3	3	100%	18.06	7	8	88%

For the most current Fantasy Football Consistency information, visit www.BigGuyFantasySports.com

CONSISTENCY PROFILES – RUNNING BACKS (continued)

LATAVIUS MURRAY

The other Murray had a decent season for the Raiders last season, but they didn't believe he was worth a long-term contract and let him go to the Vikings in the offseason. You have to believe the Vikings would make him the main back. However, they drafted Dalvin Cook, so it's anyone's guess at this point. The word is there will be a very short leash for Murray. Be cautious!

3 YEAR CONSISTENCY HISTORY

		Total FP	RANK	CG	GP	CR	RANK
Latavius Murray	2016	210.20	13	9	14	64%	T11
	2015	206.80	9	9	16	56%	25
	2014	84.70	49	4	15	27%	57

TIER DRAFT RANK – RB3 – C

AT VALUE: Murray is slightly undervalued at ADP RB42/pick 129. The ADP drop says the starting job for Murray nay disappear quickly in Minnesota. I'd stay away from this one.

QUALITY GAMES BY WEEK – 2016

Player Name	1	2	3	4	5	6	7	8	9	10	11	12	13	14	15	16	17	Total
Latavius Murray	+	+					+	+	+	B	+	+	+	+				9

CONSISTENCY VS DEFENSES (2015-2016)

	Good Defenses (Top 10)				Average Defenses				Bad Defenses (Bottom 10)				Total			
	FPG	CG	GP	CR	FPG	CG	GP	CR	FPG	CG	GP	CR	FPG	CG	GP	CR
Home	16.41	6	7	86%	17.50	3	4	75%	17.30	2	3	67%	16.91	11	14	79%
Away	8.10	1	5	20%	9.93	1	6	17%	16.02	5	5	100%	11.26	7	16	44%

ADRIAN PETERSON

Adrian Peterson changed teams in the offseason, heading to the Big Easy! If Peterson would have signed with a team that didn't have a top running back to compete with, he would be ranked much higher. However, Peterson has to compete with Mark Ingram for touches. Therefore, at this point I'm cautious with his rank, as are most experts.

3 YEAR CONSISTENCY HISTORY

		Total FP	RANK	CG	GP	CR	RANK
Adrian Peterson	2016	11.00	122	0	3	0%	99
	2015	266.70	2	12	16	75%	7
	2014	11.30	126	1	1	100%	1

TIER DRAFT RANK – RB2 – B

AT VALUE: It's hard to value Peterson's ADP of RB30/pick 79. Honestly, I would be happy to draft him at this spot. However, I'm thinking this ADP will continue to shrink. Be careful.

QUALITY GAMES BY WEEK – 2016

Player Name	1	2	3	4	5	6	7	8	9	10	11	12	13	14	15	16	17	Total
Adrian Peterson																		0

CONSISTENCY VS DEFENSES (2014-2016)

	Good Defenses (Top 10)				Average Defenses				Bad Defenses (Bottom 10)				Total			
	FPG	CG	GP	CR	FPG	CG	GP	CR	FPG	CG	GP	CR	FPG	CG	GP	CR
Home	6.55	0	2	0%	15.98	3	4	75%	12.85	2	4	50%	12.84	5	10	50%
Away	17.50	2	2	100%	14.63	5	6	83%	18.90	1	2	50%	16.06	8	10	80%

For the most current Fantasy Football Consistency information, visit www.BigGuyFantasySports.com

CONSISTENCY PROFILES – RUNNING BACKS (continued)

BILAL POWELL
Not much has changed in New York. Powell remains the 1A to Forte's #1 rank and should be drafted as such. Powell certainly was consistent last season in his limited and complimentary role to Forte. I would expect more of the same in 2017. Neither will provide a great return unless they're drafted late.

3 YEAR CONSISTENCY HISTORY

		Total FP	RANK	CG	GP	CR	RANK
Bilal Powell	2016	199.00	17	7	16	44%	33
	2015	135.10	34	6	11	55%	29
	2014	40.30	87	0	15	0%	89

TIER DRAFT RANK – RB3 – C

AT VALUE: Powell's value is based mostly on his handcuff role behind aging Matt Forte. Powell's ADP is RB26/pick 69. Therefore, there is value as Forte's backup.

QUALITY GAMES BY WEEK – 2016

Player Name	1	2	3	4	5	6	7	8	9	10	11	12	13	14	15	16	17	Total
Bilal Powell			+	+				+		+	B			+	+		+	7

CONSISTENCY VS DEFENSES (2014-2016)

	Good Defenses (Top 10)				Average Defenses				Bad Defenses (Bottom 10)				Total			
	FPG	CG	GP	CR	FPG	CG	GP	CR	FPG	CG	GP	CR	FPG	CG	GP	CR
Home	11.40	3	5	60%	16.23	2	3	67%	9.70	2	6	33%	11.71	7	14	50%
Away	9.50	1	3	33%	11.10	1	3	33%	15.49	4	7	57%	13.09	6	13	46%

THOMAS RAWLS
Rawls may be the third wheel in the running back triangle in Seattle with Eddie Lacy and third-down back, C.J. Prosise. Rawls would be worth a handcuff to Eddie Lacy, as Lacy hasn't been reliable over the past couple of years. Keep an eye on the preseason to see how this situation works out.

3 YEAR CONSISTENCY HISTORY

		Total FP	RANK	CG	GP	CR	RANK
Thomas Rawls	2016	75.50	60	2	9	22%	61
	2015	129.60	37	5	13	38%	48
	2014	DNP	DNP	DNP	DNP	DNP	DNP

TIER DRAFT RANK – RB5 – D

HANDCUFF: Rawls' value right now is as Eddie Lacy's handcuff. Even then, Rawls' consistency has never been that strong. So, be careful by not reaching too high for him this year.

QUALITY GAMES BY WEEK – 2016

Player Name	1	2	3	4	5	6	7	8	9	10	11	12	13	14	15	16	17	Total
Thomas Rawls					B						+		+					2

CONSISTENCY VS DEFENSES (2015-2016)

	Good Defenses (Top 10)				Average Defenses				Bad Defenses (Bottom 10)				Total			
	FPG	CG	GP	CR	FPG	CG	GP	CR	FPG	CG	GP	CR	FPG	CG	GP	CR
Home	2.35	0	4	0%	13.36	3	5	60%	24.65	1	2	50%	11.41	4	11	36%
Away	16.00	2	3	67%	1.48	0	4	0%	6.43	0	4	0%	7.24	2	11	18%

For the most current Fantasy Football Consistency information, visit www.BigGuyFantasySports.com

CONSISTENCY PROFILES – RUNNING BACKS (continued)

JALEN RICHARD

Richard would have been competing with DeAndre Washington in Oakland for the main back role, with the departure of Latavius Murray. However, Marshawn Lynch and the Raiders had other ideas. Therefore, Richard and Washington are relegated to third-down and occasional roles when Lynch needs rest.

3 YEAR CONSISTENCY HISTORY

		Total FP	RANK	CG	GP	CR	RANK
Jalen Richard	2016	115.60	41	4	16	25%	57
	2015	DNP	DNP	DNP	DNP	DNP	DNP
	2014	DNP	DNP	DNP	DNP	DNP	DNP

TIER DRAFT RANK – RB5 – D

UNDRAFTABLE: Richard has little to no value in most drafts this year. He may be a decent handcuff to Lynch, but even then, his fantasy value is marginal at best in 2017.

QUALITY GAMES BY WEEK – 2016

Player Name	1	2	3	4	5	6	7	8	9	10	11	12	13	14	15	16	17	Total
Jalen Richard	+				+					B	+					+		4

CONSISTENCY VS DEFENSES (2016)

	Good Defenses (Top 10)				Average Defenses				Bad Defenses (Bottom 10)				Total			
	FPG	CG	GP	CR	FPG	CG	GP	CR	FPG	CG	GP	CR	FPG	CG	GP	CR
Home	11.70	1	2	50%	7.77	1	3	33%	7.97	1	3	33%	8.83	3	8	38%
Away	1.63	0	3	0%	7.00	0	2	0%	8.70	1	3	33%	5.63	1	8	13%

THEO RIDDICK

The Lions backfield is just Abdullah and Riddick. Riddick fills the third-down back role extremely well as evidenced by his 25th place ranking in total points and 17th place rank in consistency. He missed six games, so health is a concern, but there's no reason to believe that the Lions will use Abdullah as a receiver with Riddick. He's an excellent late round value in PPR drafts.

3 YEAR CONSISTENCY HISTORY

		Total FP	RANK	CG	GP	CR	RANK
Theo Riddick	2016	161.80	25	6	10	60%	17
	2015	181.00	17	9	16	56%	T24
	2014	94.70	46	4	14	29%	58

TIER DRAFT RANK – RB3 – C

UNDERVALUED: Riddick showed that his value in a PPR format last season was around the RB2 mark. His current ADP is RB35/pick 95. This is great value as your RB3/flex player.

QUALITY GAMES BY WEEK – 2016

Player Name	1	2	3	4	5	6	7	8	9	10	11	12	13	14	15	16	17	Total
Theo Riddick	+		+		+			+		B	+		+					6

CONSISTENCY VS DEFENSES (2015-2016)

	Good Defenses (Top 10)				Average Defenses				Bad Defenses (Bottom 10)				Total			
	FPG	CG	GP	CR	FPG	CG	GP	CR	FPG	CG	GP	CR	FPG	CG	GP	CR
Home	14.16	3	5	60%	13.90	2	4	50%	15.57	3	3	100%	14.43	8	12	67%
Away	12.96	2	5	40%	8.98	1	4	25%	13.80	4	5	80%	12.12	7	14	50%

For the most current Fantasy Football Consistency information, visit www.BigGuyFantasySports.com

CONSISTENCY PROFILES – RUNNING BACKS (continued)

CHARLES SIMS

Sims was thought to be the handcuff to Doug Martin. He's not. Therefore, Sims' value is practically zero at this point unless Rodgers gets hurt in preseason. To be honest, I'd completely stay away from the Tampa Bay backfield this year until someone holds the spot down for a few weeks with some consistency.

3 YEAR CONSISTENCY HISTORY

		Total FP	RANK	CG	GP	CR	RANK
Charles Sims	2016	69.60	63	2	7	29%	53
	2015	166.40	23	6	15	40%	43
	2014	DNP	DNP	DNP	DNP	DNP	DNP

TIER DRAFT RANK – RB4 – D

UNDRAFTABLE: Jacquizz Rodgers has been marked as Doug Martin's handcuff and so Sims value is zero at this point. Stay clear of Sims and grab Rodgers as of this point.

QUALITY GAMES BY WEEK – 2016

Player Name	1	2	3	4	5	6	7	8	9	10	11	12	13	14	15	16	17	Total
Charles Sims	+		+			B												2

CONSISTENCY VS DEFENSES (2015-2016)

	Good Defenses (Top 10)				Average Defenses				Bad Defenses (Bottom 10)				Total			
	FPG	CG	GP	CR	FPG	CG	GP	CR	FPG	CG	GP	CR	FPG	CG	GP	CR
Home	14.73	2	3	67%	10.25	1	4	25%	10.20	1	3	33%	11.58	4	10	40%
Away	12.30	2	3	67%	7.57	0	3	0%	10.15	2	6	33%	10.04	4	12	33%

DARREN SPROLES

Sproles is a great PPR value. The Eagles did pick up Blount in the offseason, but that's no competition to Sproles third-down role. He's worth a late round pick in a PPR format based on his 24th ranking in PPR scoring. He will fill in great for those bye weeks or as a flex spot starter.

3 YEAR CONSISTENCY HISTORY

		Total FP	RANK	CG	GP	CR	RANK
Darren Sproles	2016	162.50	24	6	15	40%	38
	2015	149.50	29	7	16	44%	T40
	2014	147.60	26	6	15	40%	41

TIER DRAFT RANK – RB5 – D

UNDERVALUED: Sproles' ADP is around RB50/pick 154, what's not to like about drafting him as your RB5 and get RB3 value in a PPR format? Fantasy owners will forget about him. Don't be them!

QUALITY GAMES BY WEEK – 2016

Player Name	1	2	3	4	5	6	7	8	9	10	11	12	13	14	15	16	17	Total
Darren Sproles			+	B				+		+			+	+		+		6

CONSISTENCY VS DEFENSES (2014-2016)

	Good Defenses (Top 10)				Average Defenses				Bad Defenses (Bottom 10)				Total			
	FPG	CG	GP	CR	FPG	CG	GP	CR	FPG	CG	GP	CR	FPG	CG	GP	CR
Home	6.68	1	4	25%	11.26	3	7	43%	10.04	5	13	38%	9.83	9	24	38%
Away	8.73	2	6	33%	12.80	5	10	50%	7.20	2	6	33%	10.16	9	22	41%

For the most current Fantasy Football Consistency information, visit www.BigGuyFantasySports.com

CONSISTENCY PROFILES – RUNNING BACKS (continued)

JAMES STARKS

Starks is still looking for a team this offseason. Unless Starks falls into a great situation, there's not much Fantasy value here to be found. Keep an eye on him this preseason. Starks could certainly end up back in Green Bay if the Ty Montgomery experiment doesn't work out.

3 YEAR CONSISTENCY HISTORY

		Total FP	RANK	CG	GP	CR	RANK
James Starks	2016	58.90	66	3	9	33%	47
	2015	172.30	20	7	16	44%	T40
	2014	77.30	57	2	16	13%	73

TIER DRAFT RANK – RB5 – D

UNDRAFTABLE: Starks needs a great situation during this offseason to fall into Fantasy value. If he does, he may be worth a waiver wire pickup. He's undraftable at this point.

QUALITY GAMES BY WEEK – 2016

Player Name	1	2	3	4	5	6	7	8	9	10	11	12	13	14	15	16	17	Total
James Starks				B						+	+	+						3

CONSISTENCY VS DEFENSES (2014-2016)

	Good Defenses (Top 10)				Average Defenses				Bad Defenses (Bottom 10)				Total			
	FPG	CG	GP	CR	FPG	CG	GP	CR	FPG	CG	GP	CR	FPG	CG	GP	CR
Home	4.97	1	9	11%	11.63	4	7	57%	12.10	2	4	50%	8.73	7	20	35%
Away	6.02	1	9	11%	7.03	3	6	50%	6.27	1	6	17%	6.38	5	21	24%

JONATHAN STEWART

Another season and another year that Stewart only played 13 games. The Panthers decided they have had enough and drafted top rookie, Christian McCaffery, to be the heir apparent to Stewart and be a top third-down option for Cam Newton and company. Stewart's value will be near the goal-line and in standard leagues.

3 YEAR CONSISTENCY HISTORY

		Total FP	RANK	CG	GP	CR	RANK
Jonathan Stewart	2016	150.40	27	6	13	46%	31
	2015	166.80	22	9	13	69%	13
	2014	148.30	25	6	13	46%	29

TIER DRAFT RANK – RB4 – D

AT VALUE: I believe Stewarts' current ADP of RB44/pick 126 is right where I would expect him to be with the drafting of Christian McCaffery. Stewart will be worth a late-round pick and that's it.

QUALITY GAMES BY WEEK – 2016

Player Name	1	2	3	4	5	6	7	8	9	10	11	12	13	14	15	16	17	Total
Jonathan Stewart						+	B	+				+		+	+		+	6

CONSISTENCY VS DEFENSES (2014-2016)

	Good Defenses (Top 10)				Average Defenses				Bad Defenses (Bottom 10)				Total			
	FPG	CG	GP	CR	FPG	CG	GP	CR	FPG	CG	GP	CR	FPG	CG	GP	CR
Home	14.30	3	4	75%	13.04	3	5	60%	8.76	3	11	27%	10.94	9	20	45%
Away	9.63	1	4	25%	10.30	3	5	60%	15.67	8	10	80%	12.98	12	19	63%

For the most current Fantasy Football Consistency information, visit www.BigGuyFantasySports.com

CONSISTENCY PROFILES – RUNNING BACKS (continued)

CHRIS THOMPSON

Thompson is part of the Redskins three-headed backfield with Rob Kelley and rookie, Samaje Perine. Thompson does fulfill the third-down back role which can be helpful in a PPR format. However, he's probably not going to be the handcuff to Rob Kelley. So, if you're looking for a waiver wire pickup in a PPR league, he's worth a look.

3 YEAR CONSISTENCY HISTORY

		Total FP	RANK	CG	GP	CR	RANK
Chris Thompson	2016	149.50	28	4	16	25%	54
	2015	92.60	55	2	13	15%	83
	2014	15.90	117	1	2	50%	32

TIER DRAFT RANK – RB5 – D

UNDRAFTABLE: Thompson's value is limited to a PPR league at best. His 28th ranking in total points highlights that, but his consistency ranking of 54th says it's not worth it.

QUALITY GAMES BY WEEK – 2016

Player Name	1	2	3	4	5	6	7	8	9	10	11	12	13	14	15	16	17	Total
Chris Thompson	+			+			+		B							+		4

CONSISTENCY VS DEFENSES (2016)

	Good Defenses (Top 10)				Average Defenses				Bad Defenses (Bottom 10)				Total			
	FPG	CG	GP	CR	FPG	CG	GP	CR	FPG	CG	GP	CR	FPG	CG	GP	CR
Home	8.40	0	2	0%	9.73	1	4	25%	7.45	1	2	50%	8.83	2	8	25%
Away	5.53	0	3	0%	12.46	2	5	40%	0	0	0	0%	9.86	2	8	25%

SPENCER WARE

Spencer Ware is now the main back in Kansas City with the departure of Jamaal Charles in the offseason. Ware was primarily the main back last season and showed a modest 50% Clutch Rating. His 16th in total points ranking and 22nd ranking in consistency, means he can be a solid late RB2 pick. He did miss two games last season, so grab Charcandrick West as handcuff.

3 YEAR CONSISTENCY HISTORY

		Total FP	RANK	CG	GP	CR	RANK
Spencer Ware	2016	199.90	16	7	14	50%	22
	2015	82.80	60	4	11	36%	52
	2014	DNP	DNP	DNP	DNP	DNP	DNP

TIER DRAFT RANK – RB2 – A

AT VALUE: Ware's current ADP is RB19/pick 54. This is fair as the main back in KC. Remember, Charcandrick West is the handcuff. If it's a deep league, grab both. If not, grab Ware first.

QUALITY GAMES BY WEEK – 2016

Player Name	1	2	3	4	5	6	7	8	9	10	11	12	13	14	15	16	17	Total
Spencer Ware	+	+			B	+	+					+	+		+			7

CONSISTENCY VS DEFENSES (2015-2016)

	Good Defenses (Top 10)				Average Defenses				Bad Defenses (Bottom 10)				Total			
	FPG	CG	GP	CR	FPG	CG	GP	CR	FPG	CG	GP	CR	FPG	CG	GP	CR
Home	10.20	0	1	0%	13.87	3	6	50%	9.87	2	6	33%	11.74	5	13	38%
Away	6.13	2	4	50%	6.93	0	3	0%	16.96	3	5	60%	10.84	5	12	42%

For the most current Fantasy Football Consistency information, visit www.BigGuyFantasySports.com

CONSISTENCY PROFILES – RUNNING BACKS (continued)

CHARCANDRICK WEST

West will be the solid handcuff to Ware in 2017 since Charles departed. West wasn't used as much in 2016 as he was in 2015, but regardless he's the backup unless Ware gets hurt. West should be a late-round pick as his ADP is that of a very late-round pick. If you draft Ware, make sure you grab West.

3 YEAR CONSISTENCY HISTORY

		Total FP	RANK	CG	GP	CR	RANK
Charcandrick West	2016	94.10	51	1	15	7%	84
	2015	134.80	35	4	15	27%	63
	2014	DNP	DNP	DNP	DNP	DNP	DNP

TIER DRAFT RANK – RB5 – D

HANDCUFF VALUE: West's value is being the handcuff to Spencer Ware. If it's a deep league, draft both. If not, grab Ware. He is the better pick as he will be the main starter.

QUALITY GAMES BY WEEK – 2016

Player Name	1	2	3	4	5	6	7	8	9	10	11	12	13	14	15	16	17	Total
Charcandrick West					B												+	1

CONSISTENCY VS DEFENSES (2015-2016)

	Good Defenses (Top 10)				Average Defenses				Bad Defenses (Bottom 10)				Total			
	FPG	CG	GP	CR	FPG	CG	GP	CR	FPG	CG	GP	CR	FPG	CG	GP	CR
Home	5.07	0	3	0%	10.10	2	6	33%	5.35	0	6	0%	7.19	2	15	13%
Away	7.87	1	6	17%	12.28	2	4	50%	4.94	0	5	0%	8.07	3	15	20%

TERRANCE WEST

West was solid as a starter on and off last season. He was supposed to be behind Kenneth Dixon in 2017, but Dixon's season ended with an injury in July. Now West becomes the main starter along with Danny Woodhead, who was signed in the offseason by the Ravens for the third down role.

3 YEAR CONSISTENCY HISTORY

		Total FP	RANK	CG	GP	CR	RANK
Terrance West	2016	171.00	23	5	16	31%	49
	2015	23.90	105	0	6	0%	113
	2014	114.70	41	5	14	36%	52

TIER DRAFT RANK – RB3 – C

UNDERVALUED: West's value skyrocketed with the season-ending injury to Kenneth Dixon. West will be the main starter with Danny Woodhead being the third-down back.

QUALITY GAMES BY WEEK – 2016

Player Name	1	2	3	4	5	6	7	8	9	10	11	12	13	14	15	16	17	Total
Terrance West				+		+					+		+		+			5

CONSISTENCY VS DEFENSES (2015-2016)

	Good Defenses (Top 10)				Average Defenses				Bad Defenses (Bottom 10)				Total			
	FPG	CG	GP	CR	FPG	CG	GP	CR	FPG	CG	GP	CR	FPG	CG	GP	CR
Home	4.10	0	2	0%	7.86	1	5	20%	14.68	2	4	50%	9.65	3	11	27%
Away	11.10	1	4	25%	7.33	1	4	25%	5.00	0	3	0%	8.06	2	11	18%

For the most current Fantasy Football Consistency information, visit www.BigGuyFantasySports.com

CONSISTENCY PROFILES – RUNNING BACKS (continued)

JAMES WHITE

White should remain the third-down back for the Patriots heading into 2017. Last year, White had a solid consistent season as he finished 26th in total points and 34th in consistency. He should be close to this again in 2017 as the compliment to Mike Gillislee. White should be a good value based on his ADP.

3 YEAR CONSISTENCY HISTORY

		Total FP	RANK	CG	GP	CR	RANK
James White	2016	161.70	26	7	16	44%	34
	2015	122.60	40	5	14	36%	49
	2014	11.10	128	0	3	0%	105

TIER DRAFT RANK – RB3 – C

UNDERVALUED: White's current ADP is RB41/pick 119. Based on his 2016, White is undervalued. He's a very good RB4 that can easily earn RB3/flex numbers. Grab him late.

QUALITY GAMES BY WEEK – 2016

Player Name	1	2	3	4	5	6	7	8	9	10	11	12	13	14	15	16	17	Total
James White				+	+	+	+		B		+			+		+		7

CONSISTENCY VS DEFENSES (2014-2016)

	Good Defenses (Top 10)				Average Defenses				Bad Defenses (Bottom 10)				Total			
	FPG	CG	GP	CR	FPG	CG	GP	CR	FPG	CG	GP	CR	FPG	CG	GP	CR
Home	6.30	1	6	17%	15.12	5	6	83%	8.44	1	5	20%	10.04	7	17	41%
Away	8.88	2	6	33%	5.58	1	4	25%	8.18	2	6	33%	7.79	5	16	31%

DANNY WOODHEAD

Woodhead missed most of last season due to injury, but he's healthy and back as the third-down back for the Baltimore Ravens. With Kenneth Dixon out, Woodhead will be relied upon all season. Woodhead is just two years away from a Top 15 season in total points and consistency. He should provide good value in 2017.

3 YEAR CONSISTENCY HISTORY

		Total FP	RANK	CG	GP	CR	RANK
Danny Woodhead	2016	27.10	94	1	2	50%	25
	2015	233.40	5	10	15	67%	T14
	2014	12.20	124	1	3	33%	51

TIER DRAFT RANK – RB2 – B

UNDERVALUED: Woodhead provides great value at his current ADP of RB31/pick 80. He should be a big part of the offense with Terrance West. Great value!

QUALITY GAMES BY WEEK – 2016

Player Name	1	2	3	4	5	6	7	8	9	10	11	12	13	14	15	16	17	Total
Danny Woodhead	+										B							1

CONSISTENCY VS DEFENSES (2014-2016)

	Good Defenses (Top 10)				Average Defenses				Bad Defenses (Bottom 10)				Total			
	FPG	CG	GP	CR	FPG	CG	GP	CR	FPG	CG	GP	CR	FPG	CG	GP	CR
Home	5.78	0	4	0%	19.3	3	3	100%	28.97	3	3	100%	16.79	6	10	60%
Away	8.46	2	5	40%	6.9	1	3	33%	20.90	2	2	100%	10.48	5	10	50%

For the most current Fantasy Football Consistency information, visit www.BigGuyFantasySports.com

CONSISTENCY PROFILES – RUNNING BACKS (continued)

T.J. YELDON

Yeldon is just two years away from an excellent rookie season where he had a 75% Clutch Rating. However, the Jags picked up Chris Ivory and both had marginal consistency in 2016. To make matters worse, the Jags drafted Leonard Fournette and now there is a three-headed backfield in Jacksonville. I'd stay away from this situation.

3 YEAR CONSISTENCY HISTORY

		Total FP	RANK	CG	GP	CR	RANK
T.J. Yeldon	2016	139.70	33	7	15	47%	30
	2015	155.90	27	9	12	75%	8
	2014	DNP	DNP	DNP	DNP	DNP	DNP

TIER DRAFT RANK – RB5 – D

UNDRAFTABLE: One could argue that Yeldon is the handcuff to Fournette, but I'm not sure of that. Either way, Yeldon isn't worth drafting at this point. Keep an eye on him this in preseason.

QUALITY GAMES BY WEEK – 2016

Player Name	1	2	3	4	5	6	7	8	9	10	11	12	13	14	15	16	17	Total
T.J. Yeldon	+	+		+	B				+				+	+	+			7

CONSISTENCY VS DEFENSES (2015-2016)

	Good Defenses (Top 10)				Average Defenses				Bad Defenses (Bottom 10)				Total			
	FPG	CG	GP	CR	FPG	CG	GP	CR	FPG	CG	GP	CR	FPG	CG	GP	CR
Home	10.12	2	5	40%	10.37	2	3	67%	11.20	4	6	67%	10.64	8	14	57%
Away	10.17	2	3	67%	10.73	4	8	50%	15.20	2	2	100%	11.28	8	13	62%

WIDE RECEIVERS

Each major position (QB, RB, WR and TE) tracked for consistency purposes will have the following sections: Year in Review; Consistently Clutch and the Consistency Profiles. The Year in Review is exactly that, a review of the top four tiers on Fantasy consistency at each position. The Consistently Clutch article will highlight how consistent the top Fantasy players have been for the past three seasons. Finally, the Consistency Profiles will provide you with a profile of each player's consistency for each of the top returning Fantasy players.

Is the Fantasy world changing for wide receivers? Last year, there were only three receivers over 300 points and all three were barely over (307, 306 and 300, respectively). This is only half of the six receivers over 300 in 2015. In fact, this is lowest number of 300 point receivers since there were only three in 2012. So, therefore, it's very important to identify the consistent receivers more than just the high scoring receivers.

In my honest opinion, it is the wide receivers that can provide the necessary consistency to make your team better in 2017. The running backs are a little more obvious with which ones are consistent and which ones are not. However, the wide receivers, are not so obvious. For example, last season, receivers like Julio Jones and Doug Baldwin were ranked sixth and eighth respectively in total points. However, their consistency was 64% and 56% respectively. That is a terrible Clutch Rate for two Top 10 scorers!

On the other hand, Jarvis Landry and Julian Edelman were ranked 13th and 14th respectively and yet, they both earned a 75% Clutch Rate (which was tied for sixth place in consistency). So, which two were the better receivers to own last season? I believe the answer is consistently…obvious?

There are top receivers who are very consistent, but there are always consistent receivers that can be drafted in the mid-late rounds that can help take your team to playoffs and Fantasy Championships.

If you have any questions, please don't hesitate to email me at bob@bigguyfantasysports.com or hit me up on Twitter @bob_lung.

2017 PREVIEW – WIDE RECEIVERS

Let's look at those wide receivers ranked in their projected Tier for 2017 and show you their 2016 total points and consistency and where they ranked in those categories in 2016.

So, let's start with the top tier of wide receivers.

TIER ONE

Player Name	Total Points	Pts Rank	Total CG	Total GP	CR %	2016 Rank	2017 Tier	2017 Rank
Antonio Brown	307.30	1	12	15	80%	3	WR1A	1
Jordy Nelson	306.70	2	15	16	94%	1	WR1A	2
Odell Beckham	298.60	4	12	16	75%	6	WR1A	3
Julio Jones	259.90	6	9	14	64%	21	WR1A	4
Jarvis Landry	233.50	13	12	16	75%	8	WR1A	5
Dez Bryant	182.10	38	9	12	75%	11	WR1A	6
A.J. Green	186.40	34	7	10	70%	12	WR1A	7
Michael Thomas	259.70	7	12	15	80%	4	WR1A	8

The top Tier is reserved for those receivers who have the ability to earn an Expected Clutch Rating of 80%+ in 2017. All of these receivers have once in their careers earned this high Clutch Rating. This includes last year's rookie, Michael Thomas. He takes over the top spot in the Saints offense with the departure of Brandin Cooks. Antonio Brown is a Top 5 overall pick in 2017 and Jordy Nelson shouldn't be too far behind. His current ADP is WR7/pick14, so you can wait a little bit if you want. If you notice Julio Jones low Clutch Rate of 64% in 2016, then you'll understand my concern for his ability to reach 80% in 2017. Jones has earned 80% in the past, but the Falcons never did very well as a team when that happened. They went to the Super Bowl when Matt Ryan used ALL of his weapons in 2016. So, be cautious in taking Julio too high in 2017.

TIER TWO

Player Name	Total Points	Pts Rank	Total CG	Total GP	CR %	2016 Rank	2017 Tier	2017 Rank
T.Y. Hilton	271.80	5	11	16	69%	14	WR1B	9
Mike Evans	300.10	3	11	16	69%	13	WR1B	10
DeAndre Hopkins	197.40	27	9	16	56%	32	WR1B	11
Keenan Allen	DNP	DNP	DNP	DNP	DNP	DNP	WR1B	12
Amari Cooper	226.90	16	10	16	63%	23	WR2A	13
Demaryius Thomas	228.30	15	11	16	69%	16	WR2A	14
Michael Crabtree	237.30	12	11	16	69%	15	WR2A	15
Golden Tate	223.10	17	11	16	69%	17	WR2A	16

2017 PREVIEW – WIDE RECEIVERS (continued)

This Tier is a combination of WR1B and WR2A. Their Expected Clutch Ratings for 2017 should be between 65-69% (WR2A) and 70-80% (WR1B). I believe of the WR1B foursome, T.Y. Hilton is most reliable pick. Very little has changed on his team for 2017, while Mike Evans and Keenan Allen both have new weapons on their teams which may hurt their targets this year. DeAndre Hopkins will have either Tom "Nacho Man" Savage or a rookie in DeShaun Watson. There's room for improvement, but I'm still a little worried.

The Raiders' combo of Amari Cooper and Michael Crabtree are great Fantasy receivers. The difference is Cooper's ADP of WR9 and Crabtree's ADP of WR21, even though Crabtree's Clutch Rating was better than Cooper's (69% vs 63%). So, you see the value there, right? Golden Tate's ADP is currently at WR24, which makes him currently undervalued as well.

TIER THREE

Player Name	Total Points	Pts Rank	Total CG	Total GP	CR %	2016 Rank	2017 Tier	2017 Rank
Donte Moncrief	102.60	76	7	9	78%	5	WR2B	17
Julian Edelman	232.30	14	12	16	75%	9	WR2B	18
Brandin Cooks	246.30	11	12	16	75%	7	WR2B	19
Larry Fitzgerald	246.90	9	13	16	81%	2	WR2B	20
Tyreek Hill	202.00	22	10	16	63%	26	WR2B	21
Jamison Crowder	193.50	30	10	16	63%	28	WR2B	22
Willie Snead	192.00	32	9	15	60%	30	WR2B	23
Davante Adams	246.70	10	10	16	63%	22	WR2B	24
Allen Robinson	197.30	28	9	16	56%	33	WR3A	25
Doug Baldwin	253.75	8	9	16	56%	31	WR3A	26
Kelvin Benjamin	199.10	25	10	16	63%	27	WR3A	27
Emmanuel Sanders	212.60	20	7	16	44%	55	WR3A	28

So, the first part of this Tier is WR2B. There are receivers who should earned an ECR of 60-65%. Now, if you're wondering why there are four receivers who earned OVER 75% last year in this group, then you're not alone! Let's start with Donte Moncrief. He's very consistent WHEN he's on the field. There's the problem. His current ADP is WR28. If you can draft him as your WR3, fantastic! He's worth it! Julian Edelman and Brandin Cook have the same problem! They play for the same team now! If I had to pick between them, I'd take Edelman, because there's a history between him and Brady. Cook hasn't earned that trust just yet. Lastly, Larry Fitzgerald is still a solid pick as your WR2 or WR3. However, I do not believe he's going to end the season ranked second in consistency in 2017, like he did in 2016.

One quick consistency stat for Tyreek Hill. Over the last eight games of 2016, only TWO receivers earned more Clutch Games than Hill. His current ADP is WR26. He's a very solid WR2 pick, but even better WR3 pick.

In the Tier WR3A, I believe if anyone can have a comeback season, it's Allen Robinson in Jacksonville. Blake Bortles is working very hard to improve his mechanics. That should improve Robinson's consistency in 2017. The others have too much risk for me especially since they have dropped in consistency from 2015 to 2016.

TIER FOUR

Player Name	Total Points	Pts Rank	Total CG	Total GP	CR %	2016 Rank	2017 Tier	2017 Rank
Sammy Watkins	83.00	91	3	8	38%	71	WR3B	29
Alshon Jeffery	146.10	55	8	12	67%	19	WR3B	30
Terrelle Pryor	209.80	21	8	16	50%	39	WR3B	31
Stefon Diggs	193.30	31	7	13	54%	36	WR3B	32
Brandon Marshall	156.70	49	5	15	33%	73	WR3B	32
Rishard Matthews	213.50	19	10	16	63%	25	WR3B	33
Eric Decker	40.40	121	2	3	67%	20	WR3B	35
Taylor Gabriel	140.00	58	6	12	50%	46	WR3B	36

All of these receivers have an ECR of around 50-54%. Not great, but not terrible. Some of these receivers, I believe have a potential for a higher ceiling. Alshon Jeffery and Brandon Marshall were former teammates in the NFC East and now they are opponents. Jeffery is the true #1 receiver in Philadelphia while Marshall is second fiddle to Odell Beckham Jr. We'll see if either one has any Fantasy consistency left in the tank for 2017. I'll pick Jeffery over Marshall at this point. Taylor Gabriel earned all six of his Clutch Games in the last nine games last year, his current ADP is WR70! He's a great sleeper at this point!

Well, there are your Expected Clutch Rankings for 2017 with some consistency rankings for the wide receivers in 2016 to support it. If you didn't make the playoffs and you had Julio Jones or Mike Evans on your team and can't understand why, I hope this helped clear things up.

CONSISTENTLY CLUTCH – WIDE RECEIVERS

When it comes to Consistently Clutch receivers, Antonio Brown is in a class by himself. If it wasn't for Ben Roethlisberger being injured so often, Brown may be perfectly consistent every season! Other receivers only wish they could as consistent as AB.

It's one thing to be clutch during one season in Fantasy Football. However, it's those players who are consistently clutch that make up the real Fantasy studs. These players are the ones that should be drafted in the early rounds of most drafts. A consistently clutch player has normally remained consistently healthy as well, which is just as important as their consistent performance.

The Top 36 most consistent wide receivers and the number of Clutch Games earned each year are listed below. They are divided into four tiers with a three-year and two-year totals and associated rank. I'll analyze each tier and provide some insight on the players within that tier.

Tier One – The Elite (Ranks 1 - 6)

Player Name	2014	2015	2016	Total	3 yr rank	2 yr total	2 yr rank
Antonio Brown	16	13	12	41	1	25	2
Demaryius Thomas	13	13	11	37	2	24	4
Julio Jones	12	14	9	35	3	23	5
Odell Beckham	11	11	12	34	4	23	6
Jarvis Landry	9	13	12	34	5	25	3
DeAndre Hopkins	11	13	9	33	6	22	7

Antonio Brown could honestly have a top tier all to his own! He should be the #1 receiver off the board again in 2017. Brown, along with Demaryius Thomas and Odell Beckham are the only three who have earned the coveted Triple-Double over the past three seasons. Other elite receivers are close like Julio Jones, Jarvis Landry and DeAndre Hopkins, who are all one Clutch Game away from this honor. Either way, these are the elite receivers in Fantasy, due to their consistency. Hopkins is the only one who still scares me heading into 2017 due to the current quarterback situation. Once again, this year, I expect to see Jarvis Landry at an ADP that is way undervalued. Currently, he is sitting at WR17 in the MFL ADP rankings and yet, his consistency the past three seasons shows he's WR5 and his two-year ranking is WR3. Keep this in the back of your mind heading into draft season this year.

CONSISTENTLY CLUTCH – WIDE RECEIVERS (continued)

Tier Two – The Above Average (Ranks 7 – 17)

Player Name	2014	2015	2016	Total	3 yr rank	2 yr total	2 yr rank
Larry Fitzgerald	5	13	13	31	7	26	1
T.Y. Hilton	11	9	11	31	8	20	12
Emmanuel Sanders	14	10	7	31	9	17	20
Golden Tate	11	9	11	31	10	20	13
Julian Edelman	10	7	12	29	11	19	17
Mike Evans	9	9	11	29	12	20	14
A.J. Green	9	13	7	29	13	20	15
Jordy Nelson	14	DNP	15	29	14	15	27
Michael Crabtree	6	11	11	28	15	22	8
Alshon Jeffery	13	7	8	28	16	15	28
Allen Robinson	6	13	9	28	17	22	9

Let's separate this into the normally Tier 1 receivers who are here because of injuries, to them and/or their quarterbacks, ruining one season and then the rest of the remaining players. Those players include Larry Fitzgerald, T.Y. Hilton, A.J. Green and Jordy Nelson. Larry Fitzgerald was practically left for dead heading into 2015. He was drafted as WR3 on many of my teams heading into that season. However, after back-to-back years with 13 Clutch Games, his value is right back up there as one of the most consistent receivers in the game. T.Y. Hilton's issue in 2015 was obviously the loss of Andrew Luck for most of the season and Matt Hasselbeck having to play quarterback. Luck was back last season and so was Hilton's consistency. A.J. Green's injury took him out for six games in 2016 and should return healthy in 2017. He could be undervalued, so keep an eye on his ADP this summer. Edelman and Nelson had season-ending injuries in 2015 and come back 100% healthy for 2016 and their consistency returned for them as well. Nelson ended the season as the most consistent receiver with a 94% Clutch Rating.

Emmanuel Sanders was hurt by the quarterback situation in Denver. Demaryius Thomas was okay but it didn't seem that Sanders meshed well with the revolving door at quarterback. Interesting enough was the fact that Sanders ranked 20th in total points, but 55th in consistency. I'm not expecting any improvement here, so stay clear of Sanders in 2017. Golden Tate may surprise folks as being tied with Fitzgerald and Hilton in Clutch Games over the past three seasons, but I'm not. Tate was one Clutch Game away from a Triple-Double and there's no reason to believe that he won't be in double-digits in 2017 as well. With his current ADP hovering WR32, he's looking like a great value again in 2017.

Mike Evans has earned two LESS Clutch Games over the past three years than Tate and yet his current ADP AGAIN this season is WR5 or BETTER!!! Every year, he's around 10 Clutch Games, which is above average, but he's nowhere near the Top 5 in consistency (last year he ranked 13th). Michael Crabtree, Alshon Jeffery and Allen Robinson have the potential to be consistent, but I really need to see their ADP before I decide to draft them. If I can get them as the second WR on my teams, I'd be much happier.

CONSISTENTLY CLUTCH – WIDE RECEIVERS (continued)

Tier Three – The Average (Ranks 18 – 28)

Player Name	2014	2015	2016	Total	3 yr rank	2 yr total	2 yr rank
Jeremy Maclin	12	10	5	27	18	15	29
Brandin Cooks	5	9	12	26	19	21	10
Eric Decker	9	15	2	26	20	17	21
Pierre Garcon	5	9	12	26	21	21	11
Brandon Marshall	6	15	5	26	22	20	16
Dez Bryant	13	3	9	25	23	12	42
Randall Cobb	13	6	6	25	24	12	43
Anquan Boldin	10	7	7	24	25	14	34
Doug Baldwin	5	9	9	23	26	18	18
Kenny Britt	6	7	10	23	27	17	22
Jordan Matthews	7	9	7	23	28	16	25

This tier is a group of receivers that mainly consist of receivers who have had (or been close to) a double-digit season or two, but had one or two inconsistent years to offset it. The question for 2017 is can any of these receivers regain their double-digit Clutch Games this year? I believe Dez Bryant is the only receiver who will reach that goal in 2017. The other receivers are either heading in the wrong direction in their career or went to a team were their consistency will be tough to repeat. Yes, I'm talking to you, Brandin Cooks. To reach double-digit Clutch Games in 2017, Cooks is going to have to take them away from Julian Edelman. The Patriots have only had two receivers earn double-digit Clutch Games, in the same year, once (2009) with Randy Moss and Wes Welker. I honestly can't see that happening again. The rest of these receivers have too many question marks to make me feel confident they will be extremely consistent this year. However, be that as it may, there could be some good value here, if their ADP makes them undervalued. We'll take a closer look at this as we get closer to August.

Tier Four – The Below Average (Ranks 29 - 36)

Player Name	2014	2015	2016	Total	3 yr rank	2 yr total	2 yr rank
Mike Wallace	11	3	8	22	29	11	50
Allen Hurns	6	10	5	21	30	15	30
Kenny Stills	8	3	10	21	31	13	37
John Brown	5	11	4	20	32	15	31
Michael Floyd	7	8	5	20	33	13	38
DeSean Jackson	9	4	7	20	34	11	51
Kelvin Benjamin	9	DNP	10	19	35	10	56
Sammy Watkins	7	9	3	19	36	12	45

CONSISTENTLY CLUTCH – WIDE RECEIVERS (continued)

This tier is much like Tier 3. I'll start with the talented receivers worth drafting. This list consists of Kelvin Benjamin, Sammy Watkins and John Brown. Each of them are Clutch receivers and are worth drafting, just keep an eye on their ADP's this summer to see where the best value is.

The next level of talent are receivers who have the potential to be consistent in 2017 but just don't reach too high for them. These are receivers like Allen Hurns and Kenny Stills. They both earned 10+ Clutch Games once over the past two years, but are just difficult to trust to repeat it this season. Michael Floyd and DeSean Jackson have never been consistent and I'm not counting on them to find consistency in 2017. Stay away.

There are your most consistent wide receivers backs over the past three seasons. Keep this information handy as you prepare for your drafts this season. Clutch is good but consistently clutch is great!

CONSISTENCY PROFILES – WIDE RECEIVERS

The Consistency Profiles were created for the same reason that we have Fantasy profiles: to have a quick summary of a player's performance at a glance. The following Consistency Profiles for the wide receivers are listed in alphabetical order by last name for easy reference. Each player's profile will have the following information:

1. Three-year historical breakdown per season of the following:
   a. Fantasy points total
   b. Clutch Games earned
   c. Games played
   d. Clutch Rating (CR – Clutch Games/Games Played)

2. Tier Draft Rank (Expected Clutch Rate)
   a. This number ties to the Tier Draft List in this book. This is where I have ranked the running back based on Fantasy points and consistency for the 2017 redraft leagues. The Tiers equate to Expected Clutch Rate (ECR) in this manner:
      i. WR1A = 80%+ ECR
      ii. WR1B = 70-80% ECR
      iii. WR2A = 65-70% ECR
      iv. WR2B = 60-65% ECR
      v. WR3A = 55-60% ECR
      vi. WR3B = 50-55% ECR

3. Clutch Games by Week for 2016
   a. "+" means a Clutch Game was earned that week
   b. "B" means it was the player's Bye Week.

4. Three-year historical breakdown of the player's consistency by the following game scenarios:
   a. Home versus a good defense (Top 10 NFL defensive ranking)
   b. Home versus an average defense (NFL defense rankings 11-22)
   c. Home versus a bad defense (Bottom 10 NFL defensive rankings)
   d. Totals for all home games
   e. Away versus a good defense (Top 10 NFL defensive ranking)
   f. Away versus an average defense (NFL defense rankings 11-22)
   g. Away versus a bad defense (Bottom 10 NFL defensive rankings)
   h. Totals for all away games

These profiles are designed to allow quick access to how consistent a player has been over the past one, two or three seasons. In addition, the game scenarios will assist you when you're making those tough decisions on your weekly lineups. You can focus on how consistent your players have been over the past three seasons in those scenarios and change your lineup accordingly.

These profiles' descriptions will change as we get closer to the August draft dates but the historical information will not change until the season begins. If you want to access this information by inputting your own league' scoring method, you can go to the Tools section on www.BigGuyFantasySports.com on any device and have this information at your fingertips at any time.

CONSISTENCY PROFILES – WIDE RECEIVERS

DAVANTE ADAMS

Last season, Adams quietly took Randall Cobb's spot as the #2 receiver for the Packers. He ended the season 10th in total points but only had a rank of 22nd in consistency with a 63% Clutch Rate. While the Packers have talked about getting Cobb more involved in the offense in 2017, Adams should still be a solid pick in 2017.

3 YEAR CONSISTENCY HISTORY

		Total FP	RANK	CG	GP	CR	RANK
Davante Adams	2016	246.70	10	10	16	63%	22
	2015	104.30	65	3	13	23%	81
	2014	100.60	74	3	16	19%	88

TIER DRAFT RANK – WR2 – B
AT VALUE: Adams' ADP is currently around WR21/ pick 43. This is close to his current Tier Draft rank. He should be a solid WR2 pick. Don't worry about the Packers coach speak.

CLUTCH GAMES BY WEEK – 2016

Player Name	1	2	3	4	5	6	7	8	9	10	11	12	13	14	15	16	17	Total
Davante Adams	+			B	+		+	+	+	+		+		+		+	+	10

CONSISTENCY VS DEFENSES (2016)

	Good Defenses (Top 10)				Average Defenses				Bad Defenses (Bottom 10)				Total			
	FPG	CG	GP	CR	FPG	CG	GP	CR	FPG	CG	GP	CR	FPG	CG	GP	CR
Home	14.25	3	4	75%	17.97	1	3	33%	14.10	1	1	100%	15.63	5	8	63%
Away	9.80	1	2	50%	18.88	3	4	75%	13.3	1	2	50%	15.21	5	8	63%

KEENAN ALLEN

For the second year in a row, Allen had a season-ending injury. The Chargers drafted Mike Williams but loss him to injury already! This allows Allen to put up WR1 numbers in 2017. He was on pace for some amazing numbers in 2015 until he missed half of the year. I'd rather draft Allen as my WR2 with the ability to get WR1 Fantasy numbers.

3 YEAR CONSISTENCY HISTORY

		Total FP	RANK	CG	GP	CR	RANK
Keenan Allen	2016	12.30	167	1	1	100%	NA
	2015	163.50	41	7	8	88%	T3
	2014	179.30	35	6	14	43%	49

TIER DRAFT RANK – WR2 – A
UNDERVALUED: Allen's current ADP is WR17/pick 34. The loss of Mike Williams makes him a solid WR2 pick for your Fantasy team. He could put up WR1 numbers easily in 2017.

CLUTCH GAMES BY WEEK – 2016

Player Name	1	2	3	4	5	6	7	8	9	10	11	12	13	14	15	16	17	Total
Keenan Allen	+										B							1

CONSISTENCY VS DEFENSES (2014-2016)

	Good Defenses (Top 10)				Average Defenses				Bad Defenses (Bottom 10)				Total			
	FPG	CG	GP	CR	FPG	CG	GP	CR	FPG	CG	GP	CR	FPG	CG	GP	CR
Home	6.98	2	5	40%	21.90	3	3	100%	18.23	4	4	100%	14.46	9	12	75%
Away	20.40	3	5	60%	15.4	2	4	50%	9.00	1	2	50%	16.51	6	11	55%

For the most current Fantasy Football Consistency information, visit www.BigGuyFantasySports.com

TAVON AUSTIN

Austin remains the WR2 for the Rams, but when the WR1 is Robert Woods, maybe Austin isn't that far off. Regardless, the Rams passing offense will remain marginal, at best. As you will note below, Austin hasn't been very consistent in the past, so there's no reason to believe, he'll be consistent in 2017.

3 YEAR CONSISTENCY HISTORY

Tavon Austin		Total FP	RANK	CG	GP	CR	RANK
Tavon Austin	2016	148.80	51	6	15	40%	T62
	2015	196.70	28	6	16	38%	54
	2014	90.30	83	2	15	13%	104

TIER DRAFT RANK – WR6 – D

UNDRAFTABLE: Austin's ADP is WR70/pick 201. He'll have an occasional big game and then a few duds. The Rams offense doesn't provide much firepower, so I wouldn't draft Austin.

CLUTCH GAMES BY WEEK – 2016

Player Name	1	2	3	4	5	6	7	8	9	10	11	12	13	14	15	16	17	Total
Tavon Austin			+		+		+	B				+		+		+		6

CONSISTENCY VS DEFENSES (2015-2016)

	Good Defenses (Top 10)				Average Defenses				Bad Defenses (Bottom 10)				Total			
	FPG	CG	GP	CR	FPG	CG	GP	CR	FPG	CG	GP	CR	FPG	CG	GP	CR
Home	7.15	0	2	0%	11.08	1	4	25%	19.15	1	2	50%	12.11	2	8	25%
Away	17.28	3	4	75%	6.95	1	2	50%	8.4	1	2	50%	12.48	5	8	63%

DOUG BALDWIN

For the second straight season, Baldwin was Top 10 in total points, but had a 56% Clutch Rate. This ranked him 27th and 31st respectively over those two years. Yet, once again this season, Baldwin's being ranked as a Top 12 receiver. He's not based on consistency. Check out the home/away split below as well! He sucks on the road!

3 YEAR CONSISTENCY HISTORY

Doug Baldwin		Total FP	RANK	CG	GP	CR	RANK
Doug Baldwin	2016	253.80	8	9	16	56%	T31
	2015	268.90	10	9	16	56%	27
	2014	167.30	44	5	16	31%	67

TIER DRAFT RANK – WR3 – B

OVERVALUED: Baldwin's ADP is currently at WR12/pick 24. No disrespect to Mr. Baldwin; but there ain't a chance in hell that I'm drafting you that high! Let someone else take him.

CLUTCH GAMES BY WEEK – 2016

Player Name	1	2	3	4	5	6	7	8	9	10	11	12	13	14	15	16	17	Total
Doug Baldwin	+		+		B		+		+	+	+		+		+	+		9

CONSISTENCY VS DEFENSES (2015-2016)

	Good Defenses (Top 10)				Average Defenses				Bad Defenses (Bottom 10)				Total			
	FPG	CG	GP	CR	FPG	CG	GP	CR	FPG	CG	GP	CR	FPG	CG	GP	CR
Home	20.73	3	4	75%	18.71	6	7	86%	18.76	4	5	80%	19.23	13	16	81%
Away	15.63	3	6	50%	16.16	2	5	40%	8.08	0	5	0%	13.44	5	16	31%

For the most current Fantasy Football Consistency information, visit www.BigGuyFantasySports.com

COLE BEASLEY

Beasley seemed to connect well with Dak Prescott last season. This led to his total points rank of 33rd. However, his consistency was only a 44% Clutch Rate, which ranked 55th. Beasley is a solid backup especially when the Cowboys are on the road against bad defenses or home against Top 10 defenses.

3 YEAR CONSISTENCY HISTORY

		Total FP	RANK	CG	GP	CR	RANK
Cole Beasley	2016	189.00	33	7	16	44%	T55
	2015	135.60	50	4	16	25%	70
	2014	103.00	72	4	16	25%	74

TIER DRAFT RANK – WR6 – D

AT VALUE: Beasley's ADP is WR60/pick 171. His value comes as a backup to Dez Bryant and Terrance Williams. He may be drafted in deeper leagues, but he may go undrafted in most formats.

CLUTCH GAMES BY WEEK – 2016

Player Name	1	2	3	4	5	6	7	8	9	10	11	12	13	14	15	16	17	Total
Cole Beasley	+	+	+		+	+	B		+		+							7

CONSISTENCY VS DEFENSES (2016)

	Good Defenses (Top 10)				Average Defenses				Bad Defenses (Bottom 10)				Total			
	FPG	CG	GP	CR	FPG	CG	GP	CR	FPG	CG	GP	CR	FPG	CG	GP	CR
Home	15.70	2	2	100%	11.35	2	4	50%	9.70	0	2	0%	12.03	4	8	50%
Away	6.20	0	2	0%	8.10	0	2	0%	16.05	3	4	75%	11.60	3	8	38%

ODELL BECKHAM

Beckham is a very good wide receiver. His consistency and total points improved last season. However, he scares me because of his immaturity both on and off the field. Add in the addition of Brandon Marshall and rookie tight end, David Engram and all of a sudden, Beckham is sharing targets. I believe he is a Top 10 receiver, but he's not Top 3 in my opinion.

3 YEAR CONSISTENCY HISTORY

		Total FP	RANK	CG	GP	CR	RANK
Odell Beckham	2016	298.60	4	12	16	75%	6
	2015	319.30	5	11	15	73%	16
	2014	297.00	7	11	12	92%	2

TIER DRAFT RANK – WR1 – A

AT VALUE: Beckham's current ADP is WR2/overall pick 5. That's a tad high for me overall. I'd rather take him in the late first round but I doubt he'll ever far that far.

CLUTCH GAMES BY WEEK – 2016

Player Name	1	2	3	4	5	6	7	8	9	10	11	12	13	14	15	16	17	Total
Odell Beckham	+	+	+		+	+		B	+	+		+	+	+	+	+		12

CONSISTENCY VS DEFENSES (2014-2016)

	Good Defenses (Top 10)				Average Defenses				Bad Defenses (Bottom 10)				Total			
	FPG	CG	GP	CR	FPG	CG	GP	CR	FPG	CG	GP	CR	FPG	CG	GP	CR
Home	24.88	5	5	100%	19.16	6	8	75%	24.89	8	9	89%	22.80	19	22	86%
Away	11.37	1	3	33%	18.54	5	7	71%	22.66	9	11	82%	19.68	15	21	71%

For the most current Fantasy Football Consistency information, visit www.BigGuyFantasySports.com

KELVIN BENJAMIN

Benjamin started last season with seven Clutch Games out of his first nine games, but the second half was terrible with only three more Clutch Games over his last seven. He ended the year ranked in the Top 25 in both total points and consistency. The Panthers have called out Benjamin for being overweight this offseason, so be aware this summer of his status.

3 YEAR CONSISTENCY HISTORY

		Total FP	RANK	CG	GP	CR	RANK
Kelvin Benjamin	2016	199.10	25	10	16	63%	T22
	2015	DNP	DNP	DNP	DNP	DNP	DNP
	2014	227.80	15	9	16	56%	26

TIER DRAFT RANK – WR3 – A

AT VALUE: I believe Benjamin's current ADP of WR30/pick 64 is a fair spot for him. I won't draft him before that. Keep an eye on his weight this preseason as well. Be careful.

CLUTCH GAMES BY WEEK – 2016

Player Name	1	2	3	4	5	6	7	8	9	10	11	12	13	14	15	16	17	Total
Kelvin Benjamin	+	+		+	+	+	B		+	+		+				+	+	10

CONSISTENCY VS DEFENSES (2014-2016)

	Good Defenses (Top 10)				Average Defenses				Bad Defenses (Bottom 10)				Total			
	FPG	CG	GP	CR	FPG	CG	GP	CR	FPG	CG	GP	CR	FPG	CG	GP	CR
Home	7.33	1	4	25%	12.43	1	3	33%	15.22	6	9	67%	12.73	8	16	50%
Away	14.03	3	4	75%	14.53	3	3	100%	13.73	7	9	78%	13.96	13	16	81%

TRAVIS BENJAMIN

Benjamin was signed by the Chargers in 2015 to be a compliment to Keenan Allen. He filled in nicely in the second half of 2015 when Allen went down with an injury. However, last season, injuries to Benjamin and the emergence of Tyrell Williams led to Benjamin's demise. He may be cut this offseason as the Chargers drafted Mike Williams.

3 YEAR CONSISTENCY HISTORY

		Total FP	RANK	CG	GP	CR	RANK
Travis Benjamin	2016	138.40	59	5	14	36%	72
	2015	195.80	29	8	16	50%	38
	2014	68.50	94	2	16	13%	108

TIER DRAFT RANK – WR8 – D

UNDRAFTABLE: Benjamin's current ADP of around WR85 says he's not worth drafting at this point. He's now the fourth receiver for the Chargers, so there's not much hope there.

CLUTCH GAMES BY WEEK – 2016

Player Name	1	2	3	4	5	6	7	8	9	10	11	12	13	14	15	16	17	Total
Travis Benjamin		+	+		+			+			B				+			5

CONSISTENCY VS DEFENSES (2016)

	Good Defenses (Top 10)				Average Defenses				Bad Defenses (Bottom 10)				Total			
	FPG	CG	GP	CR	FPG	CG	GP	CR	FPG	CG	GP	CR	FPG	CG	GP	CR
Home	17.05	1	2	50%	1.50	0	1	0%	8.93	1	3	33%	10.40	2	6	33%
Away	7.60	1	2	50%	-0.20	0	1	0%	12.20	2	5	40%	9.50	3	8	38%

For the most current Fantasy Football Consistency information, visit www.BigGuyFantasySports.com

ANQUAN BOLDIN

Currently, Anquan Boldin has no team to play for. He certainly dropped off last season but it had just as much to do with the 49ers offense as Boldin as a player. If Boldin can hook up with the right team (Patriots, etc.), the he may have some flex player value on Fantasy teams. For now, he's not worth anything.

3 YEAR CONSISTENCY HISTORY

		Total FP	RANK	CG	GP	CR	RANK
Anquan Boldin	2016	173.40	41	7	16	44%	58
	2015	171.90	40	7	14	50%	43
	2014	219.60	19	10	16	63%	20

TIER DRAFT RANK – WR7 – D

UNDRAFTABLE: As I mentioned already, Boldin's value is undecided because he is still a free agent. If he signs with a team that will use him, he still has some value as a WR4/5.

CLUTCH GAMES BY WEEK – 2016

Player Name	1	2	3	4	5	6	7	8	9	10	11	12	13	14	15	16	17	Total
Anquan Boldin		+			+	+				B	+	+			+		+	7

CONSISTENCY VS DEFENSES (2016)

	Good Defenses (Top 10)				Average Defenses				Bad Defenses (Bottom 10)				Total			
	FPG	CG	GP	CR	FPG	CG	GP	CR	FPG	CG	GP	CR	FPG	CG	GP	CR
Home	16.53	2	3	67%	12.50	2	3	67%	13.75	2	2	100%	14.33	6	8	75%
Away	4.90	0	3	0%	8.70	0	2	0%	8.90	1	3	33%	7.35	1	8	13%

KENNY BRITT

Not everyone can be ranked in the Top 26 in both total points and consistency in the prior year and then sign with a new team and watch your ADP get worse! But, in can happen when your new team is the Cleveland Browns. Britt earned a big contract with an excellent season last year with the Rams. Can he produce these numbers again? Doubtful. But he may have value.

3 YEAR CONSISTENCY HISTORY

		Total FP	RANK	CG	GP	CR	RANK
Kenny Britt	2016	198.20	26	10	15	67%	18
	2015	122.10	55	7	16	44%	48
	2014	142.20	54	6	16	38%	57

TIER DRAFT RANK – WR5 – D

AT VALUE: With his current ADP of around WR50/pick 130. Britt may provide some value as a late round pick. Corey Coleman can't stay healthy, so Britt may be the only decent option at WR.

CLUTCH GAMES BY WEEK – 2016

Player Name	1	2	3	4	5	6	7	8	9	10	11	12	13	14	15	16	17	Total
Kenny Britt	+	+		+	+	+		B	+	+		+	+	+				10

CONSISTENCY VS DEFENSES (2016)

	Good Defenses (Top 10)				Average Defenses				Bad Defenses (Bottom 10)				Total			
	FPG	CG	GP	CR	FPG	CG	GP	CR	FPG	CG	GP	CR	FPG	CG	GP	CR
Home	11.35	1	2	50%	13.70	2	2	100%	9.00	1	3	33%	11.01	4	7	57%
Away	11.97	2	3	67%	25.25	2	2	100%	11.57	2	3	67%	15.14	6	8	75%

For the most current Fantasy Football Consistency information, visit www.BigGuyFantasySports.com

CONSISTENCY PROFILES – WIDE RECEIVERS (continued)

ANTONIO BROWN

It's hard to believe when I tell you Antonio Brown had a "down" year in 2016. But he did. He earned 75 less Fantasy points than 2015 and had his lowest Clutch Rate in the past three years. He ended the season "only" third in consistency with an 80% Clutch Rating. Enough with the sarcasm, Brown should be the top receiver in your league and third overall pick!

3 YEAR CONSISTENCY HISTORY

		Total FP	RANK	CG	GP	CR	RANK
Antonio Brown	2016	307.30	1	12	15	80%	3
	2015	382.20	1	13	16	81%	T5
	2014	382.30	1	16	16	100%	1

CLUTCH GAMES BY WEEK – 2016

Player Name	1	2	3	4	5	6	7	8	9	10	11	12	13	14	15	16	17	Total
Antonio Brown	+		+	+	+		+	B	+	+	+	+	+	+		+		12

CONSISTENCY VS DEFENSES (2014-2016)

	Good Defenses (Top 10)				Average Defenses				Bad Defenses (Bottom 10)				Total			
	FPG	CG	GP	CR	FPG	CG	GP	CR	FPG	CG	GP	CR	FPG	CG	GP	CR
Home	22.81	7	8	88%	22.58	6	8	75%	33.43	7	7	100%	25.96	20	23	87%
Away	18.29	7	7	100%	19.10	7	8	88%	21.53	7	9	78%	19.78	21	24	88%

JOHN BROWN

Brown finally becomes the WR2 for the Cardinals with the departure of Michael Floyd. Brown's 2016 was marred by health issues which limited his output. Just two years ago, Brown ranked in the Top 24 in total points and consistency. I'm not saying he's a WR2 for this year, but you can draft him as a WR4/5 and get WR3 value out of him.

3 YEAR CONSISTENCY HISTORY

		Total FP	RANK	CG	GP	CR	RANK
John Brown	2016	103.70	74	4	15	27%	86
	2015	209.50	24	11	15	73%	T16
	2014	147.00	53	5	16	31%	69

CLUTCH GAMES BY WEEK – 2016

Player Name	1	2	3	4	5	6	7	8	9	10	11	12	13	14	15	16	17	Total
John Brown			+	+				+	B						+			4

CONSISTENCY VS DEFENSES (2014-2016)

	Good Defenses (Top 10)				Average Defenses				Bad Defenses (Bottom 10)				Total			
	FPG	CG	GP	CR	FPG	CG	GP	CR	FPG	CG	GP	CR	FPG	CG	GP	CR
Home	11.91	6	10	60%	14.50	4	5	80%	10.31	3	8	38%	11.92	13	23	57%
Away	3.90	0	7	0%	15.11	5	7	71%	5.89	2	9	22%	8.09	7	23	30%

DEZ BRYANT

When healthy, Bryant has been one of the best and most consistent receivers in the game. However, the health part is still an issue. He should be 100% this season, so I see no reason in drafting him as a WR1A this year. Bryant's 75% Clutch Rate last season showed he's ready to be back near the top of the rankings!

3 YEAR CONSISTENCY HISTORY

		Total FP	RANK	CG	GP	CR	RANK
Dez Bryant	2016	182.10	38	9	12	75%	11
	2015	89.10	79	3	9	33%	60
	2014	316.00	4	13	16	81%	6

TIER DRAFT RANK – WR1 – A

UNDERVALUED: Currently Bryant's ADP is WR10/pick 19. While he was only ranked 11th in consistency last year, two years he was Top 6 in both total points and consistency.

CLUTCH GAMES BY WEEK – 2016

Player Name	1	2	3	4	5	6	7	8	9	10	11	12	13	14	15	16	17	Total
Dez Bryant		+	+				B	+		+	+	+	+		+	+		9

CONSISTENCY VS DEFENSES (2014-2016)

	Good Defenses (Top 10)				Average Defenses				Bad Defenses (Bottom 10)				Total			
	FPG	CG	GP	CR	FPG	CG	GP	CR	FPG	CG	GP	CR	FPG	CG	GP	CR
Home	10.02	2	6	33%	18.85	5	6	83%	15.05	7	8	88%	14.68	14	20	70%
Away	10.23	1	3	33%	13.98	2	4	50%	20.70	8	10	80%	17.27	11	17	65%

MARTAVIS BRYANT

Bryant is back and safe, for now. If Bryant can gel with Roethlisberger, like he did in 2015, then Bryant should have some solid value heading into 2017. However, I'm not sold that he can earn a 73% but I do believe he can be a good value as a WR3/4 on your team. But his ADP is getting close to the WR2 range. Be careful.

3 YEAR CONSISTENCY HISTORY

		Total FP	RANK	CG	GP	CR	RANK
Martavis Bryant	2016	DNP	DNP	DNP	DNP	DNP	DNP
	2015	172.20	39	8	11	73%	18
	2014	130.10	60	5	10	50%	38

TIER DRAFT RANK – WR3 - B

OVERVALUED: Bryant's current ADP is WR27/pick 56. That's a little high for me, but not unreasonable. However, if he keeps moving towards the WR2, be safe. He missed all of 2016.

CLUTCH GAMES BY WEEK – 2016

Player Name	1	2	3	4	5	6	7	8	9	10	11	12	13	14	15	16	17	Total
Martavis Bryant																		0

CONSISTENCY VS DEFENSES (2014-2016)

	Good Defenses (Top 10)				Average Defenses				Bad Defenses (Bottom 10)				Total			
	FPG	CG	GP	CR	FPG	CG	GP	CR	FPG	CG	GP	CR	FPG	CG	GP	CR
Home	17.22	3	5	60%	15.47	2	3	67%	16.65	3	4	75%	16.59	8	12	67%
Away	17.53	4	4	100%	11.45	1	2	50%	3.40	0	3	0%	11.47	5	9	56%

For the most current Fantasy Football Consistency information, visit www.BigGuyFantasySports.com

CONSISTENCY PROFILES – WIDE RECEIVERS (continued)

RANDALL COBB

The changing of the "guard" is happening in Green Bay and Cobb is being moved out of the WR2 for the Packers. Cobb and Jordy Nelson were among the most dominant 1-2 punches in Fantasy Football at the position. However, Davante Adams has taken over the WR2 for the Packers and Cobb is an occasional highlight throughout the season.

3 YEAR CONSISTENCY HISTORY

		Total FP	RANK	CG	GP	CR	RANK
Randall Cobb	2016	148.30	54	6	13	46%	52
	2015	202.90	26	6	16	38%	53
	2014	295.40	8	13	16	81%	7

TIER DRAFT RANK – WR4 – C

AT VALUE: His ADP is WR38/pick 92. However, you look at his Clutch Rating of 46%, which ranked him 52nd and you must question if WR38 is too high? He's a nice backup value!

CLUTCH GAMES BY WEEK – 2016

Player Name	1	2	3	4	5	6	7	8	9	10	11	12	13	14	15	16	17	Total
Randall Cobb	+			B	+	+	+				+		+					6

CONSISTENCY VS DEFENSES (2014-2016)

	Good Defenses (Top 10)				Average Defenses				Bad Defenses (Bottom 10)				Total			
	FPG	CG	GP	CR	FPG	CG	GP	CR	FPG	CG	GP	CR	FPG	CG	GP	CR
Home	18.26	7	9	78%	14.84	6	9	67%	13.00	2	5	40%	15.78	15	23	65%
Away	12.07	4	9	44%	9.36	2	7	29%	18.27	5	6	83%	12.90	11	22	50%

BRANDIN COOKS

After a couple of very inconsistent seasons, Cooks finally "broke out" last year with a 75% Clutch Rate, which ranked him seventh. However, this offseason, he went to the Patriots. Many Fantasy experts saw this as a great thing. I disagree. Rarely has a deep receiver in New England been consistent. Julian Edelman is Brady's favorite, so Cooks' inconsistency figures to return.

3 YEAR CONSISTENCY HISTORY

		Total FP	RANK	CG	GP	CR	RANK
Brandin Cooks	2016	246.30	11	12	16	75%	7
	2015	253.60	14	9	16	56%	T27
	2014	139.30	56	5	10	50%	37

TIER DRAFT RANK – WR2 – B

OVERVALUED: Cooks' current ADP is WR13/pick 25. If you read the profile note above, you know why I'm not drafting him that high in 2016 and neither should you.

CLUTCH GAMES BY WEEK – 2016

Player Name	1	2	3	4	5	6	7	8	9	10	11	12	13	14	15	16	17	Total
Brandin Cooks	+	+			B	+	+	+	+	+	+		+	+	+	+		12

CONSISTENCY VS DEFENSES (2014-2016)

	Good Defenses (Top 10)				Average Defenses				Bad Defenses (Bottom 10)				Total			
	FPG	CG	GP	CR	FPG	CG	GP	CR	FPG	CG	GP	CR	FPG	CG	GP	CR
Home	15.12	4	5	80%	16.98	8	10	80%	19.83	5	6	83%	17.35	17	21	81%
Away	14.73	3	6	50%	7.62	1	6	17%	15.63	7	9	78%	13.09	11	21	52%

For the most current Fantasy Football Consistency information, visit www.BigGuyFantasySports.com

CONSISTENCY PROFILES – WIDE RECEIVERS (continued)

AMARI COOPER

I love Amari Cooper as a player and truly believe SOMEDAY he will be a Top 12 Fantasy receiver! However, if Michael Crabtree is healthy and in Oakland, Cooper and Crabtree will both be 1A in Derek Carr's book. Last season, Crabtree ranked higher in both total points AND consistency and his ADP is around 30 spots later.

3 YEAR CONSISTENCY HISTORY

		Total FP	RANK	CG	GP	CR	RANK
Amari Cooper	2016	226.90	16	10	16	63%	23
	2015	214.70	21	8	16	50%	37
	2014	DNP	DNP	DNP	DNP	DNP	DNP

CLUTCH GAMES BY WEEK – 2016

Player Name	1	2	3	4	5	6	7	8	9	10	11	12	13	14	15	16	17	Total
Amari Cooper	+	+			+	+		+	+	B	+		+			+	+	10

CONSISTENCY VS DEFENSES (2015-2016)

	Good Defenses (Top 10)				Average Defenses				Bad Defenses (Bottom 10)				Total			
	FPG	CG	GP	CR	FPG	CG	GP	CR	FPG	CG	GP	CR	FPG	CG	GP	CR
Home	11.26	3	7	43%	19.96	4	5	80%	12.30	3	4	75%	14.24	10	16	63%
Away	6.92	1	5	20%	11.77	3	6	50%	21.72	4	5	80%	13.36	8	16	50%

MICHAEL CRABTREE

This guy gets no respect from the Fantasy world. In 2015, he ranked in the Top 20 in total points and consistency and his ADP was WR35. In 2016, he ranks in the Top 15 in both and his ADP is WR21. He ranks better in both categories ahead of Amari Cooper, who's ADP is 30 spots ahead of Crabtree. Take Crabtree as your WR2 for great value!

3 YEAR CONSISTENCY HISTORY

		Total FP	RANK	CG	GP	CR	RANK
Michael Crabtree	2016	237.30	12	11	16	69%	15
	2015	231.20	17	11	16	69%	T20
	2014	162.20	46	6	16	38%	54

CLUTCH GAMES BY WEEK – 2016

Player Name	1	2	3	4	5	6	7	8	9	10	11	12	13	14	15	16	17	Total
Michael Crabtree	+	+	+	+	+		+	+		B		+	+		+	+		11

CONSISTENCY VS DEFENSES (2015-2016)

	Good Defenses (Top 10)				Average Defenses				Bad Defenses (Bottom 10)				Total			
	FPG	CG	GP	CR	FPG	CG	GP	CR	FPG	CG	GP	CR	FPG	CG	GP	CR
Home	10.64	2	7	29%	18.44	5	5	100%	12.00	3	4	75%	13.42	10	16	63%
Away	17.08	3	5	60%	16.98	6	6	100%	13.30	3	5	60%	15.86	12	16	75%

For the most current Fantasy Football Consistency information, visit www.BigGuyFantasySports.com

VICTOR CRUZ

Honestly, Cruz is done. However, I listed him for one more year since he went to the Bears in the offseason. Maybe there's some salsa left in the tank in 2017. The Bears' receiving depth is limited and maybe, just maybe, Cruz could help the Bears and someone's Fantasy team some bye week. But he's not draftable, so pick him up on the waiver wire, if you need him.

3 YEAR CONSISTENCY HISTORY

		Total FP	RANK	CG	GP	CR	RANK
Victor Cruz	2016	103.60	75	3	15	20%	98
	2015	DNP	DNP	DNP	DNP	DNP	DNP
	2014	62.70	96	3	6	50%	39

TIER DRAFT RANK – WR7 – D

UNDRAFTABLE: As mentioned above, Cruz is undraftable at this point. The stars, moons and planets must align perfectly for Cruz to have any Fantasy value in 2017. Stay away at this point.

CLUTCH GAMES BY WEEK – 2016

Player Name	1	2	3	4	5	6	7	8	9	10	11	12	13	14	15	16	17	Total
Victor Cruz	+	+						B								+		3

CONSISTENCY VS DEFENSES (2014-2016)

	Good Defenses (Top 10)				Average Defenses				Bad Defenses (Bottom 10)				Total			
	FPG	CG	GP	CR	FPG	CG	GP	CR	FPG	CG	GP	CR	FPG	CG	GP	CR
Home	6.10	0	1	0%	8.23	2	6	33%	9.43	1	3	33%	8.38	3	10	30%
Away	8.30	0	3	0%	9.93	2	3	67%	5.56	1	5	20%	7.50	3	11	27%

JAMISON CROWDER

I will admit my mistakes, and I will pat myself on the back for those good picks, and Crowder was one of my best picks last year. His consistent second half in 2015 led me to believe that he was starting to create some chemistry with Kirk Cousins. He did, and ended last season ranked in the Top 30 in both total points and consistency.

3 YEAR CONSISTENCY HISTORY

		Total FP	RANK	CG	GP	CR	RANK
Jamison Crowder	2016	193.50	30	10	16	63%	28
	2015	131.60	52	5	16	31%	64
	2014	DNP	DNP	DNP	DNP	DNP	DNP

TIER DRAFT RANK – WR2 – B

UNDERVALUED: With Crowder's current ADP at around WR29/pick 63, he's a nice value pick as your WR3 in 2017. Garcon and Jackson are gone, so Crowder should be consistent.

CLUTCH GAMES BY WEEK – 2016

Player Name	1	2	3	4	5	6	7	8	9	10	11	12	13	14	15	16	17	Total
Jamison Crowder	+	+	+			+	+	+	B	+	+	+	+					10

CONSISTENCY VS DEFENSES (2015-2016)

	Good Defenses (Top 10)				Average Defenses				Bad Defenses (Bottom 10)				Total			
	FPG	CG	GP	CR	FPG	CG	GP	CR	FPG	CG	GP	CR	FPG	CG	GP	CR
Home	9.00	1	2	50%	8.74	3	8	38%	9.53	3	6	50%	9.07	7	16	44%
Away	9.67	3	6	50%	13.53	5	8	63%	6.90	0	2	0%	11.25	8	16	50%

For the most current Fantasy Football Consistency information, visit www.BigGuyFantasySports.com

CONSISTENCY PROFILES – WIDE RECEIVERS (continued)

ERIC DECKER

Decker was just signed by the Titans and will be a nice security blanket for Marcus Mariota on those tough third downs. However, there are a ton of mouths to feed in Tennessee now. I believe Decker in Tennessee is good for Mariota, but not good for Decker, nor the rest of the Titans receivers. Keep an eye on the preseason to see who starts clicking with Mariota early.

3 YEAR CONSISTENCY HISTORY

		Total FP	RANK	CG	GP	CR	RANK
Eric Decker	2016	40.40	121	2	3	67%	20
	2015	254.70	13	15	15	100%	1
	2014	200.20	26	9	15	60%	23

TIER DRAFT RANK – WR6 – D

UNDERVALUED: Decker was an extremely consistent receiver in 2015. However, he's now the third or fourth option for Mariota in Tennessee. His value is probably going to be low. I'd buy.

CLUTCH GAMES BY WEEK – 2016

Player Name	1	2	3	4	5	6	7	8	9	10	11	12	13	14	15	16	17	Total
Eric Decker	+	+									B							2

CONSISTENCY VS DEFENSES (2014-2016)

	Good Defenses (Top 10)				Average Defenses				Bad Defenses (Bottom 10)				Total			
	FPG	CG	GP	CR	FPG	CG	GP	CR	FPG	CG	GP	CR	FPG	CG	GP	CR
Home	12.20	4	5	80%	12.36	3	5	60%	13.33	5	6	83%	12.68	12	16	75%
Away	13.92	4	5	80%	21.23	6	6	100%	15.92	5	6	83%	17.21	15	17	88%

STEFON DIGGS

Diggs did not step up and take the #1 role in Minnesota as expected. Adam Thielen did. Diggs improved by one Clutch Game in 2016 and ended the season ranked as a WR3 in both total points and consistency. However, he only earned three Clutch Games in the second half of the year once Bradford locked in with Thielen.

3 YEAR CONSISTENCY HISTORY

		Total FP	RANK	CG	GP	CR	RANK
Stefon Diggs	2016	193.30	31	7	13	54%	36
	2015	149.30	45	6	13	46%	45
	2014	DNP	DNP	DNP	DNP	DNP	DNP

TIER DRAFT RANK – WR4 – C

OVERVALUED: Diggs' current ADP is at WR28/pick 60. Based on last year's performance in the second half, he's overvalued. I'd rather draft Thielen 45 spots later and get better consistency.

CLUTCH GAMES BY WEEK – 2016

Player Name	1	2	3	4	5	6	7	8	9	10	11	12	13	14	15	16	17	Total
Stefon Diggs	+	+				B		+	+	+			+			+		7

CONSISTENCY VS DEFENSES (2015-2016)

	Good Defenses (Top 10)				Average Defenses				Bad Defenses (Bottom 10)				Total			
	FPG	CG	GP	CR	FPG	CG	GP	CR	FPG	CG	GP	CR	FPG	CG	GP	CR
Home	10.70	1	4	25%	15.28	4	5	80%	14.13	1	3	33%	13.47	6	12	50%
Away	8.80	1	3	33%	13.09	4	8	50%	16.63	2	3	67%	12.93	7	14	50%

For the most current Fantasy Football Consistency information, visit www.BigGuyFantasySports.com

CONSISTENCY PROFILES – WIDE RECEIVERS (continued)

JULIAN EDELMAN

The numbers below speak for themselves. Each year, he's ranked a little higher in consistency as Brady gets more and more comfortable with Edelman. The addition of Brandin Cooks will NOT hurt Edelman's consistency. If anything, he may help Edelman by stretching the defense for Edelman and Gronk underneath.

3 YEAR CONSISTENCY HISTORY

		Total FP	RANK	CG	GP	CR	RANK
Julian Edelman	2016	232.30	14	12	16	75%	9
	2015	174.50	35	7	9	78%	13
	2014	222.60	17	10	14	71%	14

TIER DRAFT RANK – WR2 – B

UNDERVALUED: Edelman's current ADP is WR25/pick 55. As you see, his consistency is right in front of you and he's undervalued since Cook's being ranked higher. Edelman = WR2!

CLUTCH GAMES BY WEEK – 2016

Player Name	1	2	3	4	5	6	7	8	9	10	11	12	13	14	15	16	17	Total
Julian Edelman	+	+					+	+	B	+	+	+	+	+	+	+	+	12

CONSISTENCY VS DEFENSES (2014-2016)

	Good Defenses (Top 10)				Average Defenses				Bad Defenses (Bottom 10)				Total			
	FPG	CG	GP	CR	FPG	CG	GP	CR	FPG	CG	GP	CR	FPG	CG	GP	CR
Home	15.24	5	8	63%	12.82	3	6	50%	16.00	5	6	83%	14.74	13	20	65%
Away	16.52	4	5	80%	18.27	9	9	100%	17.52	3	5	60%	17.61	16	19	84%

MIKE EVANS

Mike Evans is one of the reasons I put the hard work into this book. To highlight overvalued players based on their inconsistency versus their ADP. Mike Evans is ranked WAY TOO HIGH heading into this year. His Clutch Rating says he's a WR2, but his ADP is around WR4 and pick 7 overall! Nope, not me!

3 YEAR CONSISTENCY HISTORY

		Total FP	RANK	CG	GP	CR	RANK
Mike Evans	2016	300.10	3	11	16	69%	13
	2015	205.70	25	9	14	64%	25
	2014	245.10	13	9	15	60%	21

TIER DRAFT RANK – WR1 – B

OVERVALUED: For two straight years, Evans has earned a Clutch Rating in the 60-69% range. That ranks him in the high WR2 range. His ADP is WR4/pick 7. I just can't do it!

CLUTCH GAMES BY WEEK – 2016

Player Name	1	2	3	4	5	6	7	8	9	10	11	12	13	14	15	16	17	Total
Mike Evans	+	+	+	+	+	B	+		+		+	+				+	+	11

CONSISTENCY VS DEFENSES (2014-2016)

	Good Defenses (Top 10)				Average Defenses				Bad Defenses (Bottom 10)				Total			
	FPG	CG	GP	CR	FPG	CG	GP	CR	FPG	CG	GP	CR	FPG	CG	GP	CR
Home	18.44	4	5	80%	12.31	4	10	40%	18.17	4	7	57%	15.57	12	22	55%
Away	17.63	4	4	100%	15.91	4	8	50%	19.15	9	11	82%	17.76	17	23	74%

For the most current Fantasy Football Consistency information, visit www.BigGuyFantasySports.com

CONSISTENCY PROFILES – WIDE RECEIVERS (continued)

LARRY FITZGERALD

I said I would admit when I was wrong and this was one of them. Even after, Fitzgerald had a great 2015, I couldn't see him hitting those numbers again. He didn't hit them, he improved on them! He ended the year ranked ninth in total points and second in consistency. So, here comes 2017. Can he do it again? Doubtful, but I might be looking at him for my WR3 this year.

3 YEAR CONSISTENCY HISTORY

		Total FP	RANK	CG	GP	CR	RANK
Larry Fitzgerald	2016	246.90	9	13	16	81%	2
	2015	284.50	7	13	16	81%	T5
	2014	153.40	51	5	14	36%	60

TIER DRAFT RANK – WR2 – B

UNDERVALUED: Fitzgerald's current ADP is around the WR26/pick 52 mark. This surprises me after the last two years. Draft him as your WR3 and get great value out of him!

CLUTCH GAMES BY WEEK – 2016

Player Name	1	2	3	4	5	6	7	8	9	10	11	12	13	14	15	16	17	Total
Larry Fitzgerald	+	+	+	+	+	+	+	+	B	+	+		+		+		+	13

CONSISTENCY VS DEFENSES (2014-2016)

	Good Defenses (Top 10)				Average Defenses				Bad Defenses (Bottom 10)				Total			
	FPG	CG	GP	CR	FPG	CG	GP	CR	FPG	CG	GP	CR	FPG	CG	GP	CR
Home	11.69	5	11	45%	13.56	4	5	80%	21.98	8	8	100%	15.51	17	24	71%
Away	11.88	3	6	50%	17.89	6	7	86%	12.90	5	9	56%	14.21	14	22	64%

DEVIN FUNCHESS

Funchess is currently #2 on the Panthers depth chart, but his ADP is already worse than rookie, Curtis Samuel. Funchess got worse in his second year and injuries didn't help that. Currently, Funchess is undraftable in a standard 12-team league as his ADP is WR80. Nothing to see here.

3 YEAR CONSISTENCY HISTORY

		Total FP	RANK	CG	GP	CR	RANK
Devin Funchess	2016	84.10	89	3	13	23%	90
	2015	108.30	62	4	16	25%	72
	2014	DNP	DNP	DNP	DNP	DNP	DNP

TIER DRAFT RANK – WR7 – D

UNDRAFTABLE: With his current ADP at WR80/pick 236, Funchess is basically a waiver wire pickup whenever you're desperate sometime during the season. For now, let him go.

CLUTCH GAMES BY WEEK – 2016

Player Name	1	2	3	4	5	6	7	8	9	10	11	12	13	14	15	16	17	Total
Devin Funchess						+	B			+				+				3

CONSISTENCY VS DEFENSES (2015-2016)

	Good Defenses (Top 10)				Average Defenses				Bad Defenses (Bottom 10)				Total			
	FPG	CG	GP	CR	FPG	CG	GP	CR	FPG	CG	GP	CR	FPG	CG	GP	CR
Home	4.65	0	2	0%	14.48	3	4	75%	6.90	2	8	25%	8.74	5	14	36%
Away	4.13	0	4	0%	2.50	0	4	0%	6.21	2	7	29%	4.67	2	15	13%

For the most current Fantasy Football Consistency information, visit www.BigGuyFantasySports.com

CONSISTENCY PROFILES – WIDE RECEIVERS (continued)

TAYLOR GABRIEL

Gabriel quietly was a consistent Fantasy force in the second half of last season. He earned all six of his Clutch Games from Week 8 on. He did fairly well in the NFL playoffs for the Falcons as well. He will continue to be a threat in that offense with Julio Jones on the other side. Gabriel should be a solid backup or flex player.

3 YEAR CONSISTENCY HISTORY

		Total FP	RANK	CG	GP	CR	RANK
Taylor Gabriel	2016	140.00	58	6	12	50%	46
	2015	52.10	107	1	13	8%	109
	2014	107.10	71	3	16	19%	76

TIER DRAFT RANK – WR4 – C

UNDERVALUED: Gabriel's ADP is currently WR63/pick 180. He's certainly worth more than that. If he matches his 2016 numbers, he's a WR50, when you combine consistency and points.

CLUTCH GAMES BY WEEK – 2016

Player Name	1	2	3	4	5	6	7	8	9	10	11	12	13	14	15	16	17	Total
Taylor Gabriel								+	+	+	B	+		+	+			6

CONSISTENCY VS DEFENSES (2016)

	Good Defenses (Top 10)				Average Defenses				Bad Defenses (Bottom 10)				Total			
	FPG	CG	GP	CR	FPG	CG	GP	CR	FPG	CG	GP	CR	FPG	CG	GP	CR
Home	26.20	1	1	100%	7.90	0	1	0%	13.40	2	3	67%	14.86	3	5	60%
Away	9.40	1	2	50%	9.55	1	2	50%	9.27	1	3	33%	9.39	3	7	43%

PIERRE GARCON

Garcon had an excellent season last year in Washington. This "earned" him a trip to San Francisco to play for the 49ers. However, Garcon is really the only decent receiver in San Fran and should see most of the targets. Remember, he's reconnected with former coach, Kyle Shanahan, so draft him as a WR4 and get WR3 value from him.

3 YEAR CONSISTENCY HISTORY

		Total FP	RANK	CG	GP	CR	RANK
Pierre Garcon	2016	201.10	23	12	16	75%	10
	2015	185.70	31	9	16	56%	32
	2014	161.20	47	5	16	31%	68

TIER DRAFT RANK – WR3 – B

UNDERVALUED: With his current ADP at WR36/pick 88, Garcon should be of some value as the WR1 in San Fran. Kyle Shanahan will get value from him and so should you in 2017.

CLUTCH GAMES BY WEEK – 2016

Player Name	1	2	3	4	5	6	7	8	9	10	11	12	13	14	15	16	17	Total
Pierre Garcon	+		+		+	+		+	B	+	+		+	+	+	+	+	12

CONSISTENCY VS DEFENSES (2014-2016)

	Good Defenses (Top 10)				Average Defenses				Bad Defenses (Bottom 10)				Total			
	FPG	CG	GP	CR	FPG	CG	GP	CR	FPG	CG	GP	CR	FPG	CG	GP	CR
Home	10.67	2	3	67%	12.24	6	9	67%	9.88	4	12	33%	10.87	12	24	50%
Away	11.54	5	7	71%	10.58	6	12	50%	15.90	3	5	60%	11.97	14	24	58%

For the most current Fantasy Football Consistency information, visit www.BigGuyFantasySports.com

CONSISTENCY PROFILES – WIDE RECEIVERS (continued)

TED GINN

Ginn was his normal inconsistent/big game player in 2016 for the Panthers. He was signed by the Saints in the offseason to replace the speed of Brandin Cooks. I believe Ginn will have some value in New Orleans. The tough part will be guessing which games those will happen in. Note below, he's 75% Clutch when on the road against a bad defense. Start him then!

3 YEAR CONSISTENCY HISTORY

		Total FP	RANK	CG	GP	CR	RANK
Ted Ginn	2016	163.00	48	6	16	38%	68
	2015	183.90	34	8	15	53%	53
	2014	33.60	118	0	16	0%	118

TIER DRAFT RANK – WR6 – D

AT VALUE: With his current ADP at WR61/pick 174, why not grab him for your bench? He's always capable of big plays/games (especially against bad defenses – see below). Nice late value.

CLUTCH GAMES BY WEEK – 2016

Player Name	1	2	3	4	5	6	7	8	9	10	11	12	13	14	15	16	17	Total
Ted Ginn						+	B				+	+	+		+		+	6

CONSISTENCY VS DEFENSES (2015-2016)

	Good Defenses (Top 10)				Average Defenses				Bad Defenses (Bottom 10)				Total			
	FPG	CG	GP	CR	FPG	CG	GP	CR	FPG	CG	GP	CR	FPG	CG	GP	CR
Home	11.37	1	3	33%	11.37	1	3	33%	10.20	4	9	44%	10.67	6	15	40%
Away	8.73	1	4	25%	6.55	1	4	25%	15.73	6	8	75%	11.68	8	16	50%

A.J. GREEN

Green's demise last season was injuries. He still ranked 12th in consistency when healthy last season. He's one of the best in the game and one of the most consistent. Last season before his injury, he was on pace for career highs in targets, receptions and yards.

3 YEAR CONSISTENCY HISTORY

		Total FP	RANK	CG	GP	CR	RANK
A.J. Green	2016	186.40	34	7	10	70%	12
	2015	275.70	8	13	16	81%	T5
	2014	209.30	24	9	13	69%	19

TIER DRAFT RANK – WR1 – A

AT VALUE: When you're drafting a first-round player, he better be consistent! Green's ADP is WR5/pick 8. He's a Top 5 ranked wide receiver in consistency when healthy and he's worth it!

CLUTCH GAMES BY WEEK – 2016

Player Name	1	2	3	4	5	6	7	8	9	10	11	12	13	14	15	16	17	Total
A.J. Green	+		+	+		+	+	+	B	+								7

CONSISTENCY VS DEFENSES (2014-2016)

	Good Defenses (Top 10)				Average Defenses				Bad Defenses (Bottom 10)				Total			
	FPG	CG	GP	CR	FPG	CG	GP	CR	FPG	CG	GP	CR	FPG	CG	GP	CR
Home	11.28	4	5	80%	17.90	4	6	67%	17.18	6	8	75%	15.85	14	19	74%
Away	17.98	6	6	100%	20.23	5	9	56%	16.04	4	5	80%	18.51	15	20	75%

For the most current Fantasy Football Consistency information, visit www.BigGuyFantasySports.com

CONSISTENCY PROFILES – WIDE RECEIVERS (continued)

TYREEK HILL

Fact: there were only two wide receivers who had a better Clutch Rate than Tyreek Hill from Week 10 – 17. That was Jordy Nelson and Julian Edelman, who were perfect! Hill's 89% Clutch Rate during that time frame shows the Chiefs want to give him the ball often. The departure of Jeremy Maclin should help as well. He's an excellent value this year.

3 YEAR CONSISTENCY HISTORY

		Total FP	RANK	CG	GP	CR	RANK
Tyreek Hill	2016	202.00	22	10	16	63%	26
	2015	DNP	DNP	DNP	DNP	DNP	DNP
	2014	DNP	DNP	DNP	DNP	DNP	DNP

TIER DRAFT RANK – WR2 – B

AT VALUE: Hill's current ADP is WR20, I wouldn't reach much higher than that though. He's right where I believe would be the best value for him. If you get points for return yards, grab him!

CLUTCH GAMES BY WEEK – 2016

Player Name	1	2	3	4	5	6	7	8	9	10	11	12	13	14	15	16	17	Total
Tyreek Hill				+	B		+	+		+		+	+	+	+	+	+	10

CONSISTENCY VS DEFENSES (2016)

	Good Defenses (Top 10)				Average Defenses				Bad Defenses (Bottom 10)				Total			
	FPG	CG	GP	CR	FPG	CG	GP	CR	FPG	CG	GP	CR	FPG	CG	GP	CR
Home	11.35	1	2	50%	8.67	1	3	33%	14.00	2	3	67%	11.34	4	8	50%
Away	14.60	1	2	50%	14.80	3	3	100%	12.57	2	3	67%	13.91	6	8	75%

T.Y. HILTON

Hilton was a very consistent receiver again in 2016. He's certainly worth a WR1 pick **if Luck stays healthy** (as evident from his 2015 numbers). Nothing much has changed for the Colts in the offseason, so I would expect another Top 12 season in total points and consistency in 2017. **Update: Luck's status is extremely questionable for Week 1, be cautious!**

3 YEAR CONSISTENCY HISTORY

		Total FP	RANK	CG	GP	CR	RANK
T.Y. Hilton	2016	271.80	5	11	16	69%	14
	2015	211.40	23	9	16	56%	31
	2014	260.50	11	15	15	73%	12

TIER DRAFT RANK – WR1 – B

AT VALUE: Hilton's current ADP is WR8/pick 15. I believe this is a good spot for Hilton. I have him ranked as a WR9, but Luck's health scares me! I'd rather pass on him this year.

CLUTCH GAMES BY WEEK – 2016

Player Name	1	2	3	4	5	6	7	8	9	10	11	12	13	14	15	16	17	Total
T.Y. Hilton	+		+	+	+		+		+	B	+		+	+		+	+	11

CONSISTENCY VS DEFENSES (2014-2016)

	Good Defenses (Top 10)				Average Defenses				Bad Defenses (Bottom 10)				Total			
	FPG	CG	GP	CR	FPG	CG	GP	CR	FPG	CG	GP	CR	FPG	CG	GP	CR
Home	14.05	5	8	63%	18.9	6	9	67%	16.87	6	7	86%	16.69	17	24	71%
Away	9.44	2	7	29%	21.29	7	9	78%	12.20	5	7	71%	14.92	14	23	61%

For the most current Fantasy Football Consistency information, visit www.BigGuyFantasySports.com

CONSISTENCY PROFILES – WIDE RECEIVERS (continued)

CHRIS HOGAN

Hogan did improve on his prior year numbers, but as expected, he wasn't very consistent. The Patriots added Brandin Cooks to the mix and now Chris Hogan is listed on the depth chart right after Irving Fryar. Hogan's value right now is around zero. I wouldn't be surprised if he's cut in the offseason. He may catch on to another team but for now, he's undraftable.

3 YEAR CONSISTENCY HISTORY

		Total FP	RANK	CG	GP	CR	RANK
Chris Hogan	2016	130.90	61	6	15	40%	65
	2015	93.40	74	4	16	25%	74
	2014	107.60	69	5	16	31%	71

TIER DRAFT RANK – WR7 – D

UNDRAFTABLE: Hogan is basically undraftable at this point. If Edelman or Cooks get hurt, he'll have some value again or if he goes to another team in the offseason.

CLUTCH GAMES BY WEEK – 2016

Player Name	1	2	3	4	5	6	7	8	9	10	11	12	13	14	15	16	17	Total
Chris Hogan	+				+			+	B			+	+	+				6

CONSISTENCY VS DEFENSES (2016)

	Good Defenses (Top 10)				Average Defenses				Bad Defenses (Bottom 10)				Total			
	FPG	CG	GP	CR	FPG	CG	GP	CR	FPG	CG	GP	CR	FPG	CG	GP	CR
Home	9.55	2	4	50%	2.70	0	3	0%	9.90	0	1	0%	7.03	2	8	25%
Away	8.90	1	2	50%	11.53	2	3	67%	11.15	1	2	50%	10.67	4	7	57%

DEANDRE HOPKINS

So, I was wrong for a second year with Hopkins! After his incredible 2015 season with a terrible quarterback, I figured he would continue to thrive even with Brock Osweiler. I was wrong. His consistency and his total points were terrible in 2016. I keep hearing that Tom Savage has improved as will Hopkins. Well, I'll put him back in WR1 range, but I'm skeptical.

3 YEAR CONSISTENCY HISTORY

		Total FP	RANK	CG	GP	CR	RANK
DeAndre Hopkins	2016	197.40	27	9	16	56%	32
	2015	329.10	4	13	16	81%	T5
	2014	233.00	14	11	16	69%	16

TIER DRAFT RANK – WR1 – B

AT VALUE: His ADP and rankings are almost exact, so he's currently at value. However, I'm still a little edgy about him being this high with the quarterback situation in Houston.

CLUTCH GAMES BY WEEK – 2016

Player Name	1	2	3	4	5	6	7	8	9	10	11	12	13	14	15	16	17	Total
DeAndre Hopkins	+	+			+	+			B		+	+	+		+		+	9

CONSISTENCY VS DEFENSES (2014-2016)

	Good Defenses (Top 10)				Average Defenses				Bad Defenses (Bottom 10)				Total			
	FPG	CG	GP	CR	FPG	CG	GP	CR	FPG	CG	GP	CR	FPG	CG	GP	CR
Home	18.45	4	6	67%	11.57	4	9	44%	20.28	7	9	78%	16.55	15	24	63%
Away	11.93	2	6	33%	18.57	7	7	100%	14.60	9	11	82%	15.09	18	24	75%

For the most current Fantasy Football Consistency information, visit www.BigGuyFantasySports.com

CONSISTENCY PROFILES – WIDE RECEIVERS (continued)

ALLEN HURNS

The Jaguars passing offense was horrid in 2016! Even Allen Robinson fell victim to it. Hurns had a great 2015 and was well undervalued heading into 2016. Injuries and Blake Bortles led to Hurns demise last season. I still believe in Hurns for 2017, but it's Bortles who has to improve to help Hurns' Fantasy value increase. He's a decent backup in the late rounds.

3 YEAR CONSISTENCY HISTORY

Allen Hurns		Total FP	RANK	CG	GP	CR	RANK
Allen Hurns	2016	100.70	79	5	11	45%	54
	2015	227.00	19	10	15	67%	24
	2014	154.70	49	6	16	38%	55

TIER DRAFT RANK – WR5 – D

AT VALUE: Hurns current ADP is WR64/pick 181. I have him ranked similarly but I feel like he's a much better value as your WR5 than most will be in 2017. If he's there in round 15/16, do it!

CLUTCH GAMES BY WEEK – 2016

Player Name	1	2	3	4	5	6	7	8	9	10	11	12	13	14	15	16	17	Total
Allen Hurns	+	+		+	B	+		+										5

CONSISTENCY VS DEFENSES (2014-2016)

	Good Defenses (Top 10)				Average Defenses				Bad Defenses (Bottom 10)				Total			
	FPG	CG	GP	CR	FPG	CG	GP	CR	FPG	CG	GP	CR	FPG	CG	GP	CR
Home	8.33	2	4	50%	8.59	3	8	38%	9.66	4	9	44%	9.00	9	21	43%
Away	13.54	4	5	80%	13.25	6	10	60%	15.55	3	6	50%	13.98	13	21	62%

DESEAN JACKSON

Jackson has never been a great Fantasy receiver from a consistency perspective. He will have his big games and then disappear. He took his talents to Tampa Bay this offseason where he will team with Mike Evans and newly acquired tight end, O.J. Howard. honestly don't see him becoming any more or less consistent, so take him as a WR4 and that's fair.

3 YEAR CONSISTENCY HISTORY

DeSean Jackson		Total FP	RANK	CG	GP	CR	RANK
DeSean Jackson	2016	180.50	39	7	15	47%	51
	2015	106.80	64	4	10	40%	51
	2014	209.60	23	9	15	60%	22

TIER DRAFT RANK – WR4 – C

AT VALUE: Jackson's current ADP is WR37/pick 89. While he's got the name recognition, his past numbers are a distant memory. Don't be that owner who reaches for him.

CLUTCH GAMES BY WEEK – 2016

Player Name	1	2	3	4	5	6	7	8	9	10	11	12	13	14	15	16	17	Total
DeSean Jackson	+		+						B		+	+		+	+	+		7

CONSISTENCY VS DEFENSES (2014-2016)

	Good Defenses (Top 10)				Average Defenses				Bad Defenses (Bottom 10)				Total			
	FPG	CG	GP	CR	FPG	CG	GP	CR	FPG	CG	GP	CR	FPG	CG	GP	CR
Home	16.05	1	2	50%	16.35	4	6	67%	8.29	4	11	36%	11.65	9	19	47%
Away	10.68	2	6	33%	14.15	7	11	64%	13.93	2	4	50%	13.12	11	21	52%

For the most current Fantasy Football Consistency information, visit www.BigGuyFantasySports.com

ALSHON JEFFERY

After two seasons of solid health and consistency, Jeffery's health let him and his Fantasy owners down again by missing four games. His consistency was a solid 67% Clutch Rating though. Jeffery went to Philadelphia in the offseason and will team with Jordan Matthews, Torrey Smith and Nelson Agholor plus tight end, Zach Ertz. So, who gets "fed" the most?

3 YEAR CONSISTENCY HISTORY

		Total FP	RANK	CG	GP	CR	RANK
Alshon Jeffery	2016	146.10	55	8	12	67%	19
	2015	158.70	42	7	9	78%	14
	2014	261.60	10	13	16	81%	8

TIER DRAFT RANK – WR2 – B

OVERVALUED: Jeffery's current ADP is WR18/pick 35, which is a bit high for me. With too many weapons in Philly and Carson Wentz is in his second year, all are concerns for me in 2017.

CLUTCH GAMES BY WEEK – 2016

Player Name	1	2	3	4	5	6	7	8	9	10	11	12	13	14	15	16	17	Total
Alshon Jeffery	+	+	+		+	+		+	B						+	+		8

CONSISTENCY VS DEFENSES (2014-2016)

	Good Defenses (Top 10)				Average Defenses				Bad Defenses (Bottom 10)				Total			
	FPG	CG	GP	CR	FPG	CG	GP	CR	FPG	CG	GP	CR	FPG	CG	GP	CR
Home	18.30	5	5	100%	13.92	4	6	67%	17.26	7	7	100%	16.43	16	18	89%
Away	13.86	4	7	57%	14.6	5	7	71%	14.28	3	5	60%	14.24	12	19	63%

JULIO JONES

Jones did not live up to expectations last season! The Falcons had their best season in a long time. However, this was due to a strong running game and Matt Ryan spreading the ball around in the air…much to Julio Jones' Fantasy owners' displeasure. Kyle Shanahan left, so will the new OC go back to feeding Julio more or keep winning football games? I'm worried.

3 YEAR CONSISTENCY HISTORY

		Total FP	RANK	CG	GP	CR	RANK
Julio Jones	2016	259.90	6	9	14	64%	21
	2015	371.10	2	14	16	88%	T3
	2014	299.40	6	12	15	80%	9

TIER DRAFT RANK – WR1 – A

AT VALUE: When you're in the middle of the first round and Julio is there, what should you do? I'm torn this year! I don't think he'll be on many of my teams this year regardless of where I pick.

CLUTCH GAMES BY WEEK – 2016

Player Name	1	2	3	4	5	6	7	8	9	10	11	12	13	14	15	16	17	Total
Julio Jones	+	+		+		+	+		+	+	B		+				+	9

CONSISTENCY VS DEFENSES (2014-2016)

	Good Defenses (Top 10)				Average Defenses				Bad Defenses (Bottom 10)				Total			
	FPG	CG	GP	CR	FPG	CG	GP	CR	FPG	CG	GP	CR	FPG	CG	GP	CR
Home	13.70	2	5	40%	28.52	5	6	83%	20.52	10	11	91%	21.15	17	22	77%
Away	14.55	3	4	75%	22.91	8	9	89%	20.07	9	10	90%	20.22	20	23	87%

For the most current Fantasy Football Consistency information, visit www.BigGuyFantasySports.com

MARVIN JONES

Jones started off 2016 like a wildfire! Five straight Clutch Games and six in his first seven! Then injuries and drops set in and Jones earned only two more Clutch Game for the remainder of the season. His 38th place rank isn't bad considered the horrible second half. If he stays healthy in 2017, he could be a good value. Keep an eye on him this preseason.

3 YEAR CONSISTENCY HISTORY

		Total FP	RANK	CG	GP	CR	RANK
Marvin Jones	2016	172.30	42	8	15	53%	38
	2015	173.90	36	8	16	50%	40
	2014	DNP	DNP	DNP	DNP	DNP	DNP

TIER DRAFT RANK – WR4 – C

UNDERVALUED: Jones' current ADP is WR49/pick 125. I have a little more faith in his consistency with his health back at 100%. I like him as a WR4 in 2017. A nice value at backup.

CLUTCH GAMES BY WEEK – 2016

Player Name	1	2	3	4	5	6	7	8	9	10	11	12	13	14	15	16	17	Total
Marvin Jones	+	+	+	+	+		+			B				+			+	8

CONSISTENCY VS DEFENSES (2016)

	Good Defenses (Top 10)				Average Defenses				Bad Defenses (Bottom 10)				Total			
	FPG	CG	GP	CR	FPG	CG	GP	CR	FPG	CG	GP	CR	FPG	CG	GP	CR
Home	7.07	0	3	0%	14.73	3	3	100%	13.00	2	2	100%	11.43	5	8	63%
Away	4.97	0	3	0%	7.50	1	2	50%	25.5	2	2	100%	11.56	3	7	43%

JERMAINE KEARSE

Kearse had a decent year in 2015 and was expected to improve on that and he didn't. He's still the #2 receiver on the Seahawks' depth chart, as Tyler Lockett didn't beat him out of the spot, as expected. I wouldn't expect anything better than something in between 2015 and 2016 numbers. He's undraftable in my mind, at this point.

3 YEAR CONSISTENCY HISTORY

		Total FP	RANK	CG	GP	CR	RANK
Jermaine Kearse	2016	98.10	81	3	16	19%	102
	2015	147.50	48	8	16	50%	T37
	2014	99.20	75	1	15	7%	98

TIER DRAFT RANK – WR7 – D

UNDRAFTABLE: Kearse just doesn't have the consistency as the WR2 for the Seahawks to be worth drafting this year. Maybe you can pick him up if Baldwin or Lockett get hurt.

CLUTCH GAMES BY WEEK – 2016

Player Name	1	2	3	4	5	6	7	8	9	10	11	12	13	14	15	16	17	Total
Jermaine Kearse	+				B								+			+		3

CONSISTENCY VS DEFENSES (2014-2016)

	Good Defenses (Top 10)				Average Defenses				Bad Defenses (Bottom 10)				Total			
	FPG	CG	GP	CR	FPG	CG	GP	CR	FPG	CG	GP	CR	FPG	CG	GP	CR
Home	5.45	2	6	33%	9.39	4	9	44%	8.16	2	8	25%	7.93	8	23	35%
Away	7.43	3	9	33%	6.08	2	8	25%	6.69	0	7	0%	6.76	5	24	21%

For the most current Fantasy Football Consistency information, visit www.BigGuyFantasySports.com

CONSISTENCY PROFILES – WIDE RECEIVERS (continued)

BRANDON LAFELL

LaFell has pretty much worn out his welcome in Cincinnati. He's currently #2 on their depth chart but he's merely a placeholder for Tyler Boyd or John Ross. In the meantime, I would stay far away from LaFell on draft day in 2017 unless one or both of those youngsters get hurt.

3 YEAR CONSISTENCY HISTORY

		Total FP	RANK	CG	GP	CR	RANK
Brandon LaFell	2016	186.00	35	7	16	44%	57
	2015	89.40	78	2	11	18%	91
	2014	212.60	22	9	16	56%	27

CLUTCH GAMES BY WEEK – 2016

Player Name	1	2	3	4	5	6	7	8	9	10	11	12	13	14	15	16	17	Total
Brandon LaFell	+				+		+		B				+		+	+	+	7

CONSISTENCY VS DEFENSES (2016)

	Good Defenses (Top 10)				Average Defenses				Bad Defenses (Bottom 10)				Total			
	FPG	CG	GP	CR	FPG	CG	GP	CR	FPG	CG	GP	CR	FPG	CG	GP	CR
Home	9.45	1	2	50%	14.60	2	3	67%	9.43	1	3	33%	11.38	4	8	50%
Away	10.75	1	4	25%	15.60	2	3	67%	5.20	0	1	0%	11.88	3	8	38%

JARVIS LANDRY

Another year of great consistency for Landry and another year of disrespect from the Fantasy world. That's fine with me, because this is EXACTLY where you and I will benefit. Landry ended last season with his second straight season with 75%+ Clutch Rating! He ended the year ranked eighth and 13th in total points. Check out his current ADP below!

3 YEAR CONSISTENCY HISTORY

		Total FP	RANK	CG	GP	CR	RANK
Jarvis Landry	2016	233.50	13	12	16	75%	8
	2015	268.00	11	13	16	81%	11
	2014	189.40	30	9	16	56%	29

CLUTCH GAMES BY WEEK – 2016

Player Name	1	2	3	4	5	6	7	8	9	10	11	12	13	14	15	16	17	Total
Jarvis Landry	+	+	+	+		+	+	B		+	+		+	+	+		+	12

CONSISTENCY VS DEFENSES (2014-2016)

	Good Defenses (Top 10)				Average Defenses				Bad Defenses (Bottom 10)				Total			
	FPG	CG	GP	CR	FPG	CG	GP	CR	FPG	CG	GP	CR	FPG	CG	GP	CR
Home	13.27	9	11	82%	11.06	6	9	67%	18.58	3	4	75%	13.33	18	24	75%
Away	17.92	10	11	91%	14.23	5	6	83%	12.66	4	7	57%	15.46	19	24	79%

TYLER LOCKETT

Lockett was supposed to break out last season. He didn't. He was supposed to knock Jermaine Kearse out of the #2 spot in Seattle. He didn't. He's supposed to be a WR3 in 2017. He's not. He will be lucky to be drafted as a WR5 or WR6. He has the skills, but we'll see if he can put it together in 2017. For now, I'm looking elsewhere.

3 YEAR CONSISTENCY HISTORY

		Total FP	RANK	CG	GP	CR	RANK
Tyler Lockett	2016	124.10	65	3	14	21%	93
	2015	155.40	43	5	16	31%	62
	2014	DNP	DNP	DNP	DNP	DNP	DNP

TIER DRAFT RANK – WR5 – D

AT VALUE: Lockett's ADP is around the WR62 mark. This is at the value I have him ranked as well. That's a WR5/6 value heading into this year's Fantasy drafts. Be cautious.

CLUTCH GAMES BY WEEK – 2016

Player Name	1	2	3	4	5	6	7	8	9	10	11	12	13	14	15	16	17	Total
Tyler Lockett		+			B								+		+			3

CONSISTENCY VS DEFENSES (2015-2016)

	Good Defenses (Top 10)				Average Defenses				Bad Defenses (Bottom 10)				Total			
	FPG	CG	GP	CR	FPG	CG	GP	CR	FPG	CG	GP	CR	FPG	CG	GP	CR
Home	8.38	1	4	25%	8.24	1	7	14%	12.00	2	4	50%	9.28	4	15	27%
Away	9.22	2	6	33%	9.68	1	5	20%	9.15	1	4	25%	9.35	4	15	27%

JEREMY MACLIN

Maclin was released by the Chiefs two weeks after Andy Reid attending Maclin's wedding. Ouch! Remember, it's a business. Football that is. Anyways, Maclin was signed by the Ravens and will team up with Mike Wallace. Yawn! I would expect Maclin's consistency to be around 45-50%, so draft accordingly.

3 YEAR CONSISTENCY HISTORY

		Total FP	RANK	CG	GP	CR	RANK
Jeremy Maclin	2016	109.50	71	5	12	42%	61
	2015	244.90	15	10	15	67%	22
	2014	278.90	9	12	16	75%	11

TIER DRAFT RANK – WR5 – D

OVERVALUED: Maclin's current ADP of WR39/pick 99. Which is too high based on Flacco's injury. If Flacco gets healthy, then he's a decent backup, if you need one.

CLUTCH GAMES BY WEEK – 2016

Player Name	1	2	3	4	5	6	7	8	9	10	11	12	13	14	15	16	17	Total
Jeremy Maclin	+	+		+	B			+							+			5

CONSISTENCY VS DEFENSES (2015-2016)

	Good Defenses (Top 10)				Average Defenses				Bad Defenses (Bottom 10)				Total			
	FPG	CG	GP	CR	FPG	CG	GP	CR	FPG	CG	GP	CR	FPG	CG	GP	CR
Home	4.37	0	3	0%	16.48	5	6	83%	11.06	3	5	60%	11.95	8	14	57%
Away	12.26	2	5	40%	17.05	3	4	75%	14.40	2	4	50%	14.39	7	13	54%

For the most current Fantasy Football Consistency information, visit www.BigGuyFantasySports.com

BRANDON MARSHALL

Marshall joins his third team in four years, as he heads to the Big Apple to join Odell Beckham, Jr. and Eli Manning. It sounds like a match made in heaven. But Marshall's consistency last season dropped off quite a bit and he didn't have a #1 receiver on the item side of him. He's still good value as your WR3 on your Fantasy teams in 2017.

3 YEAR CONSISTENCY HISTORY

		Total FP	RANK	CG	GP	CR	RANK
Brandon Marshall	2016	156.70	49	5	15	33%	73
	2015	343.20	3	15	16	94%	2
	2014	181.10	34	6	13	46%	41

TIER DRAFT RANK – WR3 – B

AT VALUE: Marshall's current ADP is WR33/pick 72. I believe this is fair value for him. I wouldn't reach much higher than that though. Remember, he's 33, so his health may break down.

CLUTCH GAMES BY WEEK – 2016

Player Name	1	2	3	4	5	6	7	8	9	10	11	12	13	14	15	16	17	Total
Brandon Marshall		+		+	+			+			B	+						5

CONSISTENCY VS DEFENSES (2015-2016)

	Good Defenses (Top 10)				Average Defenses				Bad Defenses (Bottom 10)				Total			
	FPG	CG	GP	CR	FPG	CG	GP	CR	FPG	CG	GP	CR	FPG	CG	GP	CR
Home	16.30	3	5	60%	14.00	2	3	67%	18.37	5	7	71%	16.81	10	15	67%
Away	10.30	2	4	50%	19.88	4	4	100%	15.89	5	8	63%	15.49	11	16	69%

JORDAN MATTHEWS

Matthews' consistency didn't improve when Chip Kelly left, but it more had to do with rookie quarterback, Carson Wentz. The Eagles' management went out and grabbed Alshon Jeffery to be the #1 receiver and take the pressure off Matthews. But, they also picked up Torrey Smith. So, it seems very crowded at receiver in 2017. Keep expectations low for Matthews.

3 YEAR CONSISTENCY HISTORY

		Total FP	RANK	CG	GP	CR	RANK
Jordan Matthews	2016	171.40	43	7	14	50%	44
	2015	232.70	16	9	16	56%	29
	2014	202.20	25	7	16	44%	42

TIER DRAFT RANK – WR4 – C

AT VALUE: Matthews' current ADP is WR47/pick 119. He's close to my ranking as well. However, there are a number of receivers to target in Philly and I believe Matthews will be limited.

CLUTCH GAMES BY WEEK – 2016

Player Name	1	2	3	4	5	6	7	8	9	10	11	12	13	14	15	16	17	Total
Jordan Matthews	+	+	B					+	+	+	+			+				7

CONSISTENCY VS DEFENSES (2014-2016)

	Good Defenses (Top 10)				Average Defenses				Bad Defenses (Bottom 10)				Total			
	FPG	CG	GP	CR	FPG	CG	GP	CR	FPG	CG	GP	CR	FPG	CG	GP	CR
Home	10.35	1	4	25%	13.40	2	6	33%	12.72	7	13	54%	12.49	10	23	43%
Away	9.87	4	7	57%	15.87	8	10	80%	15.22	3	6	50%	13.87	15	23	65%

For the most current Fantasy Football Consistency information, visit www.BigGuyFantasySports.com

CONSISTENCY PROFILES – WIDE RECEIVERS (continued)

RISHARD MATTHEWS

Another year goes by and Matthews surprised the Fantasy world again. After Week 4, Matthews became Mariota's favorite receiver and he earned all 10 of his Clutch Games over the last 12 games! The Titans drafted Corey Davis and signed Eric Decker in the offseason. This gives Mariota many more options but I believe Matthews stays his favorite.

3 YEAR CONSISTENCY HISTORY

		Total FP	RANK	CG	GP	CR	RANK
Rishard Matthews	2016	213.50	19	10	16	63%	25
	2015	133.60	51	7	11	64%	26
	2014	37.80	114	0	14	0%	125

TIER DRAFT RANK – WR4 – C

UNDERVALUED: Matthews current ADP is WR53/pick 137. don't care who the Titans drafted or signed this offseason Matthews has Mariota's attention and that will continue in 2017.

CLUTCH GAMES BY WEEK – 2016

Player Name	1	2	3	4	5	6	7	8	9	10	11	12	13	14	15	16	17	Total
Rishard Matthews					+	+		+	+	+	+	+	B		+	+	+	10

CONSISTENCY VS DEFENSES (2015-2016)

	Good Defenses (Top 10)				Average Defenses				Bad Defenses (Bottom 10)				Total			
	FPG	CG	GP	CR	FPG	CG	GP	CR	FPG	CG	GP	CR	FPG	CG	GP	CR
Home	12.35	2	4	50%	0.00	0	0	0%	11.30	2	4	50%	11.83	4	8	50%
Away	11.15	1	2	50%	15.90	2	3	67%	16.30	3	3	100%	14.86	6	8	75%

CAMERON MEREDITH

For being on the train wreck, that was the Chicago Bears last season, Meredith was a bright spot alongside Jordan Howard. Jay Cutler is gone and Mike Glennon or Mitch Trubisky is the quarterback. That's not great, but it's not terrible. My expectation is Meredith will be around the 50% Clutch Rating again this year. Don't expect much more.

3 YEAR CONSISTENCY HISTORY

		Total FP	RANK	CG	GP	CR	RANK
Cameron Meredith	2016	183.50	37	7	14	50%	42
	2015	23.00	147	0	11	0%	150
	2014	DNP	DNP	DNP	DNP	DNP	DNP

TIER DRAFT RANK – WR4 – C

AT VALUE: Meredith's ADP is currently WR42/ pick 105. That's close to where I have him ranked as well. He's a nice backup receiver for your Fantasy team in 2017 and that's his ceiling.

CLUTCH GAMES BY WEEK – 2016

Player Name	1	2	3	4	5	6	7	8	9	10	11	12	13	14	15	16	17	Total
Cameron Meredith					+	+			B	+				+	+	+	+	7

CONSISTENCY VS DEFENSES (2014-2015)

	Good Defenses (Top 10)				Average Defenses				Bad Defenses (Bottom 10)				Total			
	FPG	CG	GP	CR	FPG	CG	GP	CR	FPG	CG	GP	CR	FPG	CG	GP	CR
Home	12.85	1	2	50%	5.35	0	2	0%	19.20	2	3	67%	13.43	3	7	43%
Away	11.55	1	2	50%	11.80	1	2	50%	14.27	2	3	67%	12.79	4	7	57%

For the most current Fantasy Football Consistency information, visit www.BigGuyFantasySports.com

DONTE MONCRIEF

Moncrief is one of those players who are extremely consistent IF they can stay healthy. Last season, Moncrief had an excellent 78% Clutch Rating. However, he only played in nine games. 2017 is another year and hopefully Moncrief can stay healthy enough to contribute. I have him as a WR2-B. He can earn it if healthy. Update: Luck's injury appears worse! Be cautious!

3 YEAR CONSISTENCY HISTORY

		Total FP	RANK	CG	GP	CR	RANK
Donte Moncrief	2016	102.60	76	7	9	78%	5
	2015	173.30	37	8	16	50%	T37
	2014	96.10	78	2	16	13%	85

TIER DRAFT RANK – WR4 – C

UNDERVALUED: Moncrief's current ADP is around WR34/pick 76. With Luck's injury looking worse every day, I can't risk taking Moncrief too high at this point. Stay away.

CLUTCH GAMES BY WEEK – 2016

Player Name	1	2	3	4	5	6	7	8	9	10	11	12	13	14	15	16	17	Total
Donte Moncrief	+							+	+	B	+	+	+			+		7

CONSISTENCY VS DEFENSES (2015-2016)

	Good Defenses (Top 10)				Average Defenses				Bad Defenses (Bottom 10)				Total			
	FPG	CG	GP	CR	FPG	CG	GP	CR	FPG	CG	GP	CR	FPG	CG	GP	CR
Home	13.24	3	5	60%	13.76	4	5	80%	13.63	3	3	100%	13.53	10	13	77%
Away	2.33	0	3	0%	11.16	3	5	60%	9.30	2	4	50%	8.33	5	12	42%

J.J. NELSON

Nelson filled in nicely for John Brown last season when he was injured. However, Brown appears to be 100% healthy again. This will put Nelson back in the #3 spot for Arizona in 2017. Nelson could be a nice handcuff late in the draft if you draft Fitzgerald or Brown. Beyond that, there's not much value.

3 YEAR CONSISTENCY HISTORY

		Total FP	RANK	CG	GP	CR	RANK
J.J. Nelson	2016	141.10	57	7	14	50%	45
	2015	52.90	106	2	11	18%	96
	2014	DNP	DNP	DNP	DNP	DNP	DNP

TIER DRAFT RANK – WR7 – D

UNDRAFTABLE: Parker's current ADP is WR71/pick 205 which is close to where I'd expect him to be. I wouldn't draft him at this point, but he's worth a pickup if injuries occur in Arizona.

CLUTCH GAMES BY WEEK – 2016

Player Name	1	2	3	4	5	6	7	8	9	10	11	12	13	14	15	16	17	Total
J.J. Nelson							+	+	B				+	+	+	+	+	7

CONSISTENCY VS DEFENSES (2016)

	Good Defenses (Top 10)				Average Defenses				Bad Defenses (Bottom 10)				Total			
	FPG	CG	GP	CR	FPG	CG	GP	CR	FPG	CG	GP	CR	FPG	CG	GP	CR
Home	5.77	1	3	33%	5.90	0	1	0%	10.30	2	3	67%	7.73	3	7	43%
Away	11.57	2	3	67%	27.90	1	1	100%	8.13	1	3	33%	12.43	4	7	57%

For the most current Fantasy Football Consistency information, visit www.BigGuyFantasySports.com

JORDY NELSON

Nelson is one of the most consistent receivers in the game. Outside of Antonio Brown, no one is better. This is why he's ranked as the #2 wide receiver on my rankings. If you disagree, look below and then look at OBJ, Julio, or anyone else that you believe is better. Those 94% and 88% Clutch Ratings are unmatched. Draft with confidence.

3 YEAR CONSISTENCY HISTORY

		Total FP	RANK	CG	GP	CR	RANK
Jordy Nelson	2016	306.70	2	15	16	94%	1
	2015	DNP	DNP	DNP	DNP	DNP	DNP
	2014	327.90	3	14	16	88%	3

TIER DRAFT RANK – WR1 – A

UNDERVALUED: Nelson's current ADP is WR7/pick 13. That's a perfect place to draft him and get the most value. Combined with Johnson, Bell or Zeke, Nelson is perfect!

CLUTCH GAMES BY WEEK – 2016

Player Name	1	2	3	4	5	6	7	8	9	10	11	12	13	14	15	16	17	Total
Jordy Nelson	+	+	+	B	+	+		+	+	+	+	+	+	+	+	+	+	15

CONSISTENCY VS DEFENSES (2014-2016)

	Good Defenses (Top 10)				Average Defenses				Bad Defenses (Bottom 10)				Total			
	FPG	CG	GP	CR	FPG	CG	GP	CR	FPG	CG	GP	CR	FPG	CG	GP	CR
Home	23.13	7	7	100%	14.68	4	5	80%	27.78	4	4	100%	21.65	15	16	94%
Away	14.44	4	5	80%	20.03	6	6	100%	19.16	4	5	80%	18.01	14	16	88%

DEVANTE PARKER

Parker has been a constant under-achiever. He's always ranked in the WR3 ADP range, but his total points and consistency do not warrant it. The hype machine is on again for 2017, but I'm still seeing it. His second half was better, but it was still only 50% consistent. I'm not drafting Parker this year and neither should you.

3 YEAR CONSISTENCY HISTORY

		Total FP	RANK	CG	GP	CR	RANK
DeVante Parker	2016	154.40	50	6	15	40%	62
	2015	93.40	73	5	15	33%	58
	2014	DNP	DNP	DNP	DNP	DNP	DNP

TIER DRAFT RANK – WR4 – C

OVERVALUED: Parker's current ADP is WR35/pick 85. That's too rich for my blood. He hasn't proved that he can be consistent enough as a WR3. I'm good with him as a backup.

CLUTCH GAMES BY WEEK – 2016

Player Name	1	2	3	4	5	6	7	8	9	10	11	12	13	14	15	16	17
DeVante Parker		+	+					B		+	+		+			+	

CONSISTENCY VS DEFENSES (2015-2016)

	Good Defenses (Top 10)				Average Defenses				Bad Defenses (Bottom 10)				Total			
	FPG	CG	GP	CR	FPG	CG	GP	CR	FPG	CG	GP	CR	FPG	CG	GP	CR
Home	6.90	1	5	20%	6.79	1	7	14%	10.10	2	4	50%	7.65	4	16	25%
Away	14.18	4	5	80%	8.10	2	5	40%	3.50	1	4	25%	8.96	7	14	50%

TERRELLE PRYOR

Pryor did just enough to get him a nice contract and head over to the Redskins. He becomes their 1A with Jamison Crowder. Remember, he earned those numbers below in Cleveland. So, being ranked 21st in total points is very good. The consistency was more the quarterback situation than Pryor. With Cousins as his quarterback, more consistent days are ahead.

3 YEAR CONSISTENCY HISTORY

		Total FP	RANK	CG	GP	CR	RANK
Terrelle Pryor	2016	209.80	21	8	16	50%	39
	2015	5.10	175	0	3	0%	180
	2014	DNP	DNP	DNP	DNP	DNP	DNP

TIER DRAFT RANK – WR3 – A

OVERVALUED: Pryor's current ADP is WR23/pick 47. I like him better as a WR3 on my teams in 2017. It's not horrible if you pick him that early, as I have him ranked 26th . Be careful.

CLUTCH GAMES BY WEEK – 2016

Player Name	1	2	3	4	5	6	7	8	9	10	11	12	13	14	15	16	17	Total
Terrelle Pryor			+	+		+		+	+		+		+	B				+	8

CONSISTENCY VS DEFENSES (2016)

	Good Defenses (Top 10)				Average Defenses				Bad Defenses (Bottom 10)				Total			
	FPG	CG	GP	CR	FPG	CG	GP	CR	FPG	CG	GP	CR	FPG	CG	GP	CR
Home	11.80	1	3	33%	10.88	3	5	60%	0.00	0	0	0%	11.23	4	8	50%
Away	9.80	0	1	0%	12.94	2	5	40%	22.75	2	2	100%	15.00	4	8	50%

ALLEN ROBINSON

Robinson probably wins the most disappointing Fantasy player last year who played all 16 games. After a Top 5 finish in consistency in 2015, Robinson was a first round pick in 2016. He ended the year ranked 28th in total points and 33rd in consistency. Ouch! I have to believe he will improve, but how much is the question. I'm very skeptical.

3 YEAR CONSISTENCY HISTORY

		Total FP	RANK	CG	GP	CR	RANK
Allen Robinson	2016	197.30	28	9	16	56%	33
	2015	304.00	6	13	16	81%	T5
	2014	114.80	65	6	10	60%	24

TIER DRAFT RANK – WR3 – A

OVERVALUED: Robinson's current ADP is WR15/pick 30. He needs to earn 2-3 more Clutch Games to be in that WR2-A range, I'm not sold. He's a little overvalued for my taste.

CLUTCH GAMES BY WEEK – 2016

Player Name	1	2	3	4	5	6	7	8	9	10	11	12	13	14	15	16	17	Total
Allen Robinson	+		+	+	B			+	+	+	+					+	+	9

CONSISTENCY VS DEFENSES (2014-2016)

	Good Defenses (Top 10)				Average Defenses				Bad Defenses (Bottom 10)				Total			
	FPG	CG	GP	CR	FPG	CG	GP	CR	FPG	CG	GP	CR	FPG	CG	GP	CR
Home	13.92	3	6	50%	17.09	7	8	88%	14.44	5	7	71%	15.30	15	21	71%
Away	11.40	3	5	60%	15.29	5	9	56%	14.31	6	7	86%	14.04	14	21	67%

For the most current Fantasy Football Consistency information, visit www.BigGuyFantasySports.com

CONSISTENCY PROFILES – WIDE RECEIVERS (continued)

EMMANUEL SANDERS

No one took the brunt of the bad quarterback situation in Denver worse than Sanders. Demaryius Thomas did okay, but Sanders' consistency took a nose dive. His total points weren't bad as he ranked 20th at the end of the year. But, the 55th ranking in consistency killed most Fantasy owners who had him as their WR2/3. Be careful here. Don't reach too high.

3 YEAR CONSISTENCY HISTORY

		Total FP	RANK	CG	GP	CR	RANK
Emmanuel Sanders	2016	212.60	20	7	16	44%	55
	2015	228.40	18	10	15	67%	23
	2014	299.80	5	14	16	88%	4

TIER DRAFT RANK – WR3 – B

AT VALUE: I believe Sanders value is about right with his current ADP at WR31/pick 66. If he hits his 2015 numbers as your WR3, that's great value. But don't reach too high for him.

CLUTCH GAMES BY WEEK – 2016

Player Name	1	2	3	4	5	6	7	8	9	10	11	12	13	14	15	16	17	Total
Emmanuel Sanders			+	+	+		+	+			B	+		+				7

CONSISTENCY VS DEFENSES (2014-2016)

	Good Defenses (Top 10)				Average Defenses				Bad Defenses (Bottom 10)				Total			
	FPG	CG	GP	CR	FPG	CG	GP	CR	FPG	CG	GP	CR	FPG	CG	GP	CR
Home	14.64	7	10	70%	13.41	5	7	71%	11.86	4	7	57%	13.47	16	24	67%
Away	16.33	4	7	57%	23.59	6	7	86%	15.34	5	9	56%	18.15	15	23	65%

MOHAMED SANU

Sanu was a solid complimentary receiver to Julio Jones in Atlanta last season. However, his consistency isn't that great. Even at his best, he only reached a 44% Clutch Rating in the past, so I wouldn't expect much more than that. Handcuff to Julio Jones if you must or pick him as your WR6 or WR7.

3 YEAR CONSISTENCY HISTORY

		Total FP	RANK	CG	GP	CR	RANK
Mohamed Sanu	2016	148.80	51	6	15	40%	63
	2015	91.50	75	4	16	25%	T70
	2014	176.10	37	7	16	44%	46

TIER DRAFT RANK – WR7 – D

AT VALUE: Sanu's current ADP is WR69/pick 198. Which is fine based on his handcuff to Jones and weak consistency. He probably won't get drafted and will be a waiver wire pickup.

CLUTCH GAMES BY WEEK – 2016

Player Name	1	2	3	4	5	6	7	8	9	10	11	12	13	14	15	16	17	Total
Mohamed Sanu	+					+		+	+		B	+					+	6

CONSISTENCY VS DEFENSES (2016)

	Good Defenses (Top 10)				Average Defenses				Bad Defenses (Bottom 10)				Total			
	FPG	CG	GP	CR	FPG	CG	GP	CR	FPG	CG	GP	CR	FPG	CG	GP	CR
Home	15.00	1	1	100%	3.90	0	2	0%	13.52	3	5	60%	11.30	4	8	50%
Away	11.50	1	2	50%	6.00	0	2	0%	7.80	1	3	33%	8.34	2	7	29%

For the most current Fantasy Football Consistency information, visit www.BigGuyFantasySports.com

STERLING SHEPARD

Based on last year's consistency numbers alone, you would think Shepard will be an excellent WR3 for 2017. However, this is the NFL and things change. The Giants must have felt Shepard was not a worthy #2 receiver for their team and they went out and grabbed Brandon Marshall in the offseason. Now, Shepard is a WR5 in most Fantasy drafts. Nice as a backup though.

3 YEAR CONSISTENCY HISTORY

		Total FP	RANK	CG	GP	CR	RANK
Sterling Shepard	2016	184.40	36	9	16	56%	34
	2015	DNP	DNP	DNP	DNP	DNP	DNP
	2014	DNP	DNP	DNP	DNP	DNP	DNP

TIER DRAFT RANK – WR5 – D

AT VALUE: Shepard's current ADP is WR56/pick 149. This is at value and is a nice backup to have, just in case Marshall gets hurt again. However, that's all Shepard is worth at this point.

CLUTCH GAMES BY WEEK – 2016

Player Name	1	2	3	4	5	6	7	8	9	10	11	12	13	14	15	16	17	Total
Sterling Shepard	+	+	+					B	+	+	+		+		+	+		9

CONSISTENCY VS DEFENSES (2016)

	Good Defenses (Top 10)				Average Defenses				Bad Defenses (Bottom 10)				Total			
	FPG	CG	GP	CR	FPG	CG	GP	CR	FPG	CG	GP	CR	FPG	CG	GP	CR
Home	6.50	0	1	0%	13.54	4	5	80%	19.00	2	2	100%	14.03	6	8	75%
Away	7.60	0	2	0%	14.90	3	3	100%	4.10	0	3	0%	9.03	3	8	38%

TORREY SMITH

Smith hasn't shown any real consistency since 2014 and what was as a high WR2. He's now the third or fourth wheel in Philadelphia. I would expect an occasional deep pass for a touchdown, but I wouldn't expect his consistency to be any better than it was last season. Therefore, he's currently undraftable.

3 YEAR CONSISTENCY HISTORY

		Total FP	RANK	CG	GP	CR	RANK
Torrey Smith	2016	64.70	101	3	12	25%	88
	2015	123.30	54	4	16	25%	T70
	2014	191.70	29	9	16	56%	28

TIER DRAFT RANK – WR7 – D

UNDRAFTABLE: Smith's career is on the downslope. He's a backup/speedster who may help the Eagles with a deep touchdown every once in a while. He's not worth drafting this year.

CLUTCH GAMES BY WEEK – 2016

Player Name	1	2	3	4	5	6	7	8	9	10	11	12	13	14	15	16	17	Total
Torrey Smith		+				+		B				+						3

CONSISTENCY VS DEFENSES (2015-2016)

	Good Defenses (Top 10)				Average Defenses				Bad Defenses (Bottom 10)				Total			
	FPG	CG	GP	CR	FPG	CG	GP	CR	FPG	CG	GP	CR	FPG	CG	GP	CR
Home	2.97	0	6	0%	7.47	2	6	33%	3.25	0	2	0%	4.94	2	14	14%
Away	3.43	0	4	0%	12.13	4	7	57%	6.77	1	3	33%	8.49	5	14	36%

WILLIE SNEAD

Snead fulfilled my prophecy for him and improved a little to be worth a WR3 last year. If he earns one more Clutch Game in 2017 than he did in 2016, he will be in the WR2 value range. With the departure of Brandin Cooks, I believe this will happen. He earned eight Clutch Games over his last 12 games. He's an excellent value this year.

3 YEAR CONSISTENCY HISTORY

		Total FP	RANK	CG	GP	CR	RANK
Willie Snead	2016	192.00	32	9	15	60%	30
	2015	185.40	32	8	15	53%	T34
	2014	DNP	DNP	DNP	DNP	DNP	DNP

<table>
<tr><td colspan="2">TIER DRAFT RANK – WR2 – B</td></tr>
</table>

UNDERVALUED: Snead's current ADP is WR32/pick 67. have him ranked at WR24. So right at the end of WR2 range So, draft him as your WR3 and get WR2 value in 2017.

CLUTCH GAMES BY WEEK – 2016

Player Name	1	2	3	4	5	6	7	8	9	10	11	12	13	14	15	16	17	Total
Willie Snead	+	+			B		+	+		+		+		+	+		+	9

CONSISTENCY VS DEFENSES (2015-2016)

	Good Defenses (Top 10)				Average Defenses				Bad Defenses (Bottom 10)				Total			
	FPG	CG	GP	CR	FPG	CG	GP	CR	FPG	CG	GP	CR	FPG	CG	GP	CR
Home	16.20	3	3	100%	12.34	4	7	57%	18.20	3	4	75%	14.84	10	14	71%
Away	11.54	2	5	40%	9.08	1	4	25%	10.80	4	7	57%	10.6	7	16	44%

KENNY STILLS

Well, here's another one I was wrong on. Stills surprised everyone and ended the year ranked 29th in consistency, even though he wa only 46th in total points. So, why do I and many other experts have him ranked so poorly. Well, in my opinion, his consistency was a based on touchdowns. He scored nine touchdowns, mostly on deep passes. Repeat? Not feeling it.

3 YEAR CONSISTENCY HISTORY

		Total FP	RANK	CG	GP	CR	RANK
Kenny Stills	2016	168.60	46	10	16	63%	29
	2015	89.00	80	3	16	19%	89
	2014	173.90	39	8	15	53%	31

<table>
<tr><td colspan="2">TIER DRAFT RANK – WR6 – D</td></tr>
</table>

AT VALUE: Stills is a great deep threat, who can provide value especially at home versus a ba defense (see below). He's a goo value drafted as your WR5/6.

CLUTCH GAMES BY WEEK – 2016

Player Name	1	2	3	4	5	6	7	8	9	10	11	12	13	14	15	16	17	Total
Kenny Stills		+	+	+			+	B		+			+		+	+	+	10

CONSISTENCY VS DEFENSES (2015-2016)

	Good Defenses (Top 10)				Average Defenses				Bad Defenses (Bottom 10)				Total			
	FPG	CG	GP	CR	FPG	CG	GP	CR	FPG	CG	GP	CR	FPG	CG	GP	CR
Home	11.40	3	5	60%	5.64	2	7	29%	11.53	3	4	75%	8.91	8	16	50%
Away	6.32	1	6	17%	11.47	4	6	67%	2.08	0	4	0%	7.19	5	16	31%

CONSISTENCY PROFILES – WIDE RECEIVERS (continued)

GOLDEN TATE

Pat on the back for me on this one. I showed Tate's consistency without Megatron in 2015 and he proved me right in 2016. He started off a little slow but once he and Stafford started clicking, his consistency was fantastic! He went 10 for 11 in the last 11 games. Not saying that he does that again, but his value as your WR2 is very good.

3 YEAR CONSISTENCY HISTORY

		Total FP	RANK	CG	GP	CR	RANK
Golden Tate	2016	223.10	19	11	16	69%	17
	2015	211.40	22	9	16	56%	T27
	2014	259.10	12	11	16	69%	15

TIER DRAFT RANK – WR2 – A

UNDERVALUED: Tate's current ADP is WR24/pick 50. I have him ranked as a higher WR2, but that's good value regardless. If he falls to you as a WR3, then grab him for sure!

CLUTCH GAMES BY WEEK – 2016

Player Name	1	2	3	4	5	6	7	8	9	10	11	12	13	14	15	16	17	Total
Golden Tate	+					+	+	+	+	B		+	+	+	+	+	+	11

CONSISTENCY VS DEFENSES (2014-2016)

	Good Defenses (Top 10)				Average Defenses				Bad Defenses (Bottom 10)				Total			
	FPG	CG	GP	CR	FPG	CG	GP	CR	FPG	CG	GP	CR	FPG	CG	GP	CR
Home	15.04	5	7	71%	12.80	5	8	63%	16.86	7	9	78%	14.98	17	24	71%
Away	15.43	7	8	88%	10.62	4	9	44%	16.46	5	7	71%	13.93	16	24	67%

ADAM THIELEN

The depth chart in Minnesota shows Stefon Diggs as the #1 receiver. Psst, not according to Sam Bradford. The second half of 2016, Thielen earned six out of eight Clutch Games while Diggs was three for six. They both will be good receivers in 2017, but as long as Bradford is quarterback, Thielen is the better value from a consistency standpoint.

3 YEAR CONSISTENCY HISTORY

		Total FP	RANK	CG	GP	CR	RANK
Adam Thielen	2016	197.20	29	8	15	53%	37
	2015	35.30	128	1	16	6%	136
	2014	27.70	128	1	16	6%	135

TIER DRAFT RANK – WR3 – B

UNDERVALUED: Thielen's ADP is WR44/pick 113. Diggs' ADP is WR28 and yet, their Fantasy numbers are very similar. The better value is right here in Thielen. Take him as your WR4.

CLUTCH GAMES BY WEEK – 2016

Player Name	1	2	3	4	5	6	7	8	9	10	11	12	13	14	15	16	17	Total
Adam Thielen					+	B			+	+	+	+	+	+		+		8

CONSISTENCY VS DEFENSES (2016)

	Good Defenses (Top 10)				Average Defenses				Bad Defenses (Bottom 10)				Total			
	FPG	CG	GP	CR	FPG	CG	GP	CR	FPG	CG	GP	CR	FPG	CG	GP	CR
Home	15.77	2	3	67%	9.37	2	3	67%	8.10	0	1	0%	11.93	4	7	57%
Away	14.10	1	1	100%	8.56	1	5	20%	28.40	2	2	100%	14.21	4	8	50%

For the most current Fantasy Football Consistency information, visit www.BigGuyFantasySports.com

DEMARYIUS THOMAS

Demaryius survived the Broncos quarterback-apocalypse. His consistency stayed in the WR2 range. Nothing has changed quarterback-wise in Denver. So, I would expect much of the same in 2017. Thomas has enough talent to help the young quarterbacks and will be an excellent WR2 on your teams.

3 YEAR CONSISTENCY HISTORY

		Total FP	RANK	CG	GP	CR	RANK
Demaryius Thomas	2016	228.30	15	11	16	69%	16
	2015	271.40	9	13	16	81%	T5
	2014	338.90	2	13	16	81%	5

TIER DRAFT RANK – WR2 – A

AT VALUE: In the past, if Thomas' ADP was WR14/pick 28, owners would have fallen over each other to draft him there. But this year is different. I believe this is a fair price for him.

CLUTCH GAMES BY WEEK – 2016

Player Name	1	2	3	4	5	6	7	8	9	10	11	12	13	14	15	16	17	Total
Demaryius Thomas		+	+	+	+		+	+		+	B	+	+	+	+			11

CONSISTENCY VS DEFENSES (2014-2016)

	Good Defenses (Top 10)				Average Defenses				Bad Defenses (Bottom 10)				Total			
	FPG	CG	GP	CR	FPG	CG	GP	CR	FPG	CG	GP	CR	FPG	CG	GP	CR
Home	15.79	8	10	80%	21.09	5	7	71%	15.90	6	7	86%	17.37	19	24	79%
Away	18.50	6	7	86%	18.89	7	8	88%	15.69	5	9	56%	17.58	18	24	75%

MICHAEL THOMAS

If you read my Rookies vs Consistency article, you will know that rookie receivers rarely (less than 6%) earn over a 60% Clutch Rate in their first year. However, only two receivers (Odell Beckham Jr. and A.J. Green) have ever earned over an 80% Clutch Rate. That was until 2016, when Michael Thomas did it for the Saints. Expect much of the same in 2017.

3 YEAR CONSISTENCY HISTORY

		Total FP	RANK	CG	GP	CR	RANK
Michael Thomas	2016	259.70	7	12	15	80%	4
	2015	DNP	DNP	DNP	DNP	DNP	DNP
	2014	DNP	DNP	DNP	DNP	DNP	DNP

TIER DRAFT RANK – WR1 – A

AT VALUE: His consistency last season warrants this high ranking for a second-year receiver. His ADP matches my thoughts as well. He's a first round/early second round pick.

CLUTCH GAMES BY WEEK – 2016

Player Name	1	2	3	4	5	6	7	8	9	10	11	12	13	14	15	16	17	Total
Michael Thomas	+		+	+	B	+	+	+	+		+	+			+	+	+	12

CONSISTENCY VS DEFENSES (2016)

	Good Defenses (Top 10)				Average Defenses				Bad Defenses (Bottom 10)				Total			
	FPG	CG	GP	CR	FPG	CG	GP	CR	FPG	CG	GP	CR	FPG	CG	GP	CR
Home	17.37	2	3	67%	13.50	1	2	50%	15.90	3	3	100%	15.85	6	8	75%
Away	13.90	1	2	50%	13.10	2	2	100%	26.30	3	3	100%	18.99	6	7	86%

For the most current Fantasy Football Consistency information, visit www.BigGuyFantasySports.com

MIKE WALLACE

Wallace's Fantasy value isn't going to be that great. However, you could do much worse with your WR6 or WR7. Wallace will be a nice all-around receiver for the Ravens with newly acquired, Jeremy Maclin. His total points ranking and almost WR3 rank in consistency shows he can be a nice backup to have. Flacco's injury has me a little more pessimistic about Wallace's value.

3 YEAR CONSISTENCY HISTORY

		Total FP	RANK	CG	GP	CR	RANK
Mike Wallace	2016	200.80	24	8	16	50%	40
	2015	98.90	71	3	16	19%	88
	2014	214.80	17	11	16	69%	17

TIER DRAFT RANK – WR5 – D

AT VALUE: Wallace's current ADP is WR51/pick 130. Wallace should be a solid backup to have as your WR5 with the ability to earn WR3/4, when needed. He may become your Flex guy.

CLUTCH GAMES BY WEEK – 2016

Player Name	1	2	3	4	5	6	7	8	9	10	11	12	13	14	15	16	17	Total
Mike Wallace	+	+			+	+	+	B	+		+		+					8

CONSISTENCY VS DEFENSES (2016)

	Good Defenses (Top 10)				Average Defenses				Bad Defenses (Bottom 10)				Total			
	FPG	CG	GP	CR	FPG	CG	GP	CR	FPG	CG	GP	CR	FPG	CG	GP	CR
Home	10.27	1	3	33%	11.98	2	4	50%	20.10	1	1	100%	12.35	4	8	50%
Away	0.00	0	0	0%	14.55	2	4	50%	10.95	2	4	50%	12.75	4	8	50%

SAMMY WATKINS

Watkins caused another year of frustration for Fantasy owners in 2016. Expectations were high based on his solid 2015 (even though he missed three games). Once again, the hype train is flying and once again, I'm not boarding it! You can if you want, but don't come crying to me when the train wrecks or pulls a hamstring.

3 YEAR CONSISTENCY HISTORY

		Total FP	RANK	CG	GP	CR	RANK
Sammy Watkins	2016	83.00	91	3	8	38%	71
	2015	218.80	20	9	13	69%	21
	2014	200.00	27	7	16	44%	43

TIER DRAFT RANK – WR3 – B

OVERVALUED: With Watkins' current ADP at WR19/pick 37, I'm staying way clear of this pick. There are much more consistent and dependable receivers at WR2 than Watkins.

CLUTCH GAMES BY WEEK – 2016

Player Name	1	2	3	4	5	6	7	8	9	10	11	12	13	14	15	16	17	Total
Sammy Watkins										B	+		+		+			3

CONSISTENCY VS DEFENSES (2014-2016)

	Good Defenses (Top 10)				Average Defenses				Bad Defenses (Bottom 10)				Total			
	FPG	CG	GP	CR	FPG	CG	GP	CR	FPG	CG	GP	CR	FPG	CG	GP	CR
Home	12.23	5	9	56%	14.23	4	7	57%	15.30	2	4	50%	13.55	11	20	55%
Away	15.34	4	8	50%	8.87	1	3	33%	13.60	3	6	50%	13.58	8	17	47%

For the most current Fantasy Football Consistency information, visit www.BigGuyFantasySports.com

MARKUS WHEATON

Wheaton underwhelmed everyone in Pittsburgh, so he went to Chicago to compete with the likes of Cameron Meredith, Kevin White, and Kendall Wright. There's some glimmer of hope, but it's small. Wheaton has to stay healthy and productive to have any chance of significant Fantasy relevance. He's undraftable at this point.

3 YEAR CONSISTENCY HISTORY

		Total FP	RANK	CG	GP	CR	RANK
Markus Wheaton	2016	15.10	158	0	3	0%	159
	2015	148.90	46	5	16	31%	63
	2014	131.30	58	6	16	38%	58

TIER DRAFT RANK – WR7 – D

UNDRAFTABLE: Wheaton is currently undraftable. However, keep an eye out on the Bears receiving core this preseason, as injuries or underperformance could lead to some playing time.

CLUTCH GAMES BY WEEK – 2016

Player Name	1	2	3	4	5	6	7	8	9	10	11	12	13	14	15	16	17	Total
Markus Wheaton								B										0

CONSISTENCY VS DEFENSES (2014-2016)

	Good Defenses (Top 10)				Average Defenses				Bad Defenses (Bottom 10)				Total			
	FPG	CG	GP	CR	FPG	CG	GP	CR	FPG	CG	GP	CR	FPG	CG	GP	CR
Home	8.16	2	5	40%	7.28	2	6	33%	8.20	2	7	29%	7.88	6	18	33%
Away	12.80	2	6	33%	5.30	0	6	0%	8.96	3	5	60%	9.02	5	17	29%

TERRANCE WILLIAMS

Williams is what he is. A nice compliment to Dez Bryant. This provides very little consistency for Fantasy purposes. Added into the mix last year was Dak Prescott's love for Cole Beasley, as evident by Williams' two Clutch Games over the second half of 2016. Williams is basically undraftable in 2017.

3 YEAR CONSISTENCY HISTORY

		Total FP	RANK	CG	GP	CR	RANK
Terrance Williams	2016	127.40	62	6	15	40%	66
	2015	154.00	44	6	16	38%	55
	2014	147.10	52	6	16	38%	56

TIER DRAFT RANK – WR7 – D

UNDRAFTABLE: With the emergence of Cole Beasley last year, Williams' value is practically nil in 2017. Therefore, he's undraftable in 2017 unless Beasley or Dez gets hurt.

CLUTCH GAMES BY WEEK – 2016

Player Name	1	2	3	4	5	6	7	8	9	10	11	12	13	14	15	16	17	Total
Terrance Williams			+	+	+	+	B							+		+		6

CONSISTENCY VS DEFENSES (2014-2016)

	Good Defenses (Top 10)				Average Defenses				Bad Defenses (Bottom 10)				Total			
	FPG	CG	GP	CR	FPG	CG	GP	CR	FPG	CG	GP	CR	FPG	CG	GP	CR
Home	6.24	1	7	14%	9.70	4	8	50%	12.13	4	9	44%	9.60	9	24	38%
Away	10.30	1	3	33%	7.88	2	6	33%	8.56	6	14	43%	8.61	9	23	39%

For the most current Fantasy Football Consistency information, visit www.BigGuyFantasySports.com

CONSISTENCY PROFILES – WIDE RECEIVERS (continued)

TYRELL WILLIAMS

Williams broke out in a big way in 2016 as he replaced Keenan Allen and surpassed Travis Benjamin as the #2 receiver for the Chargers. Bad news for Tyrell, the Chargers decided to pick Mike Williams in the first round of the NFL draft. Good news for Tyrell, Mike Williams had a season-ending injury. I like his value though as a WR4 pick in most Fantasy drafts with WR3 value.

3 YEAR CONSISTENCY HISTORY

		Total FP	RANK	CG	GP	CR	RANK
Tyrell Williams	2016	216.90	18	10	16	63%	24
	2015	17.00	157	1	5	20%	159
	2014	DNP	DNP	DNP	DNP	DNP	DNP

TIER DRAFT RANK – WR3 – B

AT VALUE: Tyrell is a great pick as your WR4 with the ability to earn WR3 consistency. Mike Williams' injury greatly improved Tyrell's ADP for this year. Draft with confidence.

CLUTCH GAMES BY WEEK – 2016

Player Name	1	2	3	4	5	6	7	8	9	10	11	12	13	14	15	16	17	Total
Tyrell Williams		+	+		+			+		+	+	B	+	+			+	+	10

CONSISTENCY VS DEFENSES (2016)

	Good Defenses (Top 10)				Average Defenses				Bad Defenses (Bottom 10)				Total			
	FPG	CG	GP	CR	FPG	CG	GP	CR	FPG	CG	GP	CR	FPG	CG	GP	CR
Home	10.45	1	2	50%	18.50	1	1	100%	12.84	3	5	60%	12.95	5	8	63%
Away	11.20	1	2	50%	8.80	0	1	0%	16.42	4	5	80%	14.16	5	8	63%

ROBERT WOODS

The Rams went after Robert Woods in the offseason to become their #1 receiver. Please read this again and let it sink in a little bit. Are you kidding me? Tavon Austin is still there...not saying he's the #1 receiver, but I'm not sure Woods is better than him either. Anyways, Woods may hit a 50% Clutch Rating, but that's still not great. Let someone else take him!

3 YEAR CONSISTENCY HISTORY

		Total FP	RANK	CG	GP	CR	RANK
Robert Woods	2016	118.90	67	4	13	31%	81
	2015	120.20	57	3	14	21%	83
	2014	164.90	45	8	16	50%	36

TIER DRAFT RANK – WR6 – D

AT VALUE: Woods' current ADP is WR59/pick 165. I guess if he's a #1 receiver for a bad team, then he'll have to catch passes, right? So, maybe he's worth a backup pick? Sure.

CLUTCH GAMES BY WEEK – 2016

Player Name	1	2	3	4	5	6	7	8	9	10	11	12	13	14	15	16	17	Total
Robert Woods			+	+		+			+	B								4

CONSISTENCY VS DEFENSES (2014-2016)

	Good Defenses (Top 10)				Average Defenses				Bad Defenses (Bottom 10)				Total			
	FPG	CG	GP	CR	FPG	CG	GP	CR	FPG	CG	GP	CR	FPG	CG	GP	CR
Home	13.04	5	9	56%	4.62	1	6	17%	5.97	1	6	17%	8.61	7	21	33%
Away	10.25	4	11	36%	5.04	0	5	0%	14.20	4	6	67%	10.14	8	22	36%

For the most current Fantasy Football Consistency information, visit www.BigGuyFantasySports.com

KENDALL WRIGHT

Wright went to the Bears in the offseason and will be competing with other wide receiver misfits for a job behind Cameron Meredith and Kevin White. White is made of glass, so there's some hope for Wright to fill in for him. However, at this point, Wright is undraftable for most Fantasy leagues.

3 YEAR CONSISTENCY HISTORY

		Total FP	RANK	CG	GP	CR	RANK
Kendall Wright	2016	90.10	85	2	11	18%	103
	2015	90.70	76	3	9	33%	59
	2014	169.90	41	6	14	43%	50

TIER DRAFT RANK – WR7 – D

UNDRAFTABLE: Wright's only hope is for an injury to Kevin White or Cameron Meredith in 2017. Wright's value is minimal at this point and should be left undrafted in 2017.

CLUTCH GAMES BY WEEK – 2016

Player Name	1	2	3	4	5	6	7	8	9	10	11	12	13	14	15	16	17	Total
Kendall Wright						+		+					B					2

CONSISTENCY VS DEFENSES (2014-2016)

	Good Defenses (Top 10)				Average Defenses				Bad Defenses (Bottom 10)				Total			
	FPG	CG	GP	CR	FPG	CG	GP	CR	FPG	CG	GP	CR	FPG	CG	GP	CR
Home	12.35	1	2	50%	12.80	3	6	50%	10.21	2	8	25%	11.45	6	16	38%
Away	8.06	1	5	20%	12.43	3	6	50%	7.51	2	7	29%	9.31	6	18	33%

TIGHT ENDS

Each major position (QB, RB, WR and TE) tracked for consistency purposes will have the following sections: Year in Review; Consistently Clutch and the Consistency Profiles. The Year in Review is exactly that, a review of the top four tiers on Fantasy consistency at each position. The Consistently Clutch article will highlight how consistent the top Fantasy players have been for the past three seasons. Finally, the Consistency Profiles will provide you with a profile of each player's consistency for each of the top returning Fantasy players.

The tight end position has some serious depth issues heading into 2017. Tier One is fine and is made up of very consistent tight ends WHEN they're healthy. Some of the Tier Two tight ends have solid potential to be consistent and have certainly proved it in the past, but after those players, it gets real dicey! You need to get one of the Top 10 tight ends below. Trust me on this one!

The belief is if you don't draft Rob Gronkowski, you're going to be scrambling for a good one. Psst, this is a lie. It appears that for the first time in years, Rob Gronkowski's ADP is NOT in the first round! Currently, it's hovering around pick 20. I still believe that's way too soon, but it's more reasonable now. This Tier of TE1A represents those tight ends that I believe will earn an Expected Clutch Rate (ECR) of 70%+. Gronkowski has certainly earned over that many times in his career when healthy as have Kelce, Olsen and Reed. Reed can be a beast in a PPR format, IF he can stay on the field. Regardless, all four of these tight ends are safe, consistent picks when healthy.

As you continue to read the articles and the Consistency Profiles for the tight ends allow yourself to make your own decisions. Remember the Clutch Games is a tool to help you when you're preparing for your Fantasy draft or with your lineup decisions.

If you have any questions, please don't hesitate to email me at bob@bigguyfantasysports.com or hit me up on Twitter @bob_lung.

2017 PREVIEW – TIGHT ENDS

Let's look at those tight ends ranked in their projected Tier for 2017 and show you their 2016 total points and consistency and where they ranked in those categories in 2016.

So, let's start with the top tier of tight ends.

TIER ONE

Player Name	Total Points	Pts Rank	Total CG	Total GP	CR %	2016 Rank	2017 Tier	2017 Rank
Rob Gronkowski	97.00	26	4	7	57%	11	TE1A	1
Travis Kelce	221.50	1	10	16	63%	3	TE1A	2
Greg Olsen	205.30	3	10	16	63%	4	TE1A	3
Jordan Reed	170.60	9	9	12	75%	2	TE1A	4

It appears that for the first time in years, Rob Gronkowski's ADP is NOT in the first round! Currently, it's hovering around pick 20. I still believe that's way too soon, but it's more reasonable now. This Tier of TE1A represents those tight ends that I believe will earn an Expected Clutch Rate (ECR) of 70%+. Gronkowski has certainly earned over that many times in his career when healthy as have Kelce, Olsen and Reed. Reed can be a beast in a PPR format, IF he can stay on the field. Regardless, all four of these tight ends are safe, consistent picks when healthy.

TIER TWO

Player Name	Total Points	Pts Rank	Total CG	Total GP	CR %	2016 Rank	2017 Tier	2017 Rank
Jimmy Graham	191.70	4	10	16	63%	5	TE1B	5
Kyle Rudolph	209.00	2	12	16	75%	1	TE1B	6
Tyler Eifert	98.40	25	5	8	63%	6	TE1B	7
Delanie Walker	187.00	5	9	15	60%	7	TE1B	8
Julius Thomas	82.90	32	5	9	56%	12	TE1B	9
Martellus Bennett	167.20	10	8	16	50%	14	TE1B	10
Zach Ertz	183.60	6	8	14	57%	9	TE1B	11
Jack Doyle	147.40	13	7	16	44%	21	TE1B	12

This Tier represents an ECR of 57-69%. I realize that is a big range, but for tight ends, that's about where the second tier usually falls out. You can see above that most of the tight ends were in that range in 2016. Kyle Rudolph was the #1 most consistent tight end in 2016 and with Sam Bradford still there as his quarterback, there's no reason to believe he can't put up a 65% ECR in 2017. Not sure, he'll hit the 75% like he did last season, but with Rudolph's current ADP of TE9/pick 90, he's certainly great value this year.

Julius Thomas is currently greatly undervalued as his current ADP is TE18/pick 160. Let us not forget that Thomas' best season were when he was in Denver and Adam Gase was his OC. Now Gase is his HC and Gase went after Thomas in the offseason to bring him to Miami. I see no reason Thomas can't hit a 60% ECR in 2017 in that offense.

TIER THREE

Player Name	Total Points	Pts Rank	Total CG	Total GP	CR %	2016 Rank	2017 Tier	2017 Rank
Hunter Henry	135.20	17	7	14	50%	15	TE2A	13
Eric Ebron	138.10	14	7	13	54%	13	TE2A	14

Yes, I realize there is only two players here, but that's because the remaining tight ends are either rookies or risky veterans. We are looking at backup tight ends at this point anyways. Hunter Henry will be a very good tight end someday. However, I'm not ready to move him into the Top 10 this year as long as Antonio Gates is still playing in San Diego, Los Angeles, for the Chargers. Let someone else take that leap of faith. Eric Ebron is supposed to "break out" every year and every year, he doesn't. Health and consistency are two of Ebron's weaknesses. Stay away from both of them by not drafting Ebron.

Well, there are your Expected Clutch Rankings for 2017 with some consistency rankings for the tight ends in 2016 to support it. If you didn't make the playoffs and you had Coby Fleener or Jason Witten on your team and can't understand why, I hope this helped clear things up.

CONSISTENTLY CLUTCH – TIGHT ENDS

Tight end's consistency is often tied to their health. Rob Gronkowski, Jordan Reed and Tyler Eifert are perfect examples of this. If you could guarantee me they would play 14-16 games per year, they would easily be the most consistent tight ends in the game. However, it's not a guarantee and other tight end options must be considered.

It's one thing to be clutch during one season in Fantasy Football. However, it's those players who are consistently clutch that make up the real Fantasy studs. These players are the ones that should be drafted in the early rounds of most drafts. A consistently clutch player has normally remained consistently healthy as well, which is just as important as their consistent performance.

The Top 20 most consistent tight ends and the number of Clutch Games earned each year are listed below. The Top 20 is divided into three tiers with a three-year and two-year totals and associated rank. I'll analyze each tier and provide some insight on the players within that tier.

Tier One – The Elite (Ranks 1 - 4)

Player Name	2014	2015	2016	Total	3 yr rank	2 yr total	2 yr rank
Greg Olsen	11	11	10	32	1	21	1
Travis Kelce	10	11	10	31	2	21	2
Delanie Walker	11	11	9	31	3	20	3
Rob Gronkowski	14	12	4	30	4	16	8

If you're surprised by Rob Gronkowski NOT being at the top of the list, don't be. We all know his health is his downfall. I truly believe this will be the first time in years that we won't see Gronk drafted in the first round of most Fantasy drafts. Travis Kelce and Greg Olsen have earned the Triple-Double and Delanie Walker missed it by just one game last season. All three of them should be on your short list of tight ends to draft in 2017.

Tier Two – The Above Average (Ranks 5 – 11)

Player Name	2014	2015	2016	Total	3 yr rank	2 yr total	2 yr rank
Jason Witten	11	10	7	28	5	17	7
Antonio Gates	11	8	8	27	6	16	9
Jimmy Graham	11	5	10	26	7	15	11
Zach Ertz	9	8	8	25	8	16	10
Jordan Reed	5	11	9	25	9	20	4
Martellus Bennett	10	4	8	22	10	12	14
Kyle Rudolph	4	6	12	22	11	18	5

Let's break this Tier down into sections. First section represents Jason Witten and Antonio Gates. Both were great in their days! A couple of the most consistent tight ends over the past 15 years. But, their time is done. Let someone else draft them. Jimmy Graham and Kyle Rudolph both earned double-digit Clutch Games last season and should be capable of repeating this feat in 2017, but don't reach too high for them. Watch their ADP's this summer. Jordan Reed is one of the most consistent tight ends in the game, WHEN he's healthy. Therefore, be cautious when drafting him. Finally, Martellus Bennett went to the Packers in the offseason. The hype could drive his ADP high! He has the talent and the team to be consistent in 2017, however, everyone thought the same thing in New England and it didn't work out. So, again, be cautious.

Tier Three – The Average (Ranks 12 – 20)

Player Name	2014	2015	2016	Total	3 yr rank	2 yr total	2 yr rank
Charles Clay	7	6	6	19	12	12	15
Gary Barnidge	0	12	6	18	13	18	6
Coby Fleener	9	4	5	18	14	9	21
Julius Thomas	7	6	5	18	15	11	16
Jared Cook	8	4	3	15	16	7	27
Dwayne Allen	8	1	5	14	17	6	34
Eric Ebron	1	6	7	14	18	13	13
Tyler Eifert	0	9	5	14	19	14	12
Jermaine Gresham	8	2	3	13	20	5	38

There are some very interesting tight ends in this group. We start with Tyler Eifert. Just like Gronk and Jordan Reed, Eifert is extremely consistent, WHEN he's on the field. Eric Ebron has been waiting to break out for a couple of years and I'm not sure if it's ever going to happen. Julius Thomas may be the surprise in 2017 as he is reunited with Adam Gase in Miami. Gase was his OC when he was a top Fantasy tight end in Denver. The others are average at best and shouldn't be drafted unless as a backup.

There are your most consistent tight ends over the past three seasons. Keep this information handy as you prepare for your drafts this season. Clutch is good but consistently clutch is great!

CONSISTENCY PROFILES – TIGHT ENDS

The Consistency Profiles were created for the same reason that we have Fantasy profiles: to have a quick summary of a player's performance at a glance. The following Consistency Profiles for the tight ends are listed in alphabetical order by last name for easy reference. Each player's profile will have the following information:

1. Three-year historical breakdown per season of the following:
    a. Fantasy points total
    b. Clutch Games earned
    c. Games played
    d. Clutch Rating (CR – Clutch Games/Games Played)

2. Tier Draft Rank (Expected Clutch Rate)
    a. This number ties to the Tier Draft List in this book. This is where I have ranked the quarterback based on Fantasy points and consistency for the 2017 redraft leagues. The Tiers equate to Expected Clutch Rate (ECR) in this manner:
        i. TE1A = 70%+ ECR
        ii. TE1B = 57-70% ECR
        iii. TE2A = 44-57% ECR

3. Clutch Games by Week for 2015
    a. "+" means a Clutch Game was earned that week
    b. "B" means it was the player's Bye Week.

4. Three-year historical breakdown of the player's consistency by the following game scenarios:
    a. Home versus a good defense (Top 10 NFL defensive ranking)
    b. Home versus an average defense (NFL defense rankings 11-22)
    c. Home versus a bad defense (Bottom 10 NFL defensive rankings)
    d. Totals for all home games
    e. Away versus a good defense (Top 10 NFL defensive ranking)
    f. Away versus an average defense (NFL defense rankings 11-22)
    g. Away versus a bad defense (Bottom 10 NFL defensive rankings)
    h. Totals for all away games

These profiles are designed to allow quick access to how consistent a player has been over the past one, two or three seasons. In addition, the game scenarios will assist you when you're making those tough decisions on your weekly lineups. You can focus on how consistent your players have been over the past three seasons in those scenarios and change your lineup accordingly.

These profiles' descriptions will change as we get closer to the August draft dates but the historical information will not change until the season begins. If you want to access this information by inputting your own league's scoring method, you can go to the Tools section on www.BigGuyFantasySports.com on any device and have this information at your fingertips at any time.

CONSISTENCY PROFILES – TIGHT ENDS

GARY BARNIDGE

Another Browns tight end with one huge year (see Jordan Cameron) and then fall off the face of the earth. Barnidge is currently unsigned. Amazing! If he signs with someone soon, then maybe there's some Fantasy value but it's doubtful. Keep an eye on the situation.

3 YEAR CONSISTENCY HISTORY

		Total FP	RANK	CG	GP	CR	RANK
Gary Barnidge	2016	128.20	19	6	16	38%	25
	2015	237.30	4	12	16	75%	5
	2014	28.60	55	0	13	0%	65

TIER DRAFT RANK – TE4 – D

NO VALUE: Barnidge has no value until he gets signed by some team. That may not help either.

QUALITY GAMES BY WEEK – 2016

Player Name	1	2	3	4	5	6	7	8	9	10	11	12	13	14	15	16	17	Total
Gary Barnidge			+	+	+		+				+		B				+	6

CONSISTENCY VS DEFENSES (2015-2016)

	Good Defenses (Top 10)				Average Defenses				Bad Defenses (Bottom 10)				Total			
	FPG	CG	GP	CR	FPG	CG	GP	CR	FPG	CG	GP	CR	FPG	CG	GP	CR
Home	11.75	4	6	67%	8.89	3	8	38%	20.95	2	2	100%	11.47	9	16	56%
Away	6.74	1	5	20%	13.06	5	8	63%	14.60	3	3	100%	11.38	9	16	56%

MARTELLUS BENNETT

Bennett leaves New England after posting a season that ranked him in the Top 10 in points and 14th in consistency, all while filling in for Gronk most of the year. So, you would think he would have been more consistent, right? Anyways, He heads off to Green Bay to replace Jared Cook and become a target for Aaron Rodgers. Not too shabby. He's a TE1 for sure.

3 YEAR CONSISTENCY HISTORY

		Total FP	RANK	CG	GP	CR	RANK
Martellus Bennett	2016	167.20	10	8	16	50%	14
	2015	114.90	22	4	11	36%	24
	2014	218.50	5	10	16	63%	7

TIER DRAFT RANK – TE1 - B

AT VALUE: Bennett's ADP is TE10/pick 93. That's a fair value for him as the Packers don't use their tight end as often as other teams. He's a good value if you wait until the eighth round.

QUALITY GAMES BY WEEK – 2016

Player Name	1	2	3	4	5	6	7	8	9	10	11	12	13	14	15	16	17	Total
Martellus Bennett		+		+	+	+			B	+				+		+	+	8

CONSISTENCY VS DEFENSES (2016)

	Good Defenses (Top 10)				Average Defenses				Bad Defenses (Bottom 10)				Total			
	FPG	CG	GP	CR	FPG	CG	GP	CR	FPG	CG	GP	CR	FPG	CG	GP	CR
Home	9.90	2	4	50%	11.87	3	3	100%	22.40	1	1	100%	12.20	6	8	75%
Away	5.00	0	2	0%	4.73	0	3	0%	15.13	2	3	67%	8.70	2	8	25%

For the most current Fantasy Football Consistency information, visit www.BigGuyFantasySports.com

CONSISTENCY PROFILES – TIGHT ENDS (continued)

CAMERON BRATE

Brate is currently the #1 tight end in Tampa Bay. However, the Bucs decided they wanted O.J. Howard to be their #1 tight end in 2017, so they drafted him. Brate is still there, but what value he brings to the Fantasy table is tough to judge. He had a nice 2016 by ending the year ranked seventh in total points, but only 17th in consistency. I'm staying away.

3 YEAR CONSISTENCY HISTORY

		Total FP	RANK	CG	GP	CR	RANK
Cameron Brate	2016	172.80	7	7	15	47%	17
	2015	69.80	35	3	13	23%	32
	2014	2.70	102	0	5	0%	102

TIER DRAFT RANK – TE2 - B

AT VALUE: Brate currently has some value as his ADP shows. He's ranked as a TE17/ pick 148. A nice backup maybe, but honestly, I'm not touching the Bucs situation this year.

QUALITY GAMES BY WEEK – 2016

Player Name	1	2	3	4	5	6	7	8	9	10	11	12	13	14	15	16	17	Total
Cameron Brate			+	+		B		+	+	+			+			+		7

CONSISTENCY VS DEFENSES (2016)

	Good Defenses (Top 10)				Average Defenses				Bad Defenses (Bottom 10)				Total			
	FPG	CG	GP	CR	FPG	CG	GP	CR	FPG	CG	GP	CR	FPG	CG	GP	CR
Home	14.07	2	3	67%	21.40	1	1	100%	11.73	2	3	67%	14.11	5	7	71%
Away	4.60	0	1	0%	14.57	2	3	67%	6.43	0	4	0%	9.25	2	8	25%

CHARLES CLAY

Clay is the top tight end in Buffalo. He held that position again last year and you see the results below. He ranked 16th in total points and 23rd in consistency. Yawn! He's a solid backup or bye week pick up but beyond that, there isn't much Charles Clay brings to the Fantasy table in 2017. I'll pass on him.

3 YEAR CONSISTENCY HISTORY

		Total FP	RANK	CG	GP	CR	RANK
Charles Clay	2016	136.80	16	6	14	43%	23
	2015	121.80	18	6	13	46%	15
	2014	136.50	15	7	14	50%	16

TIER DRAFT RANK – TE3 - C

AT VALUE: Clay's current ADP is TE27/pick 205. Based on his consistency ranking at 23rd last year, his value is right about where he's ranked at this time.

QUALITY GAMES BY WEEK – 2016

Player Name	1	2	3	4	5	6	7	8	9	10	11	12	13	14	15	16	17	Total
Charles Clay				+	+	+				B				+	+	+		6

CONSISTENCY VS DEFENSES (2015-2016)

	Good Defenses (Top 10)				Average Defenses				Bad Defenses (Bottom 10)				Total			
	FPG	CG	GP	CR	FPG	CG	GP	CR	FPG	CG	GP	CR	FPG	CG	GP	CR
Home	9.80	3	5	60%	10.95	1	2	50%	14.82	4	6	67%	12.29	8	13	62%
Away	7.51	3	7	43%	4.87	0	3	0%	7.90	1	4	25%	7.06	4	14	29%

For the most current Fantasy Football Consistency information, visit www.BigGuyFantasySports.com

CONSISTENCY PROFILES – TIGHT ENDS (continued)

JARED COOK

Cook just didn't help many Fantasy teams in Green Bay last year. So, the Packers let him go to Oakland where he will be the Raiders' starter. That's fine and he should improve on last year's numbers. However, even a 50% Clutch Rate will rank him as a TE2, so unless you need a solid backup, he's a waiver wire pickup.

3 YEAR CONSISTENCY HISTORY

		Total FP	RANK	CG	GP	CR	RANK
Jared Cook	2016	73.70	36	3	10	30%	32
	2015	87.10	28	4	16	25%	30
	2014	133.40	17	8	16	50%	15

TIER DRAFT RANK – TE2 - B

AT VALUE: Cook's current ADP is TE23/pick 180. Drafting Cook as your backup tight end in the late rounds and getting the probable starter for the Raiders is good value.

QUALITY GAMES BY WEEK – 2016

Player Name	1	2	3	4	5	6	7	8	9	10	11	12	13	14	15	16	17	Total
Jared Cook				B							+				+		+	3

CONSISTENCY VS DEFENSES (2016)

	Good Defenses (Top 10)				Average Defenses				Bad Defenses (Bottom 10)				Total			
	FPG	CG	GP	CR	FPG	CG	GP	CR	FPG	CG	GP	CR	FPG	CG	GP	CR
Home	4.70	0	3	0%	2.50	0	1	0%	0.00	0	0	0%	4.15	0	4	0%
Away	4.40	0	2	0%	8.60	2	3	67%	22.50	1	1	100%	9.52	3	6	50%

LARRY DONNELL

Donnell will be infamously known for his three-touchdown night in 2014. However, it's been downhill ever since. He was signed by the Baltimore Ravens after they had injuries decimate their depth. Donnell currently backs up Ben Watson, so there's hope he could play in 2017. Not much value at this point, but you never know.

3 YEAR CONSISTENCY HISTORY

		Total FP	RANK	CG	GP	CR	RANK
Larry Donnell	2016	31.70	57	0	8	0%	62
	2015	63.80	38	2	8	25%	31
	2014	165.00	9	9	16	56%	11

TIER DRAFT RANK – TE4 - D

AT VALUE: Donnell's value is a little better now that he signed with the Ravens. He's still a backup, but watch the preseason to see if he beats out Ben Watson for the job.

QUALITY GAMES BY WEEK – 2016

Player Name	1	2	3	4	5	6	7	8	9	10	11	12	13	14	15	16	17	Total
Larry Donnell								B										0

CONSISTENCY VS DEFENSES (2014-2016)

	Good Defenses (Top 10)				Average Defenses				Bad Defenses (Bottom 10)				Total			
	FPG	CG	GP	CR	FPG	CG	GP	CR	FPG	CG	GP	CR	FPG	CG	GP	CR
Home	11.90	1	2	50%	8.10	4	7	57%	6.19	1	8	13%	7.65	6	17	35%
Away	8.33	1	3	33%	6.22	0	5	0%	10.63	3	7	43%	8.70	4	15	27%

For the most current Fantasy Football Consistency information, visit www.BigGuyFantasySports.com

ERIC EBRON

Ebron made solid improvement again this year, but he still hasn't reached his Fantasy potential. I'm not really sure he ever will. He plays on a good team with a good quarterback, but his total points ranking and consistency always falls around 13-19. That's a TE2 folks! That's where you should draft him.

3 YEAR CONSISTENCY HISTORY

		Total FP	RANK	CG	GP	CR	RANK
Eric Ebron	2016	138.10	14	7	13	54%	13
	2015	130.70	12	6	14	43%	19
	2014	55.80	41	1	13	8%	45

TIER DRAFT RANK – TE2 - A

AT VALUE: Ebron's curren ADP is TE12/pick 109. I'd draf him as my backup, if I need one. But usually, I grab a bye week one of the waiver wire You should do this as well.

QUALITY GAMES BY WEEK – 2016

Player Name	1	2	3	4	5	6	7	8	9	10	11	12	13	14	15	16	17	Total
Eric Ebron	+		+					+	+	B	+					+	+	7

CONSISTENCY VS DEFENSES (2014-2016)

	Good Defenses (Top 10)				Average Defenses				Bad Defenses (Bottom 10)				Total			
	FPG	CG	GP	CR	FPG	CG	GP	CR	FPG	CG	GP	CR	FPG	CG	GP	CR
Home	8.56	3	5	60%	5.50	0	5	0%	5.27	1	7	14%	6.31	4	17	24%
Away	10.04	4	8	50%	8.29	2	9	22%	10.42	4	6	67%	9.45	10	23	43%

TYLER EIFERT

Eifert is a Fantasy stud WHEN he's on the field. This proved true even more in 2016, when Eifert missed half of the season. Hi consistency was certainly at a 63% Clutch Rate. He's certainly worth drafting as your TE1, but when? I'm still a little worried. I' rather draft Jimmy Graham or Kyle Rudolph, who I can rely on.

3 YEAR CONSISTENCY HISTORY

		Total FP	RANK	CG	GP	CR	RANK
Tyler Eifert	2016	98.40	25	5	8	63%	6
	2015	191.50	7	9	13	69%	T6
	2014	6.70	93	0	1	0%	95

TIER DRAFT RANK – TE1 - B

OVERVALUED: Eifert's curren ADP is TE6/pick 73. At thi ADP, he is overvalued based o his injury status. Keep an eye o his injury status and ADP thi summer before draft time.

QUALITY GAMES BY WEEK – 2016

Player Name	1	2	3	4	5	6	7	8	9	10	11	12	13	14	15	16	17	Total
Tyler Eifert								+	B	+		+	+	+				5

CONSISTENCY VS DEFENSES (2015-2016)

	Good Defenses (Top 10)				Average Defenses				Bad Defenses (Bottom 10)				Total			
	FPG	CG	GP	CR	FPG	CG	GP	CR	FPG	CG	GP	CR	FPG	CG	GP	CR
Home	14.83	2	3	67%	8.90	3	6	50%	17.58	3	4	75%	12.94	8	13	62%
Away	15.87	3	3	100%	6.97	1	3	33%	26.60	2	2	100%	15.21	6	8	75%

For the most current Fantasy Football Consistency information, visit www.BigGuyFantasySports.com

ZACH ERTZ

Ertz's Top 10 finish in total points and consistency leads me to believe he should be a Top 10 tight end heading into the 2017 season. However, the Eagles went out and added many weapons. That's good for the Eagles, but bad for Zach Ertz's Fantasy value. I still like him as a late TE1, but don't reach too high for him.

3 YEAR CONSISTENCY HISTORY

		Total FP	RANK	CG	GP	CR	RANK
Zach Ertz	2016	183.60	6	8	14	57%	9
	2015	172.30	9	8	15	53%	11
	2014	146.20	13	9	16	56%	12

TIER DRAFT RANK – TE2 - A

OVERVALUED: Ertz's current ADP is TE9/pick 91, which is a little too high for me. There are too many targets for Carson Wentz in 2017. Ertz will be too inconsistent for me.

QUALITY GAMES BY WEEK – 2016

Player Name	1	2	3	4	5	6	7	8	9	10	11	12	13	14	15	16	17	Total
Zach Ertz	+			B					+	+	+		+	+	+		+	8

CONSISTENCY VS DEFENSES (2014-2016)

	Good Defenses (Top 10)				Average Defenses				Bad Defenses (Bottom 10)				Total			
	FPG	CG	GP	CR	FPG	CG	GP	CR	FPG	CG	GP	CR	FPG	CG	GP	CR
Home	10.35	2	4	50%	11.87	2	6	33%	12.03	8	13	62%	11.70	12	23	52%
Away	11.53	4	7	57%	9.53	4	9	44%	11.10	3	6	50%	10.60	11	22	50%

COBY FLEENER

Fleener went to the Saints last season and many believed he was the second coming of Jimmy Graham. He wasn't. It was pretty obvious that Fleener and Brees did not match up very well. Therefore, heading into 2017, Fleener is right about where he should be drafted, as a TE2. A nice backup if you need one or bye week pickup.

3 YEAR CONSISTENCY HISTORY

		Total FP	RANK	CG	GP	CR	RANK
Coby Fleener	2016	137.20	15	5	16	31%	31
	2015	121.10	19	4	16	25%	28
	2014	176.40	7	9	16	56%	10

TIER DRAFT RANK – TE2 - B

AT VALUE: Fleener's ADP is around the TE14 mark. This is a fair price for him. If you have bench depth to draft a backup tight end, then Fleener provides good value.

QUALITY GAMES BY WEEK – 2016

Player Name	1	2	3	4	5	6	7	8	9	10	11	12	13	14	15	16	17	Total
Coby Fleener			+	B	+						+	+	+					5

CONSISTENCY VS DEFENSES (2016)

	Good Defenses (Top 10)				Average Defenses				Bad Defenses (Bottom 10)				Total			
	FPG	CG	GP	CR	FPG	CG	GP	CR	FPG	CG	GP	CR	FPG	CG	GP	CR
Home	7.37	1	3	33%	19.55	2	2	100%	10.17	1	3	33%	11.46	4	8	50%
Away	3.95	0	2	0%	7.80	1	2	50%	5.50	0	4	0%	5.69	1	8	13%

For the most current Fantasy Football Consistency information, visit www.BigGuyFantasySports.com

ANTONIO GATES

Gates appears to be finally riding off into the sunset. However, as long as he's on the field, Philip Rivers WILL be looking for him in the end zone! Because of this, Gates is still a worthy backup in most leagues. While handcuffs are unusual at tight end in Fantasy, Gates is a definite if you draft Hunter Henry.

3 YEAR CONSISTENCY HISTORY

		Total FP	RANK	CG	GP	CR	RANK
Antonio Gates	2016	149.80	12	8	14	57%	10
	2015	149.00	12	9	11	82%	1
	2014	223.10	3	11	16	69%	4

TIER DRAFT RANK – TE2 - B
UNDERVALUED: Gates current ADP is TE25/pick 187. As much as I love Gates for consistency, I'd feel much better with him as my backup or handcuff to Hunter Henry.

QUALITY GAMES BY WEEK – 2016

Player Name	1	2	3	4	5	6	7	8	9	10	11	12	13	14	15	16	17	Total
Antonio Gates		+			+			+	+	+	B			+		+	+	8

CONSISTENCY VS DEFENSES (2014-2016)

	Good Defenses (Top 10)				Average Defenses				Bad Defenses (Bottom 10)				Total			
	FPG	CG	GP	CR	FPG	CG	GP	CR	FPG	CG	GP	CR	FPG	CG	GP	CR
Home	13.80	6	9	67%	16.25	3	4	75%	9.94	3	7	43%	12.94	12	20	60%
Away	13.08	7	9	78%	11.82	4	5	80%	10.83	3	6	50%	12.09	14	20	70%

JIMMY GRAHAM

Graham finally became the Fantasy tight end we expected him to be in 2015. His injury status heading into 2016 made him a late risky pick, but the risk takers won that one. Graham's value is back in the TE1 range, somewhere around TE5-TE10. I like his value there, but don't reach too high.

3 YEAR CONSISTENCY HISTORY

		Total FP	RANK	CG	GP	CR	RANK
Jimmy Graham	2016	191.70	4	10	16	63%	5
	2015	120.50	20	5	11	45%	17
	2014	233.90	2	11	16	69%	3

TIER DRAFT RANK – TE1 - B
AT VALUE: Graham's current ADP is TE5/ pick 62. I like this value in the middle of the sixth round. Draft five consistent studs and then add Graham as your tight end! Brilliant!

QUALITY GAMES BY WEEK – 2016

Player Name	1	2	3	4	5	6	7	8	9	10	11	12	13	14	15	16	17	Total
Jimmy Graham			+	+	B	+	+		+			+	+	+		+	+	10

CONSISTENCY VS DEFENSES (2015-2016)

	Good Defenses (Top 10)				Average Defenses				Bad Defenses (Bottom 10)				Total			
	FPG	CG	GP	CR	FPG	CG	GP	CR	FPG	CG	GP	CR	FPG	CG	GP	CR
Home	11.38	2	4	50%	16.98	5	6	83%	11.48	2	4	50%	13.81	9	14	64%
Away	7.68	1	4	25%	12.75	3	4	75%	7.44	2	5	40%	9.15	6	13	46%

For the most current Fantasy Football Consistency information, visit www.BigGuyFantasySports.com

ROB GRONKOWSKI

Gronk has finally had his ADP fall out of the first round! Maybe, it's the past couple of years of him not earning first round value that led to this historic event! Whatever, the reason, his ADP is STILL TOO HIGH! Injuries alone should take him to the fourth round. Wait a few rounds later and grab Olsen, Graham or Reed, you'll be much happier!

3 YEAR CONSISTENCY HISTORY

		Total FP	RANK	CG	GP	CR	RANK
Rob Gronkowski	2016	97.00	26	4	7	57%	11
	2015	255.60	1	12	15	80%	3
	2014	266.40	1	14	15	93%	1

TIER DRAFT RANK – TE1 - A

OVERVALUED: Gronk is Gronk! His current ADP is TE1/pick 20. Nope! Not on my teams! There isn't enough separating him and the next tight ends to justify the pick.

QUALITY GAMES BY WEEK – 2016

Player Name	1	2	3	4	5	6	7	8	9	10	11	12	13	14	15	16	17	Total
Rob Gronkowski					+	+	+	+	B									4

CONSISTENCY VS DEFENSES (2014-2016)

	Good Defenses (Top 10)				Average Defenses				Bad Defenses (Bottom 10)				Total			
	FPG	CG	GP	CR	FPG	CG	GP	CR	FPG	CG	GP	CR	FPG	CG	GP	CR
Home	17.30	4	5	80%	18.06	5	7	71%	20.28	4	5	80%	18.49	13	17	76%
Away	16.77	7	7	100%	14.59	7	9	78%	14.00	3	4	75%	15.24	17	20	85%

TRAVIS KELCE

Don't get me wrong! I love Kelce and hope he can be my TE1 on most teams. But value is value! And right now, Kelce is overvalued. He's just as consistent as Olsen, Reed or Graham, but they are going in rounds five or six, while Kelce is going in round three. Sorry, I need consistent quarterbacks, running backs or wide receivers in round three and four.

3 YEAR CONSISTENCY HISTORY

		Total FP	RANK	CG	GP	CR	RANK
Travis Kelce	2016	221.50	1	10	16	63%	3
	2015	189.50	8	11	16	69%	7
	2014	183.20	6	10	16	63%	8

TIER DRAFT RANK – TE1 - A

OVERVALUED: Kelce's current ADP is TE2/pick 29. As mentioned above, Kelce is great, but not two to three rounds greater than the other consistent tight ends. Sorry.

QUALITY GAMES BY WEEK – 2016

Player Name	1	2	3	4	5	6	7	8	9	10	11	12	13	14	15	16	17	Total
Travis Kelce	+		+	+	B			+	+		+	+	+	+		+		10

CONSISTENCY VS DEFENSES (2014-2015)

	Good Defenses (Top 10)				Average Defenses				Bad Defenses (Bottom 10)				Total			
	FPG	CG	GP	CR	FPG	CG	GP	CR	FPG	CG	GP	CR	FPG	CG	GP	CR
Home	15.29	6	8	75%	12.81	6	8	75%	10.65	4	8	50%	12.92	16	24	67%
Away	12.02	6	10	60%	10.78	5	8	63%	12.97	4	6	67%	11.84	15	24	63%

For the most current Fantasy Football Consistency information, visit www.BigGuyFantasySports.com

VANCE MCDONALD

McDonald is the No. 1 tight end for the 49ers, but he is still not more than a TE2/3. McDonald will probably go undrafted and be available for bye week pickup. I recommend passing on McDonald in your draft this year. The only way that changes is if Kyle Shanahan appears to start throwing to him more in preseason.

3 YEAR CONSISTENCY HISTORY

		Total FP	RANK	CG	GP	CR	RANK
Vance McDonald	2016	87.10	30	4	11	36%	27
	2015	80.60	30	3	14	21%	35
	2014	5.00	97	0	8	0%	97

TIER DRAFT RANK – TE3 - C

AT VALUE: McDonald's value is very minimal for 2017. He is still the #1 tight end in San Francisco, but not enough to be draftable. Nothing to see here.

QUALITY GAMES BY WEEK – 2016

Player Name	1	2	3	4	5	6	7	8	9	10	11	12	13	14	15	16	17	Total
Vance McDonald		+						B	+		+	+						4

CONSISTENCY VS DEFENSES (2015-2016)

	Good Defenses (Top 10)				Average Defenses				Bad Defenses (Bottom 10)				Total			
	FPG	CG	GP	CR	FPG	CG	GP	CR	FPG	CG	GP	CR	FPG	CG	GP	CR
Home	7.78	2	6	33%	2.86	0	5	0%	10.40	1	2	50%	6.29	3	13	23%
Away	9.30	1	3	33%	6.44	2	7	29%	6.45	1	2	50%	7.16	4	12	33%

ZACH MILLER

Miller had two completely different halves to his season. The first eight games he earned a total of five Clutch Games. The second half he had only one Clutch Game in those eight games. His foot injury in November 2016 could cause him to not even make the Bears roster. Therefore, I would stay away from Miller and the Bears tight end situation in 2017.

3 YEAR CONSISTENCY HISTORY

		Total FP	RANK	CG	GP	CR	RANK
Zach Miller	2016	119.60	20	6	10	60%	8
	2015	107.90	23	5	15	33%	25
	2014	13.60	76	0	3	0%	76

TIER DRAFT RANK – TE2 - B

UNDRAFTABLE: Miller's current injury status has many Fantasy owners scared of his future in 2017. At this point, I'd stay away from him or anyone on the Bears tight end charts.

QUALITY GAMES BY WEEK – 2016

Player Name	1	2	3	4	5	6	7	8	9	10	11	12	13	14	15	16	17	Total
Zach Miller			+	+	+	+		+	B		+							6

CONSISTENCY VS DEFENSES (2015-2016)

	Good Defenses (Top 10)				Average Defenses				Bad Defenses (Bottom 10)				Total			
	FPG	CG	GP	CR	FPG	CG	GP	CR	FPG	CG	GP	CR	FPG	CG	GP	CR
Home	7.30	2	5	40%	6.47	1	3	33%	7.03	1	3	33%	7.00	4	11	36%
Away	6.86	2	5	40%	15.68	3	5	60%	9.45	2	4	50%	10.75	7	14	50%

CONSISTENCY PROFILES – TIGHT ENDS (continued)

GREG OLSEN

Four straight seasons of Top 7 in both total points and consistency. Olsen has the most combined Clutch Games over the past three seasons and is also first in most Clutch Games over the past two years. There aren't too many tight ends out there as dependable as Olsen. He should go in the Round 4/5 range. I'd rather take him in Round 5 in order to stock up on RB's & WR's.

3 YEAR CONSISTENCY HISTORY

		Total FP	RANK	CG	GP	CR	RANK
Greg Olsen	2016	205.30	3	10	16	63%	4
	2015	229.40	5	11	16	69%	T6
	2014	220.80	4	11	16	69%	5

TIER DRAFT RANK – TE1 - A

AT VALUE: Olsen's current ADP is TE4/ pick 45. I believe this is about right for him. I'd rather take him in Round 5, but late Round 4 is certainly viable. Very consistent every year.

QUALITY GAMES BY WEEK – 2016

Player Name	1	2	3	4	5	6	7	8	9	10	11	12	13	14	15	16	17	Total
Greg Olsen	+	+	+	+	+	+	B		+					+	+	+		10

CONSISTENCY VS DEFENSES (2013-2015)

	Good Defenses (Top 10)				Average Defenses				Bad Defenses (Bottom 10)				Total			
	FPG	CG	GP	CR	FPG	CG	GP	CR	FPG	CG	GP	CR	FPG	CG	GP	CR
Home	8.66	3	5	60%	10.35	3	6	50%	16.84	10	13	77%	13.51	16	24	67%
Away	13.52	3	5	60%	12.63	5	7	71%	14.60	8	12	67%	13.80	16	24	67%

JORDAN REED

If one could guarantee me that Reed would stay healthy for all 16 games, then I would say he's worth being picked in the early fourth round. History shows that's not possible, therefore, I list him as overvalued. He's a very consistent tight end when he's on the field. He and Cousins have great chemistry when they play together. UPDATE: Reed's toe injury appears worse than expected. Stay clear!

3 YEAR CONSISTENCY HISTORY

		Total FP	RANK	CG	GP	CR	RANK
Jordan Reed	2016	170.60	9	9	12	75%	2
	2015	248.20	2	11	14	79%	4
	2014	97.90	21	5	11	45%	18

TIER DRAFT RANK – TE1 - B

OVERVALUED: Reed was great in 2016, when healthy. However, once again, he's not healthy. Toe injury is looking worse every day now. Stay away from this for now!

QUALITY GAMES BY WEEK – 2016

Player Name	1	2	3	4	5	6	7	8	9	10	11	12	13	14	15	16	17	Total
Jordan Reed	+	+	+	+	+			+	B		+	+				+		9

CONSISTENCY VS DEFENSES (2015-2016)

	Good Defenses (Top 10)				Average Defenses				Bad Defenses (Bottom 10)				Total			
	FPG	CG	GP	CR	FPG	CG	GP	CR	FPG	CG	GP	CR	FPG	CG	GP	CR
Home	10.55	1	2	50%	15.01	5	7	71%	17.48	5	6	83%	15.41	11	15	73%
Away	11.08	4	4	100%	18.78	3	5	60%	24.75	2	2	100%	17.06	9	11	82%

For the most current Fantasy Football Consistency information, visit www.BigGuyFantasySports.com

KYLE RUDOLPH

Every once in a while, players break out with no warning. Rudolph was one of those players last season. The emergence of Sam Bradford as the Vikings' quarterback made Rudolph very Fantasy relevant as Bradford used Rudolph as his security blanket all year Bradford is still there, so I wouldn't expect much change. Great value to be had in Round 7 or 8.

3 YEAR CONSISTENCY HISTORY

		Total FP	RANK	CG	GP	CR	RANK
Kyle Rudolph	2016	209.00	2	12	16	75%	1
	2015	128.50	14	6	16	38%	23
	2014	59.10	38	4	9	44%	20

TIER DRAFT RANK – TE1 - B

UNDERVALUED: Rudolph's current ADP is TE7/pick 81. He ranked #1 last year in consistency. Even if he ends up ranked in Top 5-7, he's worth a mid-round pick.

QUALITY GAMES BY WEEK – 2016

Player Name	1	2	3	4	5	6	7	8	9	10	11	12	13	14	15	16	17	Total
Kyle Rudolph	+	+	+	+		B	+			+		+	+	+	+	+	+	12

CONSISTENCY VS DEFENSES (2015-2016)

	Good Defenses (Top 10)				Average Defenses				Bad Defenses (Bottom 10)				Total			
	FPG	CG	GP	CR	FPG	CG	GP	CR	FPG	CG	GP	CR	FPG	CG	GP	CR
Home	7.28	1	5	20%	13.14	4	7	57%	11.63	3	4	75%	10.93	8	16	50%
Away	10.47	2	3	67%	10.00	5	9	56%	10.30	3	4	75%	10.16	10	16	63%

JACOB TAMME

For reasons unknown to man nor beast, Tamme asked to test the free-agent market in the offseason and now he's currently unemployed. Well done, Jacob! At this point, Tamme has zero value in the Fantasy world. There's always a possibility that he will be signed somewhere, but his value will still be minimal.

3 YEAR CONSISTENCY HISTORY

		Total FP	RANK	CG	GP	CR	RANK
Jacob Tamme	2016	61.00	39	2	8	25%	36
	2015	130.70	13	6	15	40%	21
	2014	36.90	54	1	15	7%	52

TIER DRAFT RANK – TE3 - C

NO VALUE: Tamme has no value until he is signed by some team.

QUALITY GAMES BY WEEK – 2016

Player Name	1	2	3	4	5	6	7	8	9	10	11	12	13	14	15	16	17	Total
Jacob Tamme	+	+									B							2

CONSISTENCY VS DEFENSES (2015-2016)

	Good Defenses (Top 10)				Average Defenses				Bad Defenses (Bottom 10)				Total			
	FPG	CG	GP	CR	FPG	CG	GP	CR	FPG	CG	GP	CR	FPG	CG	GP	CR
Home	9.40	1	2	50%	14.43	1	3	33%	8.33	3	6	50%	10.19	5	11	45%
Away	3.77	0	3	0%	4.67	0	3	0%	9.05	3	6	50%	6.63	3	12	25%

For the most current Fantasy Football Consistency information, visit www.BigGuyFantasySports.com

JULIUS THOMAS

In a bad situation in Jacksonville, Thomas still ended the season ranked 12th in consistency for the second straight year. Now he is in Miami, with his former coach, Adam Gase, who led him to huge Fantasy numbers in Denver in 2012 and 2013. Thomas could end up in the Top 12 in 2017. Great value here!

3 YEAR CONSISTENCY HISTORY

		Total FP	RANK	CG	GP	CR	RANK
Julius Thomas	2016	82.90	32	5	9	56%	12
	2015	123.10	17	6	12	50%	12
	2014	163.90	11	7	13	54%	13

<table>
<tr><td colspan="3">TIER DRAFT RANK – TE1 - B</td></tr>
<tr><td>UNDERVALUED: Thomas' current ADP is TE16/pick 143. Drafting a tight end in Round 12 or 13 who may end up Top 10 in points and consistency is awesome value. Don't miss out!</td></tr>
</table>

QUALITY GAMES BY WEEK – 2016

Player Name	1	2	3	4	5	6	7	8	9	10	11	12	13	14	15	16	17	Total
Julius Thomas	+	+			B		+	+		+								5

CONSISTENCY VS DEFENSES (2015-2016)

	Good Defenses (Top 10)				Average Defenses				Bad Defenses (Bottom 10)				Total			
	FPG	CG	GP	CR	FPG	CG	GP	CR	FPG	CG	GP	CR	FPG	CG	GP	CR
Home	12.83	2	3	67%	9.70	2	3	67%	17.85	4	4	100%	13.90	8	10	80%
Away	3.80	0	2	0%	7.44	3	7	43%	3.65	0	2	0%	6.09	3	11	27%

WILL TYE

Tye was terribly inconsistent last season and is still listed as the #1 tight end for the Giants. However, the Giants drafted college star, Evan Engram. It's only a matter of time before Engram takes the top spot in New York. In the meantime, regardless of situation, Tye is undraftable at this point.

3 YEAR CONSISTENCY HISTORY

		Total FP	RANK	CG	GP	CR	RANK
Will Tye	2016	95.90	27	1	16	6%	61
	2015	106.40	24	6	12	50%	13
	2014	DNP	DNP	DNP	DNP	DNP	DNP

<table>
<tr><td colspan="3">TIER DRAFT RANK – TE3 - C</td></tr>
<tr><td>UNDRAFTABLE: Tye is basically undraftable at this point. He will probably stay the backup in New York. So, if Engram gets hurt or underperforms, Tye may start.</td></tr>
</table>

QUALITY GAMES BY WEEK – 2016

Player Name	1	2	3	4	5	6	7	8	9	10	11	12	13	14	15	16	17	Total
Will Tye								B		+								1

CONSISTENCY VS DEFENSES (2015-2016)

	Good Defenses (Top 10)				Average Defenses				Bad Defenses (Bottom 10)				Total			
	FPG	CG	GP	CR	FPG	CG	GP	CR	FPG	CG	GP	CR	FPG	CG	GP	CR
Home	9.85	3	4	75%	6.20	1	6	17%	8.48	1	4	25%	7.89	5	14	36%
Away	5.83	0	3	0%	5.60	0	4	0%	7.41	2	7	29%	6.56	2	14	14%

For the most current Fantasy Football Consistency information, visit www.BigGuyFantasySports.com

DELANIE WALKER

Walker had his first season UNDER a 73% Clutch Rate for the first time in three years. He still ended the year ranked fifth in total points and seventh in consistency. He should be a solid value in the middle rounds of most Fantasy drafts in 2017. If he is, then grab him and feel good about the pick.

3 YEAR CONSISTENCY HISTORY

		Total FP	RANK	CG	GP	CR	RANK
Delanie Walker	2016	187.00	5	9	15	60%	7
	2015	238.80	3	13	16	81%	2
	2014	176.00	8	11	15	73%	2

TIER DRAFT RANK – TE1 - B

AT VALUE: Walker's current ADP of TE8/pick 83 shows he's a little undervalued. I have him at TE7 as well, but getting him in the seventh round is still a solid pick for him.

QUALITY GAMES BY WEEK – 2016

Player Name	1	2	3	4	5	6	7	8	9	10	11	12	13	14	15	16	17	Total
Delanie Walker		+			+		+	+	+	+		+	B		+	+		9

CONSISTENCY VS DEFENSES (2014-2016)

	Good Defenses (Top 10)				Average Defenses				Bad Defenses (Bottom 10)				Total			
	FPG	CG	GP	CR	FPG	CG	GP	CR	FPG	CG	GP	CR	FPG	CG	GP	CR
Home	9.80	3	7	43%	10.76	4	5	80%	16.01	7	9	78%	12.69	14	21	67%
Away	11.83	5	7	71%	13.31	6	7	86%	13.02	6	9	67%	12.75	17	23	74%

JASON WITTEN

Witten, just like Antonio Gates, is looking to his future induction into the Pro Football Hall of Fame. So, Witten is now a decent Fantasy backup, but not much more. He finally did not earn a Top 10 ranking in consistency last season. He did make the Top 12 in total points though. Draft him as a backup this year and you should do just fine.

3 YEAR CONSISTENCY HISTORY

		Total FP	RANK	CG	GP	CR	RANK
Jason Witten	2016	153.60	11	7	16	44%	20
	2015	166.20	10	10	16	63%	10
	2014	164.30	10	11	16	69%	6

TIER DRAFT RANK – TE2 - B

AT VALUE: Witten's ADP of TE18/ pick 150 has backup written all over it. That's fair assessment of his value in 2017. If someone wants him as their starter, let them!

QUALITY GAMES BY WEEK – 2016

Player Name	1	2	3	4	5	6	7	8	9	10	11	12	13	14	15	16	17	Total
Jason Witten	+			+			B	+	+	+					+	+		7

CONSISTENCY VS DEFENSES (2014-2016)

	Good Defenses (Top 10)				Average Defenses				Bad Defenses (Bottom 10)				Total			
	FPG	CG	GP	CR	FPG	CG	GP	CR	FPG	CG	GP	CR	FPG	CG	GP	CR
Home	8.16	2	7	29%	11.16	6	8	75%	12.27	6	9	67%	10.70	14	24	58%
Away	5.67	1	3	33%	7.20	2	6	33%	11.14	10	15	67%	9.47	13	24	54%

For the most current Fantasy Football Consistency information, visit www.BigGuyFantasySports.com

2017 Draft Prep

While everything that you have read so far is certainly draft prep for your upcoming Fantasy drafts, this section is segregated specifically for this year's draft preparation. There are two sections to the draft prep. The first section is an article identifying my selection of the Consistent Undervalued Players in 2017. This article was written late July, so things may change. You can certainly follow my articles on BigGuyFantasySports.com and on Twitter (@bob_lung) for my guest appearances on podcasts and other radio shows to keep up with all of my draft prep thoughts through the preseason.

The second section of the 2017 Draft Prep is the Tiered Draft sheet. The Tiered Draft sheet was created about five years ago when my good friend and business associate asked me for help for his upcoming Fantasy draft against his son and son-in-law. He said he found it very difficult to keep up during "those quick online drafts" on Yahoo and NFL.com because you only have 90 seconds between picks. In addition, he said he struggled with what round to pick the top running backs, wide receivers, etc. So I told him that I would create a one-page Excel sheet with a detailed ranking of the players by tiers and a brief section that would explain which position to pick each round and what tier to choose from.

The Tier Draft lists will be current as of the date on the sheet below. Therefore, they won't be perfectly updated for your draft, but you can get the most current Tier Draft lists by going to www.BigGuyFantasySports.com. I will update them as there are significant changes (injuries, depth chart changes, etc.) throughout the preseason.

CONSISTENT UNDERVALUED PLAYERS - QB

Every year as Fantasy owners head into their drafts, they are always looking for the "sleepers" or undervalued players. The Clutch Games system identifies undervalued players that most systems can't. These are the players who are consistent week after week but don't normally have huge games. These players slip down and can be drafted at great value.

I will identify those picks who are undervalued based on their current ADP's. This way if you want to pick a player early, you can and still get good value based on what round you draft them. Or you can wait until the middle or late rounds and get great value just as easily. It's your call!

Let's start with the quarterbacks.

Derek Carr
There was a point in 2016, where visions of MVP danced in folks' heads about Derek Carr. However, an injury cut his season short by one game. Carr still ended the season ranked 10th in consistency with a 60% Clutch Rate. With the addition of the Beast, Marshawn Lynch, Carr should improve on that consistency. Even though he's Top 10, his current ADP is in the middle of the seventh round. That's excellent value for a late QB1.

Kirk Cousins
If you're a reader of last year's Guide and the Big Guy Fantasy Sports website, you already know of my "man crush" for Kirk Cousins. I highly touted him in this section last year and he rewarded all of us by ending the season ranked fifth in total points and tied for sixth with Drew Brees in consistency with a 69% Clutch Rate. However, his current ADP is QB12/pick 90! What? Who's determining these ADP's? Dan Snyder? Kirk is ranked sixth in the Tier Draft list. If you can pick him in rounds seven or eighth, DO IT!

Matthew Stafford
Stafford has never really been very consistent. However, he ended last season ranked seventh in total points. His 50% Clutch Rate says NO, but value is value and as a backup, Stafford has value. His current ADP is QB15/pick 108. That's the end of the 9th round. Trust me on this, there are a ton of worse quarterbacks that you could have as your backup. Stafford is one that could save your QB1's bye week.

Blake Bortles
After a fifth-place effort in consistency in 2015, Bortles was expected to continue that consistency heading into 2016, but it didn't. Everybody was talked about Bortles' horrible 2016 season, but it really wasn't that bad. Bortles ended the season ranked ninth in total points and had a 50% Clutch Rate just like Stafford. Bortles will now have a better running back in 2017 and has worked on his mechanics in the off-season. Does this mean Bortles is a Top 5 QB? But with his current ADP of QB20/pick 140, there's a ton of value to be had in 2017!

There are certainly other undervalued quarterbacks in this year's draft, but these are some of my favorite picks. Don't forget to read the profiles for those quarterbacks who are undervalued and overvalued. These players can make or break your Fantasy season, so be aware as you head into draft day! Check back at www.BigGuyFantasySports.com for updates!

CONSISTENT UNDERVALUED PLAYERS – RB

Every year as Fantasy owners head into their drafts, they are always looking for the "sleepers" or undervalued players. The Clutch Games system identifies undervalued players that most systems can't. These are the players who are consistent week after week but don't normally have huge games. These players slip down and can be drafted at great value.

I will identify those picks who are undervalued based on their current ADP's. This way if you want to pick a player early, you can and still get good value based on what round you draft them. Or you can wait until the middle or late rounds and get great value just as easily. It's your call!

Let's take a look at the running backs.

Frank Gore
There is always so much value in veteran players because everyone loves to hype the "young studs" in Fantasy Football. Well, Frank Gore was extremely helpful last year to his Fantasy teams and will be this year as well. Gore ended 2016 ranked 12th in total points and tied for eighth in consistency and yet his current ADP is RB35/pick 100. Yep, you read it correctly, he is being drafted as a late RB3 in the 7th or 8th round. Do you see the value here? I know I do!

Isaiah Crowell
Many of you know that I'm a Northeast Ohio resident and therefore, I was born a Browns fan. However, when it comes to Fantasy football, it's normally tough to tell you to draft a Browns player. This year, may be different. Crowell had a quiet, yet solid season, last year. He finished the year ranked 14th in total points and 19th in consistency with a Clutch Rate of 56%. He earned those numbers behind a HORRID offensive line! The Browns had a huge upgrade in their line in the off-season and should help Crowell earn another Clutch Game or two. His current ADP is RB16/pick 45. He's definitely worth a look as an RB2 in 2017.

Mike Gillislee
Fantasy football is much more opportunity than talent, but when it truly comes together, it's when there is both! In 2017, Mike Gillislee has both! His talent as a backup to LeSean McCoy was evident when McCoy missed some time with minor aches and pains. When called upon, Gillislee earned, or was close to, a Clutch Game every time he had eight or more carries. Now, comes the opportunity! He became the main back in New England in the offseason, replacing LeGarrette Blount. However, his current ADP is RB34/pick 97. Blount last season ended the year ranked ninth in total points and ranked 13th in a PPR league! I believe Gillislee ends the year in the Top 24. Grab him if you can!

Danny Woodhead
Woodhead missed most of last season and now has fully recovered. With the suspension of Kenneth Dixon for four games, Woodhead and Terrance West will be the main backs. Even when Dixon returns, Woodhead will be the third-down back for the Ravens. In a PPR format, Woodhead is gold. The injury is a concern, but with a current ADP of RB37/pick105, it's hard not to pick him as a RB4 for your team.

There are certainly other undervalued running backs in this year's draft, but these are some of my favorite picks. Don't forget to read the profiles for those running backs who are undervalued and overvalued. These players can make or break your Fantasy season, so be aware as you head into draft day! Check back at www.BigGuyFantasySports.com for updates!

CONSISTENT UNDERVALUED PLAYERS – WR

Every year as Fantasy owners head into their drafts, they are always looking for the "sleepers" or undervalued players. The Clutch Games system identifies undervalued players that most systems can't. These are the players who are consistent week after week but don't normally have huge games. These players slip down and can be drafted at great value.

I will identify those picks who are undervalued based on their current ADP's. This way if you want to pick a player early, you can and still get good value based on what round you draft them. Or you can wait until the middle or late rounds and get great value just as easily. It's your call!

Let's take a look at the wide receivers.

Jarvis Landry
I believe Jarvis Landry gets less respect than Rodney Dangerfield! Only three receivers have earned 25 or more Clutch Games the last two seasons. Landry, Antonio Brown and Larry Fitzgerald! And yet, Landry is once again sitting around the ADP mark of WR19/pick 35. And once again, he will be on my Fantasy teams in 2017 and he should be on your teams as well!

Larry Fitzgerald
Since I mentioned Fitzgerald's awesome consistency numbers above, let's talk about the lack of respect for this guy! Fitzgerald ranked ninth in total points last season and was all alone in second place in consistency with an 81% Clutch Rate. Yes, I realize he's getting older, as is his quarterback, but Fitzgerald's current ADP is WR32/pick 72. I can only hope that I can draft Landry as my WR2 and Fitz as my WR3!

Tyreek Hill
Only four receivers earned six straight Clutch Games over the last six games of 2016. Jordy Nelson, Julian Edelman, Golden Tate, and Tyreek Hill. This guy is lightning every time he touches the ball and the Chiefs were smart enough to feed him often. There's no reason to believe that won't continue in 2017. Hill's current ADP is WR26/pick 55. Not horribly bad, when you realize that Hill ended last season ranked 22nd in total points and tied for 22nd in consistency. Not bad, right? Except he didn't get more than five rushing attempts or targets in a game until after Week Seven! So, most of those total points and consistency came in only nine games.

Michael Crabtree
Crabtree was in the article last season and he's back again! He ended the year ranked 12th in total points and tied for 13th in consistency with a 69% Clutch Rating for the second straight season. He outscored and was more consistent than Amari Cooper! Yet, Crabtree's current ADP is WR21/pick 45, while Cooper's is WR9/pick16. Crabtree's certainly worth drafting as your WR2 or WR3 who could earn you WR1 or WR2 in points and consistency.

There are certainly other undervalued wide receivers in this year's draft, but these are some of my favorite picks. Don't forget to read the profiles for those wide receivers who are undervalued and overvalued. These players can make or break your Fantasy season, so be aware as you head into draft day! Check back at www.BigGuyFantasySports.com for updates!

CONSISTENT UNDERVALUED PLAYERS – TE

Every year as Fantasy owners head into their drafts, they are always looking for the "sleepers" or undervalued players. The Clutch Games system identifies undervalued players that most systems can't. These are the players who are consistent week after week but don't normally have huge games. These players slip down and can be drafted at great value.

I will identify those picks who are undervalued based on their current ADP's. This way if you want to pick a player early, you can and still get good value based on what round you draft them. Or you can wait until the middle or late rounds and get great value just as easily. It's your call!

Let's take a look at the tight ends.

Jimmy Graham

Jimmy Graham finally got close to the level he played at in New Orleans. He ended the season ranked fourth in total points and ranked tied for third in consistency with a 63% Clutch Rate. However, his current ADP doesn't show him being ranked up with the top tight ends. It is currently TE6/pick 65. That's middle of the sixth round, while Gronk, Kelce, Reed and Olsen are being drafted before the end of round four or earlier. I'm perfectly fine with waiting to draft Graham in round six. Great value to be had!

Julius Thomas

Do you remember the days when Julius Thomas was a Fantasy stud in Denver? Well, those days may be coming back in Miami. When Thomas last played for Adam Gase, it was when he was in Denver as the OC. Now Gase leads the Dolphins and purposely grabbed Thomas this offseason in free agency. His ADP is currently at TE18/pick 160. Thomas could easily end the season in the Top 12. There's great value here if you draft him in the late rounds.

Kyle Rudolph

Want to win a bet with your buddies? Ask them who the most consistent tight end was last season? It's doubtful anyone will answer Kyle Rudolph, but that's the right answer! Rudolph connected with new quarterback, Sam Bradford, in 2016 and that combination still exists in 2017. I'm not going to guarantee Rudolph will be #1 again, but I will guarantee he'll do better than his current ADP of TE9/pick 90. Middle of the eight round is great value for him!

Martellus Bennett

Bennett was overhyped in New England last season. He did pretty well by ending the season ranked 10th in total points, but only ranked 14th in consistency with a 50% Clutch Rate. However, in the offseason, he was picked up by the Packers (who released Jared Cook). Bennett's ADP is TE11/pick 96. So, we're talking about late eighth round pick for a starting Packers tight end? Sounds good to me!

There are certainly other undervalued tight ends in this year's draft, but these are some of my favorite picks. Don't forget to read the profiles for those tight ends who are undervalued and overvalued. These players can make or break your Fantasy season, so be aware as you head into draft day! Check back at www.BigGuyFantasySports.com for updates!

The basis of the draft list was described above in the intro section titled, 2016 Draft Prep, so here I wanted to take the opportunity to briefly explain how to use the Tier Draft list.

Overall Position Rank (RB1, RB2, etc.)

The position sections (QB, RB, WR, TE, DEF & K) are ranked in order of Fantasy and Consistency value as related to the appropriate scoring method. You should follow the rankings as you draft, but you may certainly pick those higher or lower based on your draft prep, current injury news, etc.

Starting Lineup Positional Rank (RB1, RB2, etc.)

Within each position, the players are also identified by their position and a number (1 through 7). So, for example all of the running backs with the RB1 identification are running backs that you should have on your team as your main or your first starting running back. The RB2's are those running backs who should be on your team as your second starting running backs and so on.

Quality Rank (A, B, C, etc.)

Within, each position, the players are also identified by the quality of their Fantasy value and consistency within their position. An "A" ranking is the best players available within each ranking. When using the "Draft Advisor" section, always choose the highest ranked of all three categories when making your selection.

DRAFT ADVISOR

The Draft Advisor is a simple way of recommending who to draft in each round towards building a solid team. The idea is to pick the highest ranked player in each round. The first seven rounds are critical in building your core team. By the end of round seven, you should have a starting team (depending on your league) consisting of the follow players: one starting quarterback (QB1); two starting running backs (RB1 & RB2B); three starting wide receivers (WR1, WR2, WR3) and one tight end (TE1).

Of course, if you get a higher ranked player than those listed (i.e., you get a WR1 and two WR2) then congrats. After these seven players are drafted, then you can begin to draft your backups with the highest ranked players in each position until you finalize your team with a defense and kicker near the end of your draft. I do want to point out that every league is different. There are different scoring methods like bonuses for 300+ passing games and 100+ rushing or receiving games, so please do NOT take these lists as the gospel truth. I can always email you these lists in an Excel format and you can edit them to your preferences.

The Tier Draft lists are just another tool to help you dominate your league. I hope you find them as useful a many other Fantasy owners do each year. If you need an updated version of the Tier Draft, just email at anytime at bob@bigguyfantasysports.com.

2017 TIER DRAFT LIST

DRAFT ADVISOR

Pick highest of each tier

Round	Pick	Position	Tier
1	ALL	WR1/RB1	A
2	ALL	WR1/RB1	A/B
3	ALL	WR1/RB1	A/B
4	ALL	RB/WR/QB1A	A/B
5	ALL	QB1B/RB/WR/TE	A/B
6	ALL	QB1B/RB/WR/TE	A/B
7	ALL	QB/RB/WR/TE	A/B
8	ALL	QB/RB/WR/TE	A/B

At the end of Round 7, you should have:

QB	RB	WR	TE
1	2/3	2/3	1
A/B	A/B	A/B	A/B

In rounds 8 - 12, pick your backup players

8	ALL	RB/WR	B/C
9	ALL	RB/WR	B/C
10	ALL	RB/WR	TOP
11	ALL	RB/WR	B/C
12	ALL	QB2	TOP

You should have a starting lineup at this point

13	ALL	DEF	TOP
14	ALL	RB/WR	TOP
15	ALL	RB/WR	TOP
16	ALL	K	TOP

Quarterbacks

#			Name	Team/Bye
1	QB1	A	Aaron Rodgers	GB/8
2	QB1	A	Tom Brady	NE/9
3	QB1	B	Drew Brees	NO/5
4	QB1	B	Matt Ryan	ATL/5
5	QB1	B	Kirk Cousins	WAS/5
6	QB1	B	Derek Carr	OAK/10
7	QB1	B	Marcus Mariota	TEN/8
8	QB1	B	Andrew Luck	IND/11
9	QB1	B	Dak Prescott	DAL/7
10	QB1	B	Russell Wilson	SEA/6
11	QB1	B	Cam Newton	CAR/11
12	QB1	B	Ben Roethlisberger	PIT/9
13	QB2	A	Matthew Stafford	DET/7
14	QB2	A	Philip Rivers	LAC/9
15	QB2	A	Jameis Winston	TB/11
16	QB2	A	Eli Manning	NYG/8
17	QB2	A	Andy Dalton	CIN/6
18	QB2	A	Carson Palmer	ARI/8
19	QB2	A	Blake Bortles	JAX/8
20	QB2	A	Tyrod Taylor	BUF/6
21	QB2	A	Carson Wentz	PHI/10
22	QB2	B	Ryan Tannehill	MIA/11
23	QB2	B	Sam Bradford	MIN/9
24	QB2	B	Joe Flacco	BAL/10
25	QB3	C	Brian Hoyer	SF/11
26	QB3	C	Alex Smith	KC/10
27	QB3	C	Mike Glennon	CHI/8
28	QB3	C	Trevor Siemian	DEN/5
29	QB3	C	Josh McCown	NYJ/11
30	QB3	C	Jared Goff	LAR/8

Running Backs

#			Name	Team/Bye
1	RB1	A	David Johnson	ARI/8
2	RB1	A	LeVeon Bell	PIT/9
3	RB1	A	LeSean McCoy	BUF/6
4	RB1	A	Melvin Gordon	LAC/9
5	RB1	A	Ezekiel Elliott	DAL/6
6	RB1	B	DeMarco Murray	TEN/8
7	RB1	B	Devonta Freeman	ATL/5
8	RB1	B	Jordan Howard	CHI/9
9	RB1	B	Todd Gurley	LAR/8
10	RB1	B	Lamar Miller	HOU/7
11	RB1	B	Jay Ajayi	MIA/11
12	RB1	B	Isaiah Crowell	CLE/9
13	RB2	A	Spencer Ware	KC/10
14	RB2	A	C.J. Anderson	DEN/5
15	RB2	A	Tevin Coleman	ATL/5
16	RB2	A	Mike Gillislee	NE/9
17	RB2	B	Leonard Fournette	JAX/8
18	RB2	B	Christian McCaffrey	CAR/11
19	RB2	B	Frank Gore	IND/11
20	RB2	B	Mark Ingram	NO/5
21	RB2	B	Danny Woodhead	BAL/10
22	RB2	B	Carlos Hyde	SF/11
23	RB2	B	Marshawn Lynch	OAK/10
24	RB2	B	LeGarrette Blount	PHI/10
25	RB3	C	Ty Montgomery	GB/8
26	RB3	C	Theo Riddick	DET/7
27	RB3	C	Latavius Murray	MIN/9
28	RB3	C	Adrian Peterson	NO/5
29	RB3	C	Eddie Lacy	SEA/6
30	RB3	C	Ameer Abdullah	DET/7
31	RB3	C	Derrick Henry	TEN/8
32	RB3	C	Dalvin Cook	MIN/9
33	RB3	C	Bilal Powell	NYJ/11
34	RB3	C	Joe Mixon	CIN/6
35	RB3	C	Terrance West	BAL/10
36	RB3	C	James White	NE/9
37	RB4	D	Paul Perkins	NYG/8
38	RB4	D	Giovani Bernard	CIN/6
39	RB4	D	C.J. Prosise	SEA/6
40	RB4	D	Jeremy Hill	CIN/6
41	RB4	D	Samaje Perine	WAS/5
42	RB4	D	Matt Forte	NYJ/11
43	RB4	D	Jamaal Charles	DEN/5
44	RB4	D	Doug Martin	TB/11
45	RB4	D	Duke Johnson	CLE/9
46	RB4	D	Jonathan Stewart	CAR/11
47	RB4	D	Alvin Kamara	NO/5
48	RB4	D	Jacquizz Rodgers	TB/11
49	RB5	D	Rob Kelley	WAS/5
50	RB5	D	Jamaal Williams	GB/8

Wide Receivers (Ranked 1-38)

#			Name	Team/Bye
1	WR1	A	Antonio Brown	PIT/9
2	WR1	A	Jordy Nelson	GB/8
3	WR1	A	Odell Beckham Jr	NYG/8
4	WR1	A	Julio Jones	ATL/5
5	WR1	A	A.J. Green	CIN/6
6	WR1	A	Dez Bryant	DAL/6
7	WR1	A	Jarvis Landry	MIA/11
8	WR1	A	Michael Thomas	NO/5
9	WR1	B	T.Y. Hilton	IND/11
10	WR1	B	Mike Evans	TB/11
11	WR1	B	DeAndre Hopkins	HOU/7
12	WR1	B	Amari Cooper	OAK/10
13	WR2	A	Keenan Allen	LAC/9
14	WR2	A	Demaryius Thomas	DEN/5
15	WR2	A	Michael Crabtree	OAK/10
16	WR2	A	Golden Tate	DET/7
17	WR2	B	Julian Edelman	NE/9
18	WR2	B	Larry Fitzgerald	ARI/8
19	WR2	B	Brandin Cooks	NE/9
20	WR2	B	Davante Adams	GB/8
21	WR2	B	Alshon Jeffery	PHI/10
22	WR2	B	Tyreek Hill	KC/10
23	WR2	B	Jamison Crowder	WAS/5
24	WR2	B	Willie Snead	NO/5
25	WR3	A	Allen Robinson	JAX/8
26	WR3	A	Terrelle Pryor	WAS/5
27	WR3	A	Kelvin Benjamin	CAR/11
28	WR3	A	Doug Baldwin	SEA/6
29	WR3	B	Pierre Garcon	SF/11
30	WR3	B	Emmanuel Sanders	DEN/5
31	WR3	B	Brandon Marshall	NYG/8
32	WR3	B	Martavis Bryant	PIT/9
33	WR3	B	Adam Thielen	MIN/9
34	WR3	B	Sammy Watkins	BUF/6
35	WR3	B	Tyrell Williams	LAC/9
36	WR3	B	John Brown	ARI/8
37	WR4	C	Randall Cobb	GB/8
38	WR4	C	Donte Moncrief	IND/11

Wide Receivers - (Ranked 39-75)

#			Name	Team/Bye
39	WR4	C	DeSean Jackson	TB/11
40	WR4	C	Rishard Matthews	TEN/8
41	WR4	C	Jordan Matthews	PHI/10
42	WR4	C	Corey Davis	TEN/8
43	WR4	C	Marvin Jones	DET/7
44	WR4	C	DeVante Parker	MIA/11
45	WR4	C	Josh Doctson	WAS/5
46	WR4	C	Cameron Meredith	CHI/9
47	WR4	C	Taylor Gabriel	ATL/5
48	WR4	C	Stefon Diggs	MIN/9
49	WR5	D	Mike Wallace	BAL/10
50	WR5	D	Marqise Lee	JAX/8
51	WR5	D	Allen Hurns	JAX/8
52	WR5	D	Kevin White	CHI/9
53	WR5	D	Kenny Britt	CLE/9
54	WR5	D	Sterling Shepard	NYG/8
55	WR5	D	Jeremy Maclin	BAL/10
56	WR5	D	Corey Coleman	CLE/9
57	WR5	D	Breshad Perriman	BAL/10
58	WR5	D	Will Fuller	HOU/7
59	WR5	D	Mike Williams	LAC/9
60	WR5	D	John Ross	CIN/6
61	WR6	D	Eric Decker	TEN/8
62	WR6	D	Ted Ginn	NO/5
63	WR6	D	Cole Beasley	DAL/6
64	WR6	D	Tyler Lockett	SEA/6
65	WR6	D	Robert Woods	LAR/8
66	WR6	D	JuJu Smith-Schuster	PIT/9
67	WR6	D	Kenny Stills	MIA/11
68	WR6	D	Chris Conley	KC/10
69	WR6	D	Tyler Boyd	CIN/6
70	WR6	D	Laquon Treadwell	MIN/9
71	WR6	D	Quincy Enunwa	NYJ/11
72	WR6	D	Tavon Austin	LAR/8
73	WR7	D	Devin Funchess	CAR/11
74	WR7	D	Mohamed Sanu	ATL/5
75	WR7	D	Curtis Samuel	CAR/11

Tight Ends

#			Name	Team/Bye
1	TE1	A	Rob Gronkowski	NE/9
2	TE1	A	Travis Kelce	KC/10
3	TE1	A	Greg Olsen	CAR/11
4	TE1	B	Jimmy Graham	SEA/6
5	TE1	B	Kyle Rudolph	MIN/9
6	TE1	B	Delanie Walker	TEN/8
7	TE1	B	Julius Thomas	MIA/11
8	TE1	B	Tyler Eifert	CIN/6
9	TE1	B	Martellus Bennett	GB/8
10	TE1	B	Jordan Reed	WAS/5
11	TE1	B	Hunter Henry	LAC/9
12	TE1	B	Jack Doyle	IND/11
13	TE2	A	Zach Ertz	PHI/10
14	TE2	A	Eric Ebron	DET/7
15	TE2	A	O.J. Howard	TB/11
16	TE2	B	David Njoku	CLE/9
17	TE2	B	Coby Fleener	NO/5
18	TE2	B	Evan Engram	NYG/8
19	TE2	B	Antonio Gates	LAC/9
20	TE2	B	Cameron Brate	TB/11
21	TE2	B	C.J. Fiedorowicz	HOU/7
22	TE2	B	Jared Cook	OAK/10
23	TE2	B	Jason Witten	DAL/6
24	TE2	B	Austin Hooper	ATL/5
25	TE3	C	Jesse James	PIT/9
26	TE3	C	Dwayne Allen	NE/9
27	TE3	C	Zach Miller	CHI/9
28	TE3	C	Ben Watson	BAL/10
29	TE3	C	Charles Clay	BUF/6
30	TE3	C	Tyler Higbee	LAR/8
31	TE3	C	Vance McDonald	SF/11

Defenses

1	ARI		12	SEA
2	CAR		13	HOU
3	PHI		14	NE
4	DEN		15	IND
5	MIN		16	MIA
6	KC		17	BAL
7	GB		18	WAS
8	PIT		19	ATL
9	LAR		20	BUF
10	TB		21	SD
11	NYG		22	OAK

Kickers

#	Name	Team/Bye
1	Justin Tucker	BAL/10
2	Stephen Gostkowski	NE/9
3	Dan Bailey	DAL/6
4	Matt Bryant	ATL/5
5	Mason Crosby	GB/8
6	Adam Vinatieri	IND/11
7	Matt Prater	DET/7
8	Steve Hauschka	BUF/6
9	Cairo Santos	KC/10
10	Brandon McManus	DEN/5
11	Sebastian Janikowski	OAK/10
12	Graham Gano	CAR/11

For the most current Fantasy Football Consistency information, visit www.BigGuyFantasySports.com

Made in the USA
Columbia, SC
28 August 2017